Psychology Revivals

Thinking and Reasoning

The subject of thinking is the oldest in the whole science of psychology, going back to well before the separation of the disciplines of philosophy and psychology. Originally published in 1983, this collection of up-to-date critical essays about thinking – with particular emphasis on reasoning – is written from the perspective of psychologists who are themselves actively engaged in research into the nature of human thought.

The editor's introduction identifies the major issues which have traditionally concerned students of human thought, and provides an historical background. It describes how at first the subject was studied by introspection, and how this method fell into disrepute at the end of last century. A satisfactory alternative has not yet emerged, although much recent work is based on the information-processing model, which sees the brain as a sophisticated computer. Consequently the papers presented in this volume deal with a wide range of issues, and a number of different experimental tasks and paradigms. They cover most current approaches to the theory and methodology of cognitive psychology, including problem solving, the relationship between language and thought, and reasoning.

Thinking and Reasoning

Psychological approaches

Edited by
Jonathan St. B.T. Evans

Ψ Psychology Press
Taylor & Francis Group

LONDON AND NEW YORK

First published in 1983
by Routledge & Kegan Paul plc

This edition first published in 2014 by Psychology Press
27 Church Road, Hove, BN3 2FA

and by Psychology Press
711 Third Avenue, New York, NY 10017

Psychology Press is an imprint of the Taylor & Francis Group, an informa business

Publisher's Note
The publisher has gone to great lengths to ensure the quality of this reprint but
points out that some imperfections in the original copies may be apparent.

Disclaimer
The publisher has made every effort to trace copyright holders and welcomes
correspondence from those they have been unable to contact.

A Library of Congress record exists under ISBN: 0710094604

ISBN: 978-1-84872-317-7 (hbk)
ISBN: 978-1-315-81961-7 (ebk)
ISBN: 978-1-84872-318-4 (pbk)

Thinking and reasoning
Psychological approaches

Edited by
Jonathan St B. T. Evans

Routledge & Kegan Paul
London, Boston, Melbourne and Henley

First published in 1983
by Routledge & Kegan Paul plc
39 Store Street, London WC1E 7DD,
9 Park Street, Boston, Mass. 02108, USA,
296 Beaconsfield Parade, Middle Park,
Melbourne 3206, Australia, and
Broadway House, Newtown Road,
Henley-on-Thames, Oxon RG9 1EN
Set in 10pt Baskerville by
Input Typesetting Ltd, London
and printed in Great Britain by
Redwood Burn Ltd
Trowbridge, Wiltshire

Library of Congress Cataloging in Publication Data

Main entry under title:
Thinking and reasoning.
(International library of psychology)
Bibliography: p.
Includes index.
1. Thought and thinking. 2. Reasoning (Psychology)
3. Problem solving. I. Evans, Jonathan St. B.T.,
1948– II. Series.
BF455.T524 1983 153.4 83–3264

ISBN 0-7100-9460-4

Contents

Contributors

Richard Byrne
Department of Psychology, University of St. Andrews

Jonathan St B. T. Evans
Department of Psychology, Plymouth Polytechnic

Richard A. Griggs
Department of Psychology, University of Florida

Philip N. Johnson-Laird
MRC Applied Psychology Unit, Cambridge

Stephen E. Newstead
Department of Psychology, Plymouth Polytechnic

Paul Pollard
Department of Psychology, Plymouth Polytechnic

John T. E. Richardson
Department of Psychology, Brunel University

Peter C. Wason
Psycholinguistics Research Unit, University College London

Introduction

Jonathan St B. T. Evans

This is a book about thinking with particular emphasis on reasoning. It provides a set of up-to-date and critical essays on various aspects of the subject written by a number of different authors. With one exception (Chapter 6) each was prepared specially for the present volume. The purpose of the book is to provide different views of this important subject from the perspective of psychologists who are themselves actively engaged in research into the nature of human thought.

The book should not, then, be regarded as a conventional textbook. The authors do not necessarily agree with all one another's views and the coverage of the subject of thinking is not comprehensive. There is, for example, relatively little discussion of developmental research or the problem of creative thinking. Nevertheless, the authors' interests do involve most of the major issues which have traditionally concerned students of human thought. The purpose of this introduction is to identify these issues and to provide some historical background and perspectives.

Thinking and the problem of introspection

No subject in psychology has a longer tradition of study than that of thinking, which goes back well before the separation of the disciplines of philosophy and psychology. For example, Aristotle and later British Empiricist philosophers such as Locke, Hobbes and the Mills were concerned to describe thinking as a series of associated mental images derived from perceptual experience (see Mandler and Mandler, 1964; Reeves, 1965). Implicit in this work is the definition of thinking as neither more nor less than the *contents of consciousness*. The method by which thought was studied was therefore, inevitably, that of introspection.

Introspection did not become an *issue* or a problem, however, until the late nineteenth and early twentieth centuries. Both theoretical and experimental developments cast doubt upon the validity of introspection as a method. Theoretical doubts arose from alternative views of thinking which did *not* equate the phenomena with consciousness. The idea of unconscious thinking, although not invented by Freud (see Reeves, 1965) was made famous by him. The notion that productive, creative thinking – as well as neurotic tendencies – could be unconscious in origin was proposed, for example, by Poincaré (trans. 1924) and has frequently arisen since (see e.g. Kubie, 1958; Neisser, 1963). The other major theoretical development which challenged introspection was that of Watson's behaviourism. Watson attacked all reference to unobserved mental experiences as causal factors in behaviour as *mentalistic* and unscientific. The philosophical basis for criticisms of mentalistic explanations was later expanded in the classic work of Ryle (1949).

The introspective method was also questioned as a result of attempts to use the method in systematic experiments. For example, Francis Galton (1879) studied his own introspections both in naturalistic and in laboratory situations. He became progressively disillusioned with the method and eventually concluded that 'consciousness seems to do little more than attest to the fact that the various organs of the brain do not work with perfect ease or cooperation. Its position appears to be that of a helpless spectator of but a minute fraction of a huge amount of automatic brain work.' The concept of consciousness traditionally implies both an *awareness* of the process of thought and also a control over behaviour through *intentions*. Galton was clearly questioning both of these assumptions.

The introspection experiments of the Würzburg school of psychologists, conducted around the turn of the century, also undermined traditional views on thinking (see Humphrey, 1951, for a review). In these experiments, subjects would be asked to perform simple cognitive or judgmental acts, such as generating word associations, or making psychophysical judgments. Immediately after the subject would be asked to report on his mental experiences while performing the acts. The expected mediating images, predicted by the associationist theory of thinking, frequently failed to occur. Subjects often reported either *no* accompanying experiences, or the presence of 'imageless thoughts' which were experienced but indescribable. This work suggested that at least some aspects of thought are not amenable to study by introspection.

Of course, one may believe that internal processes mediate between stimulus and response without assuming that they are available to introspection. There is a middle way between behaviourism and mentalism. Non-mentalistic methods of studying thought processes were developed in the pre-war period by Gestalt psychologists in their work on problem solving (see next section). The emergence of modern cognitive psychology in the 1960s was, however, heavily influenced by the availability of a new model – the digital computer. Much current theory is based on viewing man as an *information processing system*. The study of thinking can be seen as an attempt to understand the software of a very sophisticated computer – the human brain.

The issue of introspection has not died, however. Within cognitive psychology and social psychology, debates continue between those wishing to regard introspections as *one* useful source of evidence about mental processes and those wishing to disregard all such reports as unreliable or misleading. This debate has been marked by some recent major theoretical papers, especially those of Nisbett and Wilson (1977) and Ericsson and Simon (1980). The argument involves more than just the use of classical introspection in the sense of descriptions of mental processes. It concerns the validity of reported strategies and the interpretation of 'thinking aloud' protocols collected during problem solving. The interpretation of verbal protocols is thus a matter of major concern in contemporary study of thinking and problem solving and is the focus of BYRNE's* chapter in the present volume.

The problem of introspection is also, inevitably, addressed in RICHARDSON's chapter on mental imagery. The remarkable resurgence of interest in the study of mental imagery is one of the reasons why introspection has remained a focal problem in cognitive psychology. To many, the term 'imagery' *can* only refer to a mental experience of a perception-like character, in the absence of appropriate stimuli. Few modern psychologists are, however, content to use only self-report data, so various attempts have been made to

---

* Throughout this book, cross reference to individual chapters is
  indicated by capitalization of authors' names.

operationalize the definition of imagery and to demonstrate its functional role in cognition (see, for example, Paivio, 1971; Kosslyn,
1981). Particularly interesting is the suggestion (e.g. Paivio, 1975)
that dual systems of thinking are available: one sequential, analytic
and specialized for verbal information processing, and the other
parallel, heuristic and specialized for visual-spatial information processing. The possibility of an anatomical basis for such a duality is
becoming increasingly credible in the light of research into the
specialized function of the two hemispheres of the brain (for a recent
review, see Springer and Deutsch, 1981).

However, the explanatory value of the imagery construct is subject to strong challenge (see, for example, Pylyshyn, 1973; 1981)
and is the focus of a complex but important debate about the use
of representational concepts in cognitive psychology. The issues are
discussed and dealt with in detail in RICHARDSON's chapter.

Problem solving

The term 'problem solving' can be construed in such a way as to
include almost all the subject matter of cognitive psychology. In
practice, the use of the term is restricted to relatively complex tasks
which take a comparatively long time to complete and often give
rise to errors. For example, the term normally includes anagram
solving but does not include the problem of recognizing words
flashed briefly in a tachistoscope. The fact that both tasks are
influenced by very similar factors – such as the frequency of linguistic usage of the solution word – shows the arbitrariness of the
distinction.

Traditionally, thinking has been classified by dichotomies: many
of these distinguish free-associative, fantasy-based thinking from
purposive, goal-directed thought. The latter type of thought, concerned with problem solving, has received more attention in the
literature, perhaps because of its great amenability to experimentation. Problem solving can be further subdivided by the nature of
the problems involved. Problems with clearly defined conditions
and goals are amenable to analytic solutions; other problems require
production of a wide range of new ideas and are thus 'creative' in
nature. This distinction has been embodied in the psychometric
study of intelligence following Guilford's (1950) distinction between

convergent and divergent thinking abilities. The chapters of the present volume are primarily concerned with convergent thinking, although JOHNSON-LAIRD discusses open-ended reasoning problems.

The Gestalt school made a lasting contribution to the study of thinking as well as perception. While conducted, for the most part, before the Second World War, their work still receives major coverage in current textbooks – a longevity bestowed on very few areas of psychological research to date. The work is well known and will only be reviewed in the barest outline here.

The Gestalt school approached the study of thinking and problem solving from their background in perception. The contrast with behaviouristic treatments of thinking of the same period – based on learning principles – is stark indeed. Gestaltists emphasized the importance of perceiving the problem *structure* in an insightful manner. Authors such as Duncker (1945) and Wertheimer (1945) discuss the value of productive formulation or reformulation in the perception of problem structure as compared with the 'blind' or reproductive thinking resulting from associative (learning theory) principles.

An important concept to arise in the Gestalt work was that of mental *set* or direction of thinking. Sometimes, the idea is treated positively as in Maier's (1931) use of 'hints' in problem solving (see also Maier and Burke, 1967 and Burke, Maier and Hoffman, 1965). More often, however, the emphasis was on set, or fixed patterns of thought, as an inhibitor of productive thinking. The classic phenomena identified were Einstellung (Luchins, 1942; Luchins and Luchins, 1950) or 'mechanisation' of problem solving strategies, and 'functional fixedness' (Duncker, 1945): the inability to use an object for a function other than one fixed by previous experience in solving a problem. These phenomena continue to stimulate interest and theoretical discussion (see, for example, Kearsley, 1975).

The Gestalt ideas were developed in the information processing approach which has dominated more recent research on problem solving. The work of Newell and Simon (1972) is generally recognized as particularly significant (for a more recent review of this approach, see Simon, 1979). The essence of this work is an application of the concepts developed in artificial intelligence to the study of human problem solving. Particularly important is a distinction between errors arising in the *representation* of problem information and those arising in the *processing* of those representations. One may fail to solve a problem because one misunderstands its conditions or because one applies the wrong strategy. Problem solvers are seen as working in a *problem space*, endeavouring to find a route from the initial state to the goal state via intermediate states generated by the permissible operators of the task environment.

The Gestalt concepts are embodied within this new language. The importance of insight and 'productive reformulations' can be related directly to the idea of problem representation. Similarly, Newell and Simon's discussion of 'means-ends' analysis, and of the generation of sub-problems as a technique for solving problems, is anticipated in Duncker's (1945) famous discussion of the 'tumor problem'.

Problem solving is discussed in this book with reference to protocol analysis by BYRNE. The various reasoning tasks discussed in this book can also be viewed as specialized problem solving tasks (see Evans, 1982). In fact, the literatures on 'reasoning' and on 'problem solving' have developed separately with little cross-reference. This unhappy state of affairs is remedied to some extent by two of the chapters of the present volume. EVANS takes the concepts of selective attention and direction of thought, developed in the study of problem solving, and argues that they can explain many of the errors observed on a range of different kinds of reasoning tasks. JOHNSON-LAIRD, taking Bartlett's (1958) discussion of thinking as a 'skill' as his starting point, develops a representational model of deductive inference. Whereas EVANS emphasizes attentional limitations, JOHNSON-LAIRD discusses the importance of limitations in 'working memory' capacity. Errors in performance may result from failure to keep sufficient ideas in mind at the same time.

Language and thought

Among the classic issues not discussed so far is the problem of the relationship between language and thought. While many would reject the strong view that language determines thinking (see Whorf, 1956, and for a critique, Rosch, 1974), few would deny that it has an important influence. There is a strong Russian tradition, dating from Pavlov, in which language is seen as a means by which humans control or regulate their behaviour; whilst observable in young children as egocentric speech, in adults the process becomes internalized and vital to 'logical', problem-solving thought (cf. Vygotsky, 1962; Luria, 1959a and b; Sokolov, 1972). A behaviouristic tradition, dating from Watson (1920) also emphasizes the role of 'inner speech' in thought (see McGuigan, 1966). Finally, developmental psychologists such as Piaget and Bruner have emphasized the importance of the use of language to facilitate symbolic, representational thought (see, for example, Bruner, Olver and Greenfield, 1966).

The relationship between language and thought arises in several chapters of the present book. For example, it is clearly involved in the interpretation of verbal protocol data discussed by BYRNE. It is also involved in the discussion of verbal reasoning problems; for example, EVANS argues that linguistic presuppositions are one of the major factors determining the locus of attention in reasoning problems; NEWSTEAD AND GRIGGS stress the importance of understanding the linguistic nature of disjunctive sentences in their discussion of disjunctive thinking. At the semantic level, the importance of how the *meaning* of sentences, and the context in which they are presented, influences reasoning is discussed in several chapters, especially that by GRIGGS.

Reasoning

Reasoning occurs whenever we draw inferences, or 'go beyond the information given'. In its broadest sense, 'reasoning' can be seen as fundamental to virtually all cognitive acts from social judgments (cf. Nisbett and Ross, 1980) to language comprehension (cf. Johnson-Laird and Wason, 1977, Part V; JOHNSON-LAIRD, this volume). Suppose, for example, that you go into a bank – not your own branch – to cash a cheque. You do not strictly *know* that the woman behind the counter is a bank clerk – you *infer* it from the fact that she is sitting there and facing you with an appropriate expression. When she asks you to wait and moves out of sight, you *infer* that she is checking out your credit in some way. You *predict* that the cheque will be satisfactory and *infer* that it was when she returns and gives you the money.

The inferences described above are *pragmatic* in that they are based on knowledge of the context and are probabilistic in nature. You would be fairly sure but not certain that your inferences were correct. Whether the inferences are *logical* or not is debatable. One could argue that they are logical since they follow with certainty from some plausible assumptions. The uncertainty of the conclusion would then reflect the possible falsity of the premises. Alternatively one could argue for a broad definition of 'logic' which can deal with probabilistic truth values.

While psychologists are becoming increasingly interested in pragmatic inferences (e.g. Harris and Monaco, 1978; Fillenbaum, 1978), most research on reasoning has had a rather different focus. The prime concern seems to have been a search for evidence that people 'possess' rational rule systems to allow them to solve problems involving logical or statistical principles in a context-free manner. In the eyes of some, this search has conspicuously failed, and the evidence for non-rational biases and context-dependent processes is overwhelming (e.g. Nisbett and Ross, 1980; Evans, 1982). In the deductive reasoning field, a strong rationalist tradition has nevertheless been maintained (see, for example, Revlin and Mayer, 1978). This is less true in the area of decision making, though there has been a rationalist reaction to authors in both fields whose experiments appear to provide 'bleak implications for human rationality' (cf. Cohen, 1981). The issue of rationality arises in several chapters, especially those by JOHNSON-LAIRD and by WASON with reference to deductive reasoning and that of POLLARD AND EVANS with reference to statistical reasoning.

Reasoning paradigms are defined by their formal structure, or the normative, prescriptive system by which they can be solved. Thus *deductive reasoning* research focuses on problems which can be solved by application of formal logic. Subjects are presented with the premises of an argument and asked to generate, or more commonly evaluate a conclusion. The question is whether or not the conclusion is logically necessary on the basis of information given. Traditional formal logic may be regarded as an inadequate criterion of the 'correctness' of an inference because its logical relations do not correspond accurately to linguistic conventions (e.g. Wason and Johnson-Laird, 1972; Braine, 1978) or because of its precise rather than fuzzy concepts of truth and falsity (see NEWSTEAD AND GRIGGS, this volume). Nevertheless, research has focused primarily upon the explanation of why logical 'errors' occur, with a debate between 'rationalistic' explanations which emphasize misinterpretation of the premises rather than illogical reasons, and non-rational explanations which emphasize biases (cf. Evans, 1982).

Philosophers distinguish *inductive inferences* from deductive ones, in that the former involve the induction of general rules from particular observations, as opposed to deducing particular consequences of general rules. Consequently, certain 'rule discovery' tasks such as Wason's '2 4 6' problem (discussed by EVANS, this volume) are often referred to as inductive reasoning experiments. In fact, neither philosophically nor psychologically are deductive and inductive inferences that clearly distinct. As Popper (1959) has argued, scientific theories of general laws are actually tested in a *deductive* manner: one attempts to deduce predictions with observable consequences, whose lack of observation could *falsify* the theory. Science can be seen as involving alternate processes of induction and deduction. Observations lead to hypotheses or theories which in turn lead to predictions about future observations, and so on.

Three reasoning problems invented by Peter Wason capture this mixture of inductive (hypothesis formation) and deductive (hypothesis testing) reasoning. One, the '2 4 6' problem, has already been mentioned. The most famous is the 'selection task' or 'four-card' problem (first reported by Wason, 1966). Subjects are given a rule specifying a relationship between symbols on either side of the cards which *may or may not be true*. Subjects must decide which cards to turn over in order to find out whether it is true or false (the problem is fully described in several chapters of this book). The problem is not simply one of deductive reasoning since the subject must consider hypothetical circumstances: 'suppose that the rule were true, what would have to be on the back of each card?; suppose that a given symbol was on the back of a particular card, could this show me whether or not the rule was true?', etc.

Research on the selection task, as I have said elsewhere (Evans, 1982) has been one of the most psychologically interesting and productive in the whole field of reasoning. Two chapters of the present volume take studies of this problem as their main focus. WASON discusses it with reference to the issue of rationality. GRIGGS focuses on the question of whether realistic material facilitates logical reasoning, which brings us on to another issue in the psychology of reasoning: how does the meaning of the problem content affect reasoning, when the formal structure of the task is held constant?

There are two reasons why it is important to understand precisely how reasoning depends upon content. The first relates to the ecological validity of the experiments – what they tell us about real-life reasoning. When early experiments (Wason and Shapiro, 1971; Johnson-Laird, Legrenzi and Legrenzi, 1972) indicated facilitation by the use of thematic rather than abstract content in the selection task, a particular reaction was made by many psychologists. The apparently irrational, illogical view of people conveyed by the earlier experiments was seen to be unrepresentative of real-life reasoning. The artificial nature of the materials, it was argued, prevented subjects from showing their true capabilities. In fact, recent research, discussed in detail by GRIGGS, has suggested that the facilitation effect may be specific to the type of thematic material used and its relation to the subject's previous experience (see also Pollard, 1982). The question of what exactly leads to facilitation in the selection task and whether or not it does provide evidence for rationality are points discussed by both GRIGGS and WASON in their chapters. GRIGGS also discusses Wason's most recent invention – THOG. This also requires subjects to generate and test hypotheses but with reference to the logic of exclusive disjunction.

Quite apart from the concern with ecological validity, it is arguable that understanding the precise way in which content affects reasoning is one of the most important theoretical problems in the field. This is particularly apparent if one accepts the argument that performance is *not* governed by the possession of 'logical competence' in the sense of a general purpose rule system (cf. Evans, 1982; JOHNSON-LAIRD, this volume). Certainly, content effects need not have a facilitatory nature, as research on other reasoning paradigms has shown. For example, contextual cues can induce logically fallacious but pragmatically reasonable inferences from conditional statements (Fillenbaum, 1978). Research with classical syllogisms has also provided evidence that subjects' evaluations of logical arguments may be biased by their prior beliefs in the truth of the conclusions (see Revlin and Leirer, 1978; Evans, 1982).

A different type of reasoning which has been studied by psychologists is *statistical inference*. Psychologists themselves make statistical inferences when they use statistical tests to evaluate experimental results. They make inferences about populations on the basis of the evidence of samples. Hypotheses are tested not in a logical, true or false, manner, but in a statistical, probabilistic manner. The psychologist asks how likely are my data to have occurred if only chance variation were responsible? Such inferences form the basis for decisions: if the chance hypothesis is sufficiently unlikely it is rejected, and a decision is made to accept that an experimental effect was present. Unlike logical decisions, statistical decisions are subject to error. Ideally, this is a known error rate such as a significance level.

Studies of intuitive statistical inference require subjects to estimate probabilities, judge 'confidence' etc., without the aid of formal procedures and statistical tables, etc. Research suggests that people have inaccurate intuitions which may lead them to error even when they are formally trained (cf. Tversky and Kahneman, 1971). It is important to understand statistical inference also because many real-life decisions, and social judgments, are based on inductive inferences from samples of evidence to populations (cf. Nisbett and Ross, 1980). Finally, it is of interest to see whether or not the kinds of factor which influence deductive reasoning also underlie statistical inferences.

The field of statistical inference was at one time primarily concerned to assess man's competence as an intuitive statistician (cf. Peterson and Beach, 1967), just as so much work on deductive reasoning has assessed man as an intuitive logician. The shifting of the field away from the assessment of competence towards the understanding of performance is due in large measure to the publications of Kahneman and Tversky. Their original papers argued that people use *heuristics* which, while appropriate in some contexts, lead to systematic errors in others (e.g. Kahneman and Tversky, 1972; Tversky and Kahneman, 1973). More recently they have recognized also the extent to which performance is context and content specific (e.g. Kahneman and Tversky, 1982). The chapter by POLLARD AND EVANS focuses on research stimulated by investigation of one of their proposed heuristics: *representativeness.* POLLARD AND EVANS are not primarily concerned to assess the correctness of the original theory, but rather to ask what psychological information about the nature of human inference has been gained from the experiments conducted.

Form of the book

It will be clear from the preceding pages that the chapters of this book deal with a wide range of issues and a number of different experimental tasks or paradigms. The form of chapters is not regimented. Some focus on a particular issue in relation to a number of paradigms, others take as their focus research on a particular kind of problem and discuss the various issues arising. For this reason, it was decided not to divide the book into sections. If divided by issues, where would a single paradigm, multi-issue chapter go (and vice versa)? Efforts have been made, however, to provide continuity by cross-referencing between chapters whenever closely related material is discussed. Finally, the order in which chapters are presented is fairly arbitrary. No particular form of progression influenced the editor's choice from among the 8! possibilities available.

References

Bartlett, F. (1958), *Thinking: An Experimental and Social Study*, London, Allen & Unwin.

Braine, M. D. S. (1978), 'On the relation between the natural logic of reasoning and standard logic', *Psychological Review*, *85*, pp. 1–21.

Bruner, J. S., Goodnow, J. J. and Austin, G. A. (1956), *A Study of Thinking*, New York, Wiley.

Bruner, J. S., Olver, R. R. and Greenfield, P. M. (eds) (1966), *Studies in Cognitive Growth*, New York, Wiley.

Burke, R. J., Maier, N. R. F. and Hoffman, L. R. (1965), 'Functions of hints in problem solving', *American Journal of Psychology*, *79*, pp. 389–99.

Cohen, L. J. (1981), 'Can human irrationality be experimentally demonstrated?' *The Behavioral and Brain Sciences*, *4*, 317–70.

Duncker, K. (1945), 'On problem solving', *Psychological Monographs*, *58*, whole no. 270.

Ericsson, K. A. and Simon, H. A. (1980), 'Verbal reports as data', *Psychological Review*, *87*, pp. 215–51.

Evans, J. St. B. T. (1982), *The Psychology of Deductive Reasoning*, London, Routledge & Kegan Paul.

Fillenbaum, S. (1978), 'How to do some things with IF', in J. W. Cotton and R. L. Klatzky (eds), *Semantic factors in cognition*, New York, Wiley.

Galton, F. (1879), 'Psychometric experiments', *Brain*, *2*, pp. 148–62.

Guilford, J. P. (1950), 'Creativity', *American Psychologist*, *5*, pp. 444–54.

Harris, R. J. and Monaco, G. E. (1978), 'Psychology of pragmatic implication: information processing between the lines', *Journal of Experimental Psychology: General, 107*, pp. 1–22.

Humphrey, C. (1951), *Thinking: an introduction to its experimental psychology*, London, Methuen.

Johnson-Laird, P. N., Legrenzi, P. and Legrenzi, M. S. (1972), 'Reasoning and a sense of reality', *British Journal of Psychology, 64*, pp. 395–400.

Johnson-Laird, P. N. and Wason, P. C. (1977) (eds), *Thinking: Readings in Cognitive Science*, Cambridge, Cambridge University Press.

Kahneman, D. and Tversky, A. (1972), 'Subjective probability: A judgment of representativeness', *Cognitive Psychology, 3*, pp. 430–54.

Kahneman, D. and Tversky, A. (1982), 'On the study of statistical intuitions', *Cognition, 11*, pp. 123–42.

Kearsley, G. P. (1975), 'Problem solving set and functional fixedness: a contextual dependency hypothesis', *Canadian Psychological Review, 16*, pp. 261–8.

Kosslyn, S. M. (1981), *Image and Mind*, Cambridge, Mass., Harvard University Press.

Kubie, L. S. (1958), *Neurotic Distortions of the Creative Process*, Kansas City, Laurence.

Luchins, A. S. (1942), 'Mechanisation in problem solving', *Psychological Monographs, 54*, no. 248, pp. 1–45.

Luchins, A. S. and Luchins, E. H. (1950), 'New experimental attempts at preventing mechanisation in problem solving', *Journal of General Psychology, 42*, pp. 279–97.

Luria, A. R. (1959a), 'The directive function of speech I', *Word, 15*, pp. 341–52.

Luria, A. R. (1959b), 'The directive function of speech II', *Word, 15*, pp. 453–64.

Maier, N. R. F. (1931), 'Reasoning in humans II: The solution of a problem and its appearance in consciousness', *Journal of Comparative Psychology, 12*, pp. 181–94.

Maier, N. R. F. and Burke, R. J. (1967), 'Influence of the timing of hints on their effectiveness in problem solving', *Psychological Reports, 20*, pp. 3–8.

Mandler, J. M. and Mandler, G. (1964), *Thinking: From Association to Gestalt*, New York, Wiley.

McGuigan, F. J. (ed.) (1966), *Thinking: Studies of Covert Language Processes*, New York, Appleton-Century-Crofts.

Neisser, U. (1963), 'The multiplicity of thought', *British Journal of Psychology, 54*, pp. 1–14.

Newell, A. and Simon, H. A. (1972), *Human Problem Solving*, Englewood Cliffs, New Jersey, Prentice-Hall.

Nisbett, R. E. and Ross, L. (1980), *Human Inference: Strategies and Shortcomings of Social Judgment*, Englewood Cliffs, New Jersey, Prentice-Hall.

Nisbett, R. E. and Wilson, T. D. (1977), 'Telling more than we can know: verbal reports on mental processes', *Psychological Review*, *84*, pp. 231–59.

Paivio, A. (1971), *Imagery and Verbal Processes*, New York, Holt, Rinehart & Winston.

Paivio, A. (1975), 'Imagery and synchronic thinking', *Canadian Psychological Review*, *16*, pp. 147–63.

Peterson, C. R. and Beach, L. R. (1967), 'Man as an intuitive statistician', *Psychological Bulletin*, *68*, pp. 29–46.

Poincaré, H. (1924), 'Mathematical creation', *The Foundations of Science*, (trans. G. B. Halstead), New York, Science Press.

Pollard, P. (1982), 'Human Reasoning: Some possible effects of availability', *Cognition*, *12*, pp. 65–96.

Popper, K. (1959), *The Logic of Scientific Discovery*, London, Hutchinson.

Pylyshyn, Z. W. (1973), 'What the mind's eye tells the mind's brain: a critique of mental imagery', *Psychological Bulletin*, *80*, pp. 1–24.

Pylyshyn, Z. W. (1981), 'The imagery debate: Analogue media vs tacit knowledge', *Psychological Review*, *86*, pp. 383–94.

Reeves, J. W. (1965), *Thinking about Thinking*, London, Methuen.

Revlin, R. and Leirer, V. O. (1978), 'The effect of personal biases on syllogistic reasoning: rational decisions from personalized representations', in R. Revlin and R. E. Mayer (eds), *Human Reasoning*, New York, Wiley.

Revlin, R. and Mayer, R. E. (eds) (1978), *Human Reasoning*, New York, Wiley.

Rosch, E. (1974), 'Linguistic relativity', in A. Silverstein (ed.) *Human Communication: Theoretical Perspectives*, Hillsdale, New Jersey, Erlbaum.

Ryle, G. (1949), *The Concept of Mind*, London, Hutchinson.

Simon, H. A. (1979), 'Information processing models of cognition', *Annual Review of Psychology*, *30*, pp. 363–96.

Sokolov, A. N. (1972), *Inner Speech and Thought*, New York, Plenum.

Springer, S. P. and Deutsch, G. (1981), *Left Brain, Right Brain*, San Francisco, Freeman.

Tversky, A. and Kahneman, D. (1971), 'The belief in the law of small numbers', *Psychological Bulletin*, *76*, pp. 105–10.

Tversky, A. and Kahneman, D. (1973), 'Availability: a heuristic for judging frequency and probability', *Cognitive Psychology*, *5*, pp. 207–32.

Vygotsky, L. S. (1962), *Thought and Language*, Cambridge, Mass., MIT Press.

Wason, P. C. (1966), 'Reasoning', in B. M. Foss (ed.), *New Horizons in Psychology I*, Harmondsworth, Penguin.

Wason, P. C. and Johnson-Laird, P. N. (1970), 'A conflict between selecting and evaluating information in an inferential task', *British Journal of Psychology*, *61*, pp. 509–15.

Wason, P. C. and Johnson-Laird, P. N. (1972), *Psychology of Reasoning: Structure and Content*, London, Batsford.

Wason, P. C. and Shapiro, D. (1971), 'Natural and contrived experience in a reasoning problem', *Quarterly Journal of Experimental Psychology*, *23*, pp. 63–71.

Watson, J. B. (1920), *Behaviorism*, New York, Norton.
Wertheimer, M. (1945), *Productive Thinking*, New York, Harper & Row.
Whorf, B. J. (1956), *Language, Thought and Reality*, Cambridge, Mass.,
MIT Press.

1 The role of problem content in the selection task and in the THOG problem

Richard A. Griggs

This chapter will be concerned with the role of problem content in two tasks developed by Peter Wason. One of these, the selection task (or four-card problem), is also the topic of WASON's chapter in this volume. The second one, the THOG problem, is a more recent addition to the deductive reasoning research area and is not as well known as the selection task. In fact, the THOG problem was developed in part because of the prominence of the selection task (Wason, 1977a; 1981).

The selection task involves the logic of a conditional rule for its solution while the THOG problem involves the logic of exclusive disjunction. However, these tasks are not simply propositional logic problems. In addition to an understanding of these propositional logic rules, both tasks require the formulation and testing of hypotheses. Exactly how each task does this will become clear as they are introduced in more detail later.

Performance on the selection task, and to a lesser extent on the THOG problem because of its recent development, has figured prominently in arguments concerning human rationality (e.g. Cohen, 1981; and see WASON, this volume) and Piaget's theory of formal operations (e.g. Wason, 1977b). The factor most crucial to these arguments is the effect of problem content; specifically, the claim of facilitation in performance for thematic, realistic content. This chapter will consider this claim by first examining closely the research concerning this facilitation for the selection task. The main questions to be addressed are (1) Is there really a thematic facilitation effect? and (2) If so, what is its origin and nature? Following the selection task discussion, the recent research on the role of content in the THOG problem will be reviewed. Because published work on the THOG problem is so scarce at present, other questions concerning performance on that problem will also be discussed.

The question of thematic facilitation has also been examined in the other deductive reasoning paradigms (e.g. categorical syllogism and propositional reasoning tasks). This research has been discussed very clearly and thoroughly by Evans (1982), and thus there is no need to review it again here.

Wason's selection task

Wason's selection task involves an implication rule usually in the 'If P then Q' form and an array of four cards representing P, P̄ (not P), Q, and Q̄ (not Q). Symbolical material (e.g. letters of the alphabet and numbers) and affirmative antecedent and consequent are employed in the *basic form* of the task. For example, the subject might be presented with four cards showing E, K, 4, and 7, and the rule, 'If there is an E on one side of a card, then there is a 4 on the other side.' The subject would be instructed that each card has a letter on one side and a number on the other side and that the task is to select just those cards that are necessary to turn over in order to decide whether the rule is true or false.

The problem has been the subject of much research since its initial description in the literature (Wason, 1966; 1968), because it is extremely difficult for even highly intelligent subjects. Usually less than 10 per cent of the subjects make the correct selection (Manktelow and Evans, 1979). In an informal experiment reported by Dawes (1975) only one of five subjects with doctorates in mathematical psychology solved the task correctly! The correct answer is a selection of the P and the Q̄ cards (E and 7 in the example) since only a combination of P on one side and Q̄ on the other side can falsify the implication rule. In general, subjects make two prevalent errors: (1) although many choose the P-card, they fail to select the Q̄-card, and (2) frequently select the Q-card instead. Wason and Johnson-Laird (1972) provide a review of the early literature on this task while Evans (1982) covers this and some of the more recent literature. (See WASON's chapter in this volume for an informative, historical account of the task.)

Thematic-materials effects in the early 1970s

Beginning with Wason and Shapiro (1971/Experiment 2), several studies were published during the early 1970s claiming to demonstrate a *thematic-materials effect* – an improvement in performance brought about by the use of 'thematic' materials. Exactly what is meant by 'thematic' material is defined in each study. The words *thematic* (e.g. Wason and Shapiro, 1971), *realistic* (e.g. Johnson-Laird, Legrenzi and Sonino Legrenzi, 1972), and *concrete* (e.g. Gilhooly and Falconer, 1974) have all been used to describe such material. In general, 'thematic' material has been defined to be anything except the arbitrarily related symbols and forms (e.g. letters of the alphabet, numbers, geometric patterns, etc.) that have been used in the basic form of the task. The term *thematic* will be employed in this chapter since it has evolved to be the most frequently used term to describe this effect. Only four of the studies examining the thematic-materials effect (Wason and Shapiro, 1971; Johnson-Laird *et al.*, 1972; Bracewell and Hidi, 1974; and Van Duyne, 1974) reported substantial improvement (50 per cent or greater correct selection performance); thus, these will be described first.

Wason and Shapiro (1971/Experiment 2) used rules that were presented as claims by the experimenter about four journeys she had made on four different days of the week. The rules involved two cities (Manchester and Leeds) and two modes of transportation (train and car), such as 'Every time I go to Manchester, I travel by car.' All four possible permuted variants of the two cities and the two modes of transportation were used in rules in a between-subjects design. It should be noted that before the task was presented, subjects were given a familiarization deck of 16 cards which included the four actual selection-task cards (Manchester, Leeds, car and train). Subjects were instructed to state which cards would need to be turned over to determine the truth or falsity of the experimenter's claim. Ten of 16 subjects (62·5 per cent) made the correct selection compared to two of 16 (12·5 per cent) in an abstract condition using the basic version of the task with letters and numbers.

Johnson-Laird *et al.* (1972) employed a different thematic scenario. They asked each subject to 'imagine that he was a post-office worker sorting letters' and to 'select those envelopes that you definitely need to turn over to find out whether or not they violate the rule' (p. 397). The two thematic rules used were 'If a letter is sealed, then it has a 50 lire stamp on it' and 'A letter is sealed only if it has a 5d. stamp on it.' Invariably the methodology of this experiment has been described inaccurately in secondary sources (e.g. Wason and Johnson-Laird, 1972). Griggs and Cox (1982) should be consulted for a discussion of the methodological problems in the Johnson-Laird *et al.* study. Briefly, they stem from a blank fifth envelope present in all the experimental arrays but not usually mentioned in secondary descriptions of the study. Regardless, the performance they observed for thematic material is the highest observed in a *published* study, 39/48 (81 per cent) correct selections.

Results comparable to those of Wason and Shapiro (1971) were observed by Bracewell and Hidi (1974). Bracewell and Hidi used towns and modes of transport like Wason and Shapiro, except they examined the contributions of two factors, natural relationship v. arbitrary relationship of the terms and concrete (thematic) v. abstract terms. The concrete material/natural relationship rules (e.g. 'Every time I go to Ottawa, I travel by car') and the abstract/arbitrary relationship rules (e.g. 'Every time J is on one side, 2 is on the other side') are of main interest here. In the concrete/natural relationship problems they observed 9/12 (75 per cent) correct selections and only 1/12 (8·33 per cent) correct responses in the abstract/arbitrary relationship problems. However, as pointed out by Griggs and Cox (1982) and Manktelow (1979), a procedural difference in the Bracewell and Hidi study may have contributed partially to this effect. Bracewell and Hidi told their subjects that 'the conditional rule was not reversible.' The overall effect of this instruction seemed to be a *decrease* in inclusion of the Q-card in subjects' selections. The P and Q combination is always one of the most frequent selections for the basic version of the task. However, only 3/96 subjects in the Bracewell and Hidi study made this selection. In addition, when the order of the clauses in the implication rule was reversed (e.g. 'I travel by car every time I go to Ottawa'), the thematic materials effect completely disappeared (only 2/12 subjects correctly responded in the concrete material/natural relationship condition). Thus, it appears that the instruction about non-reversibility of the conditional rule may have interacted with content and other task and subject factors to bring about the good performance in the concrete material/natural relationship condition.

For further discussion of problems with the Bracewell and Hidi study, see Manktelow (1979).

Like Bracewell and Hidi (1974), Gilhooly and Falconer (1974) were interested in both the nature of the relationship between the terms and the nature of the terms in the selection task. They used the towns-and-modes-of-transport thematic material like Wason and Shapiro (1971) but observed a much weaker but significant effect (11/50 or 22 per cent correct selections in their concrete terms/ concrete relation condition). However, the procedures for familiarizing the subjects with the task materials differed between the Gilhooly and Falconer study and Wason and Shapiro's experiment. As indicated earlier, the familiarization deck in the Wason and Shapiro study included the four cards used in the actual selection task. Thus, subjects appear to have been exposed to the falsifying instance in each case. As Gilhooly and Falconer point out, although Wason (1968) found no effect of prior identification of a falsifying instance for an abstract form of the task and no effect was observed in the abstract condition of Wason and Shapiro (1971), exposure to the falsifying instance may have been a factor when thematic materials were involved. The relevant test card may more easily have evoked memories of the falsifying instance in the case of the more concrete material. Gilhooly and Falconer used a different familiarization technique so that this did not occur, and they observed a much weaker effect. It should be noted that Bracewell and Hidi (1974) used a familiarization deck that did not contain the problem cards and they observed substantial facilitation in their concrete material/ natural relationship condition. However, as explained above, interpretation of their data is hindered by possible effects of their instructions about the non-reversibility of the rule.

Van Duyne's (1974) thematic material consisted of student cards taken from some hypothetical register of students. On one side of a card was a student's academic subject and on the other side, his university. The four thematic rules used were 'Every student who studies physics is at Oxford,' 'If a student studies philosophy then he is at Cambridge,' 'A student doesn't study French, or he is at London,' and 'It isn't the case that a student studies psychology and isn't at Glasgow.' The four cards, respectively, for each of these rules were Physics, Spanish, Oxford, and Cambridge; Philosophy, Physics, Cambridge, and Oxford; French, Law, London, and Bristol; and Psychology, Chemistry, Glasgow, and Edinburgh. Subjects were instructed to 'select only those cards you definitely need to turn over in order to find out whether they violate the rule or not.' Only the first two rules showed significant improvement relative to abstract counterpart conditions. On the conditional rule 14/24 (58 per cent) were correct, and on the universal rule 12/24 (50 per cent).

Van Duyne (1976) should also be mentioned because of some results from an unpublished study described in this paper and by Wason (1977b). In this unpublished study, Van Duyne not only varied the abstract-thematic dimension but also the arbitrariness of the thematic rules. Van Duyne's thematic rules concerned postal matters. The arbitrary rule was 'If there is L. B. MILL on one side of the envelope, then there is PRINTED PAPER REDUCED RATE on the other side.' The non-arbitrary rule was 'If there is PRINTED PAPER REDUCED RATE on one side of the envelope, then it must be left open.' Van Duyne reports a high-level of performance (87 per cent and 98 per cent) in the two non-arbitrary, thematic conditions (white cards were used as stimulus materials in one non-arbitrary condition and real envelopes in the other) and a lower-level of correct selections (almost 50 per cent) in the arbitrary, thematic condition. The level of performance in the non-arbitrary conditions is even higher than that in the Johnson-Laird *et al.* study, except Van Duyne's study was never subsequently published and only this brief description of it is available.

One final study from this period should be noted. Lunzer (1975) mentions that Lunzer, Harrison, and Davey (1972) found an 'appreciable and highly significant' effect due to thematic material (i.e. a relationship between the color of a lorry and whether or not it was full of coal or empty). However, Lunzer must be referring to the Lunzer *et al.* data for a *reduced* presentation array ($Q, Q, \bar{Q}, \bar{Q}$ instead of the usual $P, \bar{P}, Q, \bar{Q}$), because there is clearly no effect of content for complete arrays in the Lunzer *et al.* experiments.

The elusive thematic-materials effect in the late 1970s and early 1980s

Manktelow and Evans (1979) was the first in a series of recent *failures* to replicate the earlier studies finding thematic-materials effects. Manktelow and Evans conducted five experiments including an *almost* exact replication of the Wason and Shapiro study. The first four experiments examined rules involving food and drink, such as 'If I eat haddock, then I drink gin.' No evidence for a thematic-materials effect was found in any of the four experiments (Yachanin and Tweney, 1982; and Reich and Ruth, 1982/Experiment 1, have also failed to find an effect for this type of thematic material). In Manktelow and Evans's fifth experiment, they also failed to replicate the Wason and Shapiro findings. The only methodological difference in the studies is that Manktelow and Evans showed the four days of the week for the journeys on four separate cards instead of on the four array cards as in the Wason and Shapiro study.

Except for one study (Pollard, 1981) in which a weak effect was observed, other recent attempted replications of the Wason and Shapiro study have also failed. Brown, Keats, Keats and Seggie (1980) and Griggs and Cox (1982) completely failed to find a facilitative effect for towns-and-transport thematic material. Similarly, Yachanin and Tweney (1982) using campus locations and modes of transport found no facilitation effect. Pollard (1981) found a small but significant effect (4/12 v. 0/12 correct selections in the thematic and abstract conditions, respectively). In addition, Pollard's experiment was not an exact replication. Pollard employed a very different response procedure in which 'subjects were asked to indicate their selections by entering all four values in the appropriate column of a form divided into two columns, the left-hand column headed "necessary to turn over" and the other headed "not necessary to turn over" ' (p. 25). Thus, subjects were forced to classify all four cards. In addition, unlike in Wason and Shapiro's study, the subjects were not allowed to see both sides of the cards in the familiarization deck.

Given the four recent complete failures to replicate and only Pollard's weak replication, the existence of a *reliable* thematic-materials effect for the Wason and Shapiro towns-and-transport material seems doubtful. There are four complete failures to replicate, two replications but with much weaker effects, and one replication with a substantial effect but a confounded methodology. (For an attempt to reconcile these variable findings, see Pollard, 1982.)

Recent studies have also failed to replicate the other two substantial thematic-materials effects observed in the early 1970s (Johnson-Laird *et al.*, 1972; Van Duyne, 1974). Griggs and Cox

(1982) completely failed to replicate Johnson-Laird *et al.*'s findings using American students as subjects and American and Mexican stamps and addresses in their materials. It should also be noted that Leahey (1977) failed to find good performance for Johnson-Laird *et al.*'s postal problem with American subjects and materials (Leahey, personal communication).

Yachanin and Tweney (1982) failed to replicate Van Duyne's (1974) findings for rules involving schools and major fields of study for hypothetical students. Yachanin and Tweney observed only 1/80 correct selections for such material for the normal 'If P then Q' rule form! Thus, it seems that recent studies have found little evidence for a thematic-materials effect for towns and transport material, schools and major fields of study material, food and drink material, and postal rule material.

Where did the effect go? A memory-cuing explanation

A clue to the answer to this question can be found in the results for some recent studies by Cox and Griggs (1982), D'Andrade (described in Rumelhart, 1979; 1980), Golding (1981), and Griggs and Cox (1982), and in a reconsideration of the source of the observed facilitation in the earlier studies. Firstly, the recent findings will be considered.

Although Griggs and Cox (1982) did not replicate the findings of Wason and Shapiro (1971) and Johnson-Laird *et al.* (1972), they did observe facilitation for another type of thematic content – an implication rule that involved the legal drinking age in Florida ('If a person is drinking beer, then the person must be over 19'). The subjects were told to imagine that they were police officers responsible for ensuring the regulation was followed. The four cards represented information about four people sitting at a table. They were labeled DRINKING BEER, DRINKING COKE, 16 YEARS OF AGE, and 22 YEARS OF AGE. The task was to select those cards (people) that definitely needed to be turned over to determine whether or not they were violating the rule. The correct selection for this problem was made by 74 per cent of the subjects, while not one subject did so for a basic-form abstract problem using letters and numbers.

Griggs and Cox interpreted these results in accordance with a memory-cuing explanation (see Manktelow and Evans, 1979). Griggs and Cox argued that performance on the selection task is significantly facilitated when the presentation environment of the task permits the subject to recall past experience with the content of the problem, the relationship (rule) expressed, and a counterexample to the rule. Griggs and Cox collected questionnaire data to show that their undergraduate subjects were familiar with the content, the relationship, and counterexamples for their drinking-age problem. However, their subject population was not familiar with a relationship between sealing an envelope and the amount of postage on the envelope as were Johnson-Laird *et al.*'s British subjects in their earlier study. In Great Britain until 1968 there was a postal regulation requiring more postage for sealed letters. Thus, differences in the American and British subjects' past experiences could explain both the facilitation observed by Johnson-Laird *et al.* and the failure to replicate by Griggs and Cox.

This memory-cuing explanation is supported by some recent findings by Golding (1981). She gave British subjects an updated version of Johnson-Laird *et al.*'s postal problem followed by a standard abstract problem. The postal problem used the now-defunct British postal regulation but with current postage values, i.e. 'If a letter is sealed, then it has a 12p stamp on it.' The four selection envelopes were sealed, unsealed, a 12p stamp attached, and a 10p stamp attached. The subject was asked to 'select just those letters you definitely need to turn over to find out whether or not they break the rule.' Golding found a significant difference between subjects under 45 and over 45 years of age on the postal problem, but no difference in performance between age groups on the abstract problem. The older group was correct 59 per cent (13/22) of the time on the postal problem while the younger group was correct only 9 per cent (2/22) of the time. Golding interpreted her results in terms of subjects' experiences. She argued that the over-45 group performed better because of their past experience with the old postal system: an argument for relevant past experience bringing about facilitation. Subjects responded to the updated version of the problem in a manner that would match their responses to the *analogous* content of their *specific* experience with the old postal regulation and postage system. Her younger subjects would not have had as much or any experience with the defunct regulation.

Van Duyne's (1974) results can also be explained in terms of the subjects' experience and the specific content and relationship presented in the task (Steve Newstead, personal communication). Remember that Van Duyne used students' universities and fields of study. A significant facilitation was only observed for two (x,⊃) of the four thematic rules he examined. The 'x' rule was 'Every student who studies physics is at Oxford,' and the four selection cards were Physics, Spanish, Oxford, and Cambridge. The '⊃' rule was 'If a student studies philosophy then he is at Cambridge,' and the cards were Philosophy, Physics, Cambridge, and Oxford. Thus, the correct selection in each case (Physics and Cambridge for the 'x' rule and Philosophy and Oxford for the '⊃' rule) would be very familiar to the British subjects since Cambridge has a reputation for excellence in physics and Oxford for philosophy. Thus, the facilitation Van Duyne observed for these two rules could have been due to memory cuing of prominent counterexamples to the rules. This explanation is supported by the study of Pollard and Evans (1981) who have shown that performance is facilitated when the rule used is believed to be usually false as opposed to usually true. Their associational explanation (developed by Pollard, 1982) is equivalent to an account in terms of the availability of the counterexample. Hence, Yachanin and Tweney's (1982) failure to replicate Van Duyne's findings is perfectly understandable. Unlike Van Duyne, Yachanin and Tweney did not employ rules with the correct selections representing well-known counterexamples to the rules.

Roy D'Andrade (described in Rumelhart, 1979, 1980) has provided empirical evidence for facilitation as a result of memory cuing of *general* experience. D'Andrade has devised a thematic version of the selection task in which subjects are told to imagine that they are managers in a Sears store and are responsible for checking sales receipts to determine whether the rule 'If a purchase exceeds $30, then the receipt must be approved by the department manager' was followed. Four sales receipts were presented – one for a $15 purchase, one for a $45 purchase, one signed, and one unsigned. D'Andrade found nearly 70 per cent correct performance on this version of the task. Mandler (1980) reports that she has informally replicated D'Andrade's results several times with college students in her classes. In addition, Griggs and Cox (in press) observed good performance (85 per cent correct) for a version of D'Andrade's Sears problem.

It is highly unlikely that D'Andrade's, Mandler's, and Griggs and Cox's subjects had specific experience as Sears managers, but it is highly probable that they had experience with analogous materials and relationships; for example, store managers authorizing checks, etc. Hence, the data of Golding and D'Andrade seem to require a memory-cuing plus reasoning-by-analogy explanation. Thus, subjects do not have to have experience with the specific content of the task. What seems to be essential is that the problem cue the subjects to recall their experience with the specific situation *or* analogous situations.

The original Johnson-Laird *et al.* postal study provides more evidence for this reasoning-by-analogy process. In one thematic condition of that experiment, British subjects were given a version of the selection task using Italian stamps and the British postal rule, 'If a letter is sealed, then it has a 50 lire stamp on it.' This rule is analogous to the British one used in the other thematic condition, 'A letter is sealed only if it has a 5d. stamp on it.' The values of the stamps in each problem were directly analogous, 4d. and 5d. and 40 and 50 lire, and 5d. and 50 lire were the Q-instances in the two problems. In agreement with the reasoning-by-analogy hypothesis, no difference between these two conditions was observed. Similarly, in Van Duyne's unpublished study using postal rules, fairly good performance (almost 50 per cent correct) was even observed for the *arbitrary* postal rule. Reasoning by analogy could be the source of this result.

In further support of the memory-cuing/reasoning-by-analogy hypothesis, Cox and Griggs (1982) have found facilitation for a version of the selection task identical to their drinking-age problem except the problem involved two colors of apparel (blue and green) that people were wearing rather than people drinking beer or drinking coke. The text of the problem was as follows:

> On this task imagine you are a police officer on duty. It is your job to ensure that people conform to certain rules. The cards above have information about four people sitting at a table. On one side of a card is a person's age and on the other side of the card is the color of apparel the person is wearing. Here is a rule: IF A PERSON IS WEARING BLUE, THEN THE PERSON MUST BE OVER 19. Select those cards that you definitely need to turn over to determine whether or not the people are violating the rule.

The four cards were WEARING BLUE, WEARING GREEN, 16 YEARS OF AGE, and 22 YEARS OF AGE. Thus, this version is clearly analogous to the drinking-age problem.

When presented first, 25 per cent of the subjects (12/48) made the correct selection for this apparel-color problem. This problem is not directly related to the subjects' experience since in all likelihood they would never have been in a situation constraining the relationship of age and apparel color. However, subjects would have been in many natural situations in which the joint occurrence of their age and some other factor had to be considered. For example, the legal age for drinking as in the drinking-age problem, the legal age for driving, the legal age for voting, and so on. Thus, it is certainly plausible that the memory-cuing/reasoning-by-analogy explanation is applicable here. In further support of this explanation, when the apparel-color problem appeared second in the series of problems and followed the drinking-age problem, 18/24 (75 per cent) of the subjects made the correct selection.

Cox and Griggs also observed facilitation for a *contrapositive* version of the drinking-age rule, i.e., 'If a person is under 19 years of age, then the person must be drinking coke.' This rule is certainly less familiar to college undergraduates than the drinking-age rule, but the counterexample to this contrapositive is the same as to the drinking-age rule – a person under 19 drinking beer. Of 24 subjects, 13 (54 per cent) made the correct selection for this contrapositive problem when it was presented first.

The contrapositive rule keeps the logical relations among the values presented on the selection cards and the counterexample instance the same as in the drinking-age problem while manipulating the familiarity of the rule. Cox and Griggs also examined the *converse* of the drinking-age rule (i.e. 'If a person is over 19, then the person must be drinking beer'). This rule employs the same terms as the drinking-age rule, but the counterexample is just the opposite – a person *over* 19 drinking coke. Facilitation was even observed for this rule; 50 per cent of the subjects made the correct selection when this problem was presented first. Thus, it appears that manipulating the violating case or the wording of the rule does *not* eliminate facilitation for a rule like the drinking-age rule with which subjects are very familiar. The amount of facilitation for the variations of the well-known rule is less, but performance is still significantly better than for the basic-form abstract version of the task.

It should be made clear that the memory-cuing/reasoning-by-analogy hypothesis does *not* propose that 'logical' reasoning is facilitated. It only proposes that cued relevant experience leads the subject to make the correct selection. In fact, all the available experimental evidence indicates that logical reasoning is not facilitated. A good criterion for the presence of logical reasoning is positive transfer to the basic-form abstract version of the problem following a thematic version. There is absolutely no evidence for such transfer (see Cox and Griggs, 1982; Griggs and Cox, 1982; Johnson-Laird *et al.*, 1972; and Lunzer *et al.*, 1972). As pointed out earlier, positive transfer can result from memory cuing if the problems are related in a way that permits a subject to recall a solution to one problem and reason by analogy to solve the other problem (e.g. the two thematic postal problems in Johnson-Laird *et al.*, 1972; or the drinking-age and colored-apparel problems in Cox and Griggs, 1982).

The memory-cuing/reasoning-by-analogy hypothesis proposes that the problem content cues familiar information in long-term memory which is used to make the correct selection or if not directly applicable, is used to derive the answer by a reasoning-by-analogy process. Rumelhart (1980) makes a similar proposal but in terms of *schemata*. He argues that schemata play a major role in our reasoning processes and that 'most of our reasoning ability is tied to particular schemata related to particular bodies of knowledge' (p. 55). Rumelhart uses the facilitation for D'Andrade's Sears problem to support his argument. He states, 'Once we can "understand" the situation by encoding it in terms of a relatively rich set of schemata, the conceptual constraints of the schemata can be brought into play and the problem readily solved. It is as if the schema already contains all of the reasoning mechanisms ordinarily required in the use of the schemata. Thus, understanding the problem and solving it is nearly the same thing' (p. 57).

Mandler (1980) also proposes that much of our thinking is controlled by schemata and that schemata are constructed around specific content areas and can be 'flexibly applied to varying content within a given area' (p. 27). Like Rumelhart (1980), Mandler also cites facilitation for D'Andrade's Sears problem as evidence that our reasoning knowledge is *context-dependent*. She argues that performance on the selection task turns out to be a result only of 'knowledge of what matters in a familiar setting' (p. 32). Thus

Mandler, like Rumelhart, feels that our knowledge of reasoning is embedded in 'task-specific procedures rather than in general rules of inference' (p. 32).

The memory-cuing/reasoning-by-analogy and the schema-cuing explanations could be conceived of as processing strategies that would bypass a 'logical' reasoning mechanism (if one exists). In the next section such 'short circuiting' will be considered.

Memory cuing as cognitive short circuiting

Yachanin and Tweney (1982) have proposed that formal reasoning, such as is required in the basic-form abstract version of the selection task, may result in extra cognitive demands and thus motivate the subject to search for a 'cognitive short-circuiting' strategy or heuristic to reduce the cognitive load. The use of such a strategy would thus allow the subject to respond consistently while expending a minimum of cognitive effort. Yachanin and Tweney cite Doherty, Mynatt, Tweney and Schiavo (1979) as evidence that subjects find it easier to confirm one hypothesis than to test several alternative hypotheses, even when the relative effort is equated. Thus, Yachanin and Tweney argue that in evaluating evidence for the selection task, it may be more difficult to test two hypotheses, that the rule might be either true or false, instead of just the one that the rule is true. This would lead to verification bias (see Wason, 1968). Matching bias (Evans and Lynch, 1973) could also be conceived of as a short-circuiting strategy since it bypasses even testing one hypothesis but results in systematic responses that require only a minimum of cognitive effort (however, see EVANS, this volume, for an alternative interpretation of matching bias).

Yachanin and Tweney go on to propose that the facilitation observed by Griggs and Cox (1982) for the drinking-age problem is also the result of 'short-circuiting'. The rule content cues relevant memories from the subjects' experiences. A similar argument would also apply to D'Andrade's results, Johnson-Laird *et al.*'s (1972) findings, and Van Duyne's (1974; and unpublished, referred to by Van Duyne, 1976) results. In brief, in all the cases where a substantial facilitative effect has been observed, cognitive short circuiting could plausibly be proposed as an explanation. Admittedly, some sort of reasoning process must be postulated to explain some of the findings (e.g. Johnson-Laird *et al.*, 1972; Golding, 1981), but this reasoning would not be the formal reasoning needed to solve the basic-form abstract version of the selection task. As argued previously, strong support for this is the fact that transfer from any of the thematic versions of the task to the basic form version of the task has never been observed.

This type of criticism does not originate with Yachanin and Tweney (1982). Several people (e.g. Manktelow and Evans, 1979; Pollard, 1979; Manktelow, 1979) have criticized the Johnson-Laird *et al.* study for similar reasons. The criticism essentially amounts to the question: When is a reasoning task a reasoning task and not a memory task?

In addition, all of the studies in which substantial facilitation has been reliably observed seemed to have *changed* the original nature of the selection task. Michael Doherty (personal communication) has argued that the Griggs and Cox drinking-age problem, D'Andrade's Sears problem, and the Johnson-Laird *et al.*, postal problem all differ from the basic-form version of the task. Doherty proposes that in these versions of the task, subjects reason *from* a rule rather than as in the original task, *about* a rule. In the basic form of the task, Wason asked subjects to select only the cards necessary to determine whether the rule was true or false. Griggs and Cox, D'Andrade, and Johnson-Laird *et al.* have changed the nature of the task by making the rule a procedural rule, one to be followed, not one which is characterizable as true or false. Thus, according to Doherty, subjects are *not* seeking to assess the truth status of a putatively universal generalization, but rather are seeking only to determine if the four instances obey some procedural rule. Subjects are checking the cards to determine whether or not they conform to a hypothesis rather than as in the original task, to assess the truth status of a hypothesis. These certainly seem to be different psychological operations. Yachanin and Tweney (1982) level the same type of criticism against Griggs and Cox (1982) and Johnson-Laird *et al.* (1972).

This criticism that the selection task has been subtly changed in the studies reporting a substantial amount of facilitation seems appropriate. Contributing to this, all of these studies direct the subject toward falsification by using instructions which ask the subject to select the cases necessary to determine whether or not the rule is *violated* (Johnson-Laird *et al.*, 1972; Van Duyne, 1974;

Cox and Griggs, 1982; Griggs and Cox, in press; 1982) or similarly, those necessary to find out whether or not they *break* the rule (Golding, 1981) or those necessary to make sure the rule *was followed* (D'Andrade's study as described in Rumelhart, 1979, 1980). It is clear, however, that such an instruction is *not* a sufficient condition for facilitation (see, e.g. Bracewell, 1974; Cox and Griggs, 1982; Golding, 1981; Griggs and Cox, 1982; Johnson-Laird *et al.*, 1972). This type of instruction, though, may be a necessary condition for substantial facilitation.

Thus, as Manktelow and Evans (1979) propose, there does not appear to be any clear evidence for a *singular* thematic-materials facilitation effect. It would seem that in the cases where *substantial* facilitation has been observed, this facilitation could have resulted from the cuing of familiar relevant information in long-term memory, instructions that conceivably biased subjects' strategies, and a problem context that may have changed the nature of the original selection task. The precise role of each of these factors and how they may interact to produce facilitation remain as problems for further research. In the next section, recent research examining performance on Wason's latest problem, the THOG problem, will be considered to see if a comparable state of affairs is developing for that task.

The THOG problem

Although subjects do not seem to have great difficulty in drawing disjunctive inferences (see NEWSTEAD AND GRIGGS, this volume), the THOG problem, which involves exclusive disjunction, causes considerable difficulty (Wason, 1977a; 1978; Wason and Brooks, 1979). The standard version of the problem, as given by Wason and Brooks (1979, p. 80), is as follows, and the designs used in the problem are given in Figure 1.1.

In front of you are four designs: Blue Diamond, Red Diamond, Blue Circle, and Red Circle. You are to assume that I have written down one of the colours (blue or red) and one of the shapes (diamond or circle). Now read the following rule carefully:
If, and only if, any of the designs includes either the colour I

have written down or the shape I have written down, but not both, then it is called a THOG.

I will tell you that the Blue Diamond is a THOG.

Each of the designs can now be classified into one of the following categories:

(a) Definitely is a THOG

(b) Insufficient information to decide

(c) Definitely is not a THOG.

The correct answer is that the red diamond and blue circle are definitely not THOGs, but that the red circle is a THOG. The reason for this is that the experimenter could have written down two combinations: blue + circle or red + diamond. If blue + circle had been written down, then the red diamond is not a THOG because it possesses neither of the required properties and the blue circle is not a THOG because it contains both properties. However, the red circle possesses just one property (circularity), so it is a THOG. If red + diamond had been written down, then the red diamond design contains both properties, the blue circle neither, and the red circle just one. Hence, whichever combination had been written down, the same conclusion follows.

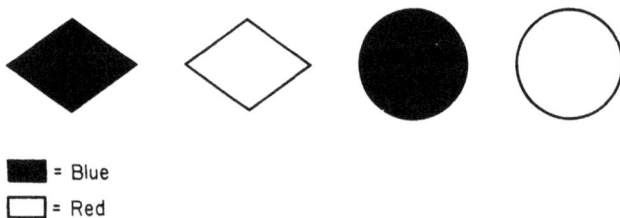

■ = Blue
☐ = Red

FIGURE 1.1 The four designs used in the standard THOG problem

In the first published research study on the problem, Wason and Brooks (1979) found that approximately 20 per cent of their undergraduate subjects gave the correct response. The errors were not random; the majority fell into a category called 'intuitive error' by Wason and Brooks. This error involves giving the mirror image of the correct response. Subjects making this error say that the red diamond and blue circle *are* THOGs or are indeterminate, while the red circle is definitely *not* a THOG.

There are two main questions that arise concerning this problem. Firstly there is the question of why subjects should find the THOG problem so difficult; and secondly there is the question of why 'intuitive errors' should be so prevalent. One possible reason for the difficulty may be in understanding the disjunctive rule. Wason (1977a) originally suggested this: 'The contradictory element within the problem, responsible for wrong solutions, is due to the logical relation (exclusive disjunction) involved in it' (p. 127). However, as Wason and Brooks (1979) have pointed out, this is unlikely to be the case. In two of their experiments, they checked whether subjects had understood the exclusive disjunctive relationship, and about 80 per cent of the subjects had. Further, the concept formation and disjunctive reasoning literatures do not indicate that subjects should have exceptional difficulty with this relationship (see NEW-STEAD AND GRIGGS, this volume).

Wason and Brooks (1979) in another of their experiments showed that the required combinatorial analysis was not beyond their subjects. When subjects wrote down a color and a shape, they were quite capable of evaluating the designs as to their consistency with the rule. Thus subjects can understand the exclusive disjunction rule and carry out the combinatorial analysis, but when both of these are required in the actual THOG problem, performance breaks down (for a discussion of similar effects in the selection task, see Evans's (1982) section on the 'therapy' experiments, pp. 160–2).

Effects of thematic content

As with the selection task, it is possible that performance on the THOG problem could be facilitated by the use of more thematic, realistic content. Newstead, Griggs and Warner (1982) checked on this possibility by devising two thematic THOG problems. In the first of these, 'style' was defined by the possession of one but only one quality – a certain type of clothing or a certain musical taste. The second problem involved restrictions on the courses third-year psychology students could take; essentially, a third-year cognitive psychology course could be taken if one and only one cognitive psychology course had been taken in previous years. Neither version of the problem produced any facilitation relative to the standard abstract THOG. These results agree with the research on content effects in the selection task. Neither type of content cued in the necessary relevant experience from memory. We concluded that these two types of realism do not produce facilitation, but this does not mean that no kind of realism will be effective.

Indeed at least one kind of realism *does* produce some facilitation. Following a suggestion of Cordell (1978), Newstead *et al.* devised a problem in which the experimenter told the subject that he would eat a meal if it contained just one of the two foods he had written down. The correct answer involved subjects saying that the experimenter would *not* eat meat and chocolate sauce or ice cream and gravy, but that he would eat ice cream and chocolate sauce. Performance was significantly better than on the abstract problem, rising to approximately 40 per cent, but it seemed to us that this was not a case of thematic material *per se* facilitating performance. Rather it was a case of the subject giving an answer based on previous experience and taking little account of the logical problem presented. Effectively, then, subjects were 'failing to accept the logical task' (Henle, 1962) or perhaps imposing their own everyday logic on a rather strange reasoning problem. If subjects are responding on the basis of prior experience, then one would expect few correct solutions when experience conflicts with logic. This was illustrated in a follow-up experiment done on school children (eight- and nine-year-olds). When the answer conformed to experience, 75 per cent of the children got the problem right; when experience conflicted with logic, *no* child gave the right answer, but instead gave the answer that was consistent with experience. Clearly, these children were very susceptible to the effects of memory cuing whether or not this was congruent with the logically correct answer. However, Newstead *et al.* did find in another experiment that it is difficult to induce *incorrect* responses in adult subjects through memory cuing. It should be noted that in the context of the THOG problem, 'memory cuing' is virtually the same thing as belief bias (responding in accordance with one's beliefs). Subjects, especially the young children, tended to give answers that conformed to their beliefs; clearly a nonlogical response bias.

Effects of problem structure

According to Wason (1978), one problem in devising a realistic THOG is that exclusive disjunction is quite rare in everyday usage. (However, exclusive disjunction is normal at least in some contexts; see NEWSTEAD AND GRIGGS, this volume). One context that Wason does regard as exclusive and which NEWSTEAD AND GRIGGS have shown to be so, is that of imperatives, what NEW-STEAD AND GRIGGS call 'choice', e.g. 'either you can have the cake with chocolate icing or the cake with chocolate filling.' Hence, Steve Newstead and I devised some realistic THOGs around such an imperative context. One of the versions we devised – the DRUG problem – is worth quoting in full:

> Dr. Robinson was instructing some trainee nurses on how to administer drugs. He was talking about kidney diseases and told the nurses that renal patients required carefully controlled intakes of calcium and potassium. The best way of administering these was by two injections daily, but patients became very sore with this number of injections. Thus, it was hospital policy to administer one drug intravenously and one orally. The doctor emphasized, 'You must give the patients potassium either in an injection or orally every day, but of course you must not give them both the potassium injection and the potassium pill. Similarly, you must give the patients calcium but not both the calcium injection and the calcium pill.'
>
> The nurses were then told, as a class exercise, to decide what brand name of drugs they would select to administer to patients. They were told to choose some combination of the drugs Deroxin and Altanin (which are intravenous drugs, one containing calcium and the other potassium) with the drugs Prisone and Triblomate (which are orally administered drugs, one of which contains calcium, the other potassium).
>
> At the next class, Dr. Robinson was surprised to find that the class had produced as answers all the possible combinations of the drugs:

	Injection	*Drug*
Answer 1	Deroxin	Prisone
Answer 2	Deroxin	Triblomate
Answer 3	Altanin	Prisone
Answer 4	Altanin	Triblomate

Dr. Robinson got as far as telling the class that the combination of Answer 1 conformed to his instructions when he was called away to do an emergency operation. Hence, the student nurses had to work out for themselves whether they were right or wrong. Subjects then had to classify the remaining three combinations as to whether or not they conformed to Dr. Robinson's instructions or whether there was insufficient information to decide.

In a series of experiments (Griggs and Newstead, 1982), this problem gave consistently good performance, roughly between 50–90 per cent accuracy. It might seem that the original hypothesis has been confirmed; i.e. that putting the THOG problem in a realistic imperative context had facilitated performance. However, we had tried two other versions involving imperatives, and these had not produced facilitation; thus it seems as though there is something specific to the DRUG problem which leads to improved performance. This led us to a detailed analysis of the structure of the various versions of the THOG problem. These structures can be represented as binary trees, revealing for the standard, abstract THOG the tree shown in Figure 1.2.

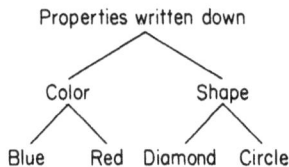

FIGURE 1.2 The proposed binary-tree representation for the standard THOG problem

If we apply a similar analysis to the DRUG problem, the structure seems more complicated, as shown in Figure 1.3.

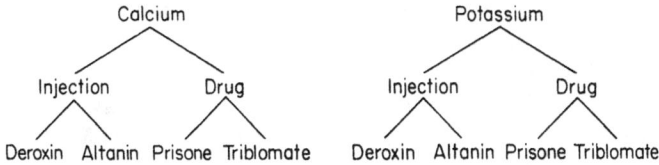

FIGURE 1.3 The proposed binary-tree representation for the DRUG problem

What is the source of this difference in structural representation? Essentially, the DRUG problem has a second 'half' added on to it. The equivalent in the standard THOG problem would be to have a second binary tree headed 'PROPERTIES NOT WRITTEN DOWN', but having the same divisions as the tree actually given. Thus what the DRUG problem effectively does is to specify not only what the written-down properties are but also what the non-written-down properties are. In the standard THOG, these properties can be inferred, but this presumably causes subjects some difficulty.

It is worthwhile at this stage to refer to the concept formation literature discussed in NEWSTEAD AND GRIGGS (this volume). There it seemed that one of the major problems with disjunctive concepts was that they required the use of negative instances, and that one way of improving performance was by drawing attention to these, either by starting off with a negative instance or through practice with negative instances. We have an exact parallel here. Subjects do not realize how important the negative information is, tending to focus on the left-hand side of the tree (Properties Written Down); while also focusing on the right-hand side of the tree (Properties Not Written Down) would make the symmetrical binary structure of the problem very clear and enable conclusions to be drawn fairly simply.

Tweney *et al*'s (1980) study on Wason's (1960) '2-4-6' problem is also relevant here. In the '2-4-6' problem, the subject is given three numbers and instructed that these numbers conform to a rule and that the task is to discover the rule by generating and testing new triads of numbers. Although the rule is a simple one (i.e. any three numbers in ascending order), subjects have a difficult time in discovering it. Tweney *et al.* (1980/Experiment 4) found that performance improved greatly on this task if instead of saying 'right' and 'wrong' they gave one name (DAX) to instances which conformed to the rule and another name (MED) to instances which did not conform to rule. As in the DRUG version of the THOG problem, defining negative instances in a positive way and giving them a name made the problem easier to handle. (EVANS, this volume, also argues that a bias to attend to positive rather than negative information can account for performance on various reasoning tasks.)

If this analysis in terms of problem structure is correct, then it should be possible to devise an abstract THOG problem with the same structure which should produce facilitation. This was done by Griggs and Newstead (1982) in a problem using shapes of different colors which were given nonsense names. Performance on the problem showed 80 per cent accuracy – if anything, higher than on the DRUG problem. We also investigated whether the improved performance on the DRUG problem would transfer to the standard THOG problem, with negative results. It seems that the underlying representations of the problems are sufficiently dissimilar that subjects do not realize the similarity, and do not utilize the negative information in the standard THOG problem in a way which parallels the use of the equivalent information in the DRUG problem. As with the selection task, facilitation does not transfer to the standard abstract problem.

Thus this research has revealed a powerful way of improving performance on the THOG problem, by making the problem structure highly explicit. Hence one source of the difficulty of the standard THOG problem is the difficulty subjects have in handling negative information. Subjects in concept formation studies have a tendency to treat disjunctives as if they were conjunctives, and it seems that this may have happened here as well. This is demonstrated by the prevalence of the 'intuitive error' in both Wason and Brooks's study and in our own work. In the standard problem, the subject is told that the blue diamond is a positive instance; and if the rule were one of conjunction rather than disjunction, then any design that was blue or diamond-shaped would be a THOG and a design with neither of these properties would not be a THOG. This corresponds, of course, to the intuitive errors that subjects make. It might also be noteworthy that the THOG problem involved a color-shape combination. Ketchum and Bourne (1980) have shown that such combinations are particularly conducive to a classification scheme corresponding to that of *inclusive* disjunction.

Bruner, Goodnow and Austin (1956) found that subjects learned disjunctive concepts more easily when the series started with a negative instance. It is possible, then, that the THOG problem would also be easier if the subject is told that a particular design is *not* a THOG, though it should be borne in mind that Bruner *et al.*'s study used inclusive disjunction while THOG uses exclusive disjunction. Griggs and Newstead (in press) have confirmed this prediction. Problems which started by indicating a figure which was *not* a THOG produced significantly better performance than the standard THOG, though performance on both problems was fairly poor.

There are a number of interesting parallels between the THOG problem and the learning of disjunctive concepts. In fact, Steve Newstead and I are drawn to the conclusion that the THOG problem is difficult for almost the same reasons that disjunctive concepts are. It involves a rule which is fairly complex logically and which involves working with negative information; this difficulty can be overcome by drawing the subject's attention to the negative information or by starting with a negative instance. And finally there is a tendency to focus on the positive instance and to assume that the attributes of this are what have been written down; this is remarkably similar to Bruner *et al.*'s 'common element fallacy' (see NEW-STEAD AND GRIGGS, this volume).

Summary

The thematic-materials effect, which appeared to be a very robust effect during the early 1970s, no longer appears so given the recent findings and a closer examination of the earlier studies. All of the studies reporting *reliable* facilitation are subject to the criticism of changing the nature of the task to check the four cards to see if they follow the given rule. In addition, these studies have employed content that allows memory cuing of past related experience and instructions that bias the subject toward falsification. Thus, the necessary and sufficient conditions for this type of facilitation are not clear and require further research to sort them out. Performance on this task appears to be the result of a complex interaction between content, task, and subject variables. However, one conclusion seems clear – there is no reliable evidence for a *pure* thematic-materials effect for the *original* form of the selection task. Simply phrasing the problem in thematic terms is not sufficient to produce reliable and substantial facilitation. Problem content that cues related past experience appears to be a necessary condition. In addition, having subjects check whether or not a procedural rule has been followed, as opposed to testing a hypothetical rule for truth or falsity, may also be necessary to achieve facilitation.

The present situation with Wason's THOG problem is quite different. Memory cuing has been demonstrated, but resulting in less facilitation. In addition, memory cuing in this case is more like the belief-bias effect in the research on categorical syllogisms (see Evans, 1982). Subjects appear to fail to accept the task and respond in accordance with their attitudes. As with the selection task, no evidence exists for a *pure* thematic-materials effect. However, performance has been facilitated for both abstract and thematic content by making the problem structure highly explicit (Griggs and New-stead, 1982). It can be asked whether this change creates a completely different problem. This is not the case. All the various THOG problems examined by Griggs and Newstead, including the standard THOG problem, are isomorphic with each other. The problem structure is just made highly explicit in the structured problems. This presumably makes the problem easier to represent in a problem space (Newell and Simon, 1972) and therefore easier to search through for the solution.

Acknowledgments

I would like to thank James Cox and Steve Newstead. Their contributions to my work on reasoning have been invaluable. Special thanks also go to Steve for his assistance in writing the THOG section of this chapter.

References

Bracewell, R. J. (1974), 'Interpretation factors in the four card selection task', paper presented at the Selection Task Conference, Trento, Italy, April (unpublished).

Bracewell, R. J. and Hidi, S. E. (1974), 'The solution of an inferential problem as a function of stimulus materials', *Quarterly Journal of Experimental Psychology, 26*, pp. 480–8.

Brown, C., Keats, J. A., Keats, D. M. and Seggie, I. (1980), 'Reasoning about implication: A comparison of Malaysian and Australian subjects', *Journal of Cross-Cultural Psychology, 11*, pp. 395–410.

Bruner, J. S., Goodnow, J. J. and Austin, G. A. (1956), *A study of thinking*, New York, Wiley.

Cohen, L. J. (1981), 'Can human irrationality be experimentally demonstrated?' *The Behavioral and Brain Sciences, 4*, pp. 317–70.

Cordell, R. L. (1978), *Mature reasoning and problem solving*, unpublished University of Nottingham M Ed dissertation.

Cox, J. R. and Griggs, R. A. (1982), 'The effects of experience on performance in Wason's selection task', *Memory and Cognition, 10*, pp. 496–502.

Dawes, R. M. (1975), 'The mind, the model, and the task', in F. Restle, R. M. Shiffrin, N. J. Castellan Jr., H. R. Lindman and D. B. Pisoni (eds), *Cognitive theory: Volume 1*, Hillsdale, New Jersey, Erlbaum.

Doherty, M. E., Mynatt, C. R., Tweney, R. D. and Schiavo, M. D. (1979), 'Pseudodiagnosticity', *Acta Psychologica, 43*, pp. 111–21.

Evans, J. St. B. T. (1982), *The psychology of deductive reasoning*, London, Routledge & Kegan Paul.

Evans, J. St. B. T. and Lynch, J. S. (1973), 'Matching bias in the selection task', *British Journal of Psychology, 64*, pp. 391–7.

Gilhooly, K. J. and Falconer, W. A. (1974), 'Concrete and abstract terms and relations in testing a rule', *Quarterly Journal of Experimental Psychology, 26*, pp. 355–9.

Golding, E. (1981), *The effect of past experience on problem solving*, paper presented at the Annual Conference of the British Psychological Society, Surrey University, April.

Griggs, R. A. and Cox, J. R. (1982), 'The elusive thematic-materials effect in Wason's selection task', *British Journal of Psychology, 73*, pp. 407–20.

Griggs, R. A. and Cox, J. R. (in press), 'The effects of problem content and negation on Wason's selection task', *Quarterly Journal of Experimental Psychology*.

Griggs, R. A. and Newstead, S. E. (1982), 'The role of problem structure in a deductive reasoning task', *Journal of Experimental Psychology: Learning, Memory, and Cognition, 8*, pp. 297–307.

Griggs, R. A. and Newstead, S. E. (in press), 'The source of intuitive errors in Wason's THOG problem', *British Journal of Psychology*.

Henle, M. (1962), 'On the relation between logic and thinking', *Psychological Review, 69*, pp. 366–78.

Johnson-Laird, P. N., Legrenzi, P. and Sonino Legrenzi, M. (1972), 'Reasoning and a sense of reality', *British Journal of Psychology, 63*, pp. 395–400.

Ketchum, R. D. and Bourne, L. E., Jr. (1980), 'Stimulus-rule interactions in concept verification', *American Journal of Psychology*, *93*, pp. 5–23.

Leahey, T. H. (1977), 'Training reasoning with implication', *The Journal of General Psychology*, *96*, pp. 63–73.

Lunzer, E. A. (1975), 'The development of advanced reasoning abilities', *Italian Journal of Psychology*, *2*, pp. 369–90.

Lunzer, E. A., Harrison, C. and Davey, M. (1972), 'The four-card problem and the generality of formal reasoning', *Quarterly Journal of Experimental Psychology*, *24*, pp. 326–39.

Mandler, J. M. (1980), *Structural invariants in development*, Center for Human Information Processing Technical Report no. 96, La Jolla, University of California, San Diego.

Manktelow, K. I. (1979), *The role of content in reasoning*, unpublished PhD thesis, Plymouth Polytechnic.

Manktelow, K. I. and Evans, J. St. B. T. (1979), 'Facilitation of reasoning by realism: Effect or non-effect?', *British Journal of Psychology*, *70*, pp. 477–88.

Newell, A. and Simon, H. A. (1972), *Human problem solving*, Englewood Cliffs, New Jersey, Prentice-Hall.

Newstead, S. E., Griggs, R. A. and Warner, S. A. (1982), 'The effects of realism on Wason's THOG problem', *Psychological Research*, *44*, pp. 85–96.

Pollard, P. (1979), *Human reasoning: Logical and nonlogical explanations*, unpublished PhD thesis, Plymouth Polytechnic.

Pollard, P. (1981), 'The effect of thematic content on the "Wason selection task" ', *Current Psychological Research*, *1*, pp. 21–9.

Pollard, P. (1982), 'Human reasoning: Some possible effects of availability', *Cognition*, *12*, pp. 65–96.

Pollard, P. and Evans, J. St. B. T. (1981), 'The effects of prior beliefs in reasoning: An associational interpretation', *British Journal of Psychology*, *72*, pp. 73–81.

Reich, S. S. and Ruth, P. (1982), 'Reasoning: Verification, falsification, and matching', *British Journal of Psychology*, *73*, pp. 395–406.

Rumelhart, D. E. (1979), *Analogical processes and procedural representations*, Center for Human Information Processing Technical Report no. 81, La Jolla, University of California, San Diego.

Rumelhart, D. E. (1980), 'Schemata: The building blocks of cognition', in R. J. Spiro, B. C. Bruce and W. F. Brewer (eds), *Theoretical issues in reading comprehension*, Hillsdale, New Jersey, Erlbaum.

Tweney, R. D., Doherty, M. E., Worner, W. J., Pliske, D. B., Mynatt, C. R., Gross, K. A. and Arkkelin, D. L. (1980), 'Strategies of rule discovery in an inference task', *Quarterly Journal of Experimental Psychology*, *32*, pp. 109–23.

Van Duyne, P. C. (1974), 'Realism and linguistic complexity in reasoning', *British Journal of Psychology*, *65*, pp. 59–67.

Van Duyne, P. C. (1976), 'Necessity and contingency in reasoning', *Acta Psychologica*, *40*, pp. 85–101.

Wason, P. C. (1960), 'On the failure to eliminate hypotheses in a conceptual task', *Quarterly Journal of Experimental Psychology, 12*, pp. 129–40.

Wason, P. C. (1966), Reasoning, in B. Foss (ed.), *New horizons in psychology*, Harmondsworth, Penguin.

Wason, P. C. (1968), 'Reasoning about a rule', *Quarterly Journal of Experimental Psychology, 20*, pp. 273–81.

Wason, P. C. (1977a), 'Self-contradictions', in P. N. Johnson-Laird and P. C. Wason (eds), *Thinking: Readings in cognitive science*, Cambridge, Cambridge University Press.

Wason, P. C. (1977b), 'The theory of formal operations – A critique', in B. A. Geber (ed.), *Piaget and knowing: Studies in genetic epistemology*, London, Routledge & Kegan Paul.

Wason, P. C. (1978), *Hypothesis testing and reasoning*, Unit 25, Block 4, Cognitive Psychology, Milton Keynes, Open University Press.

Wason, P. C. (1981), 'Understanding and the limits of formal thinking', in H. Parret and J. Bouveresse (eds), *Meaning and understanding*, New York, Walter de Gruyter.

Wason, P. C. and Brooks, P. G. (1979), 'THOG: The anatomy of a problem', *Psychological Research, 41*, pp. 79–90.

Wason, P. C. and Johnson-Laird, P. N. (1972), *Psychology of reasoning: Structure and content*, Cambridge, Mass., Harvard University Press.

Wason, P. C. and Shapiro, D. (1971), 'Natural and contrived experience in a reasoning problem', *Quarterly Journal of Experimental Psychology, 23*, pp. 63–71.

Yachanin, S. A. and Tweney, R. D. (1982), 'The effect of thematic content on cognitive strategies in the four-card selection task', *Bulletin of the Psychonomic Society, 19*, pp. 87–90.

2 Realism and rationality in the selection task

Peter C. Wason

The selection task has been attacked as subversive because it usually defies the wits of even highly intelligent individuals, and sometimes elicits patterns of behaviour which are distinctly irrational. Hence it is argued we ought to stop using it. This essay is about why we don't, and what we have discovered in the process.

It is not just that it is difficult – a five-move chess problem can be very difficult for even a competent chess problemist. And it is not just that it provokes irrationality – novel ideas in the arts (surrealism) and in the sciences (psychoanalysis) have in the past made rational individuals behave in an irrational way. By any standards, the selection task ought not to be difficult, and it certainly ought not to ensnare people in a delusion of their own making. For it possesses a simple logical structure which can readily be grasped if you don't try to solve it, and its content would hardly be expected to pose a threat to conventional wisdom. So it is something of a paradox that what looks like a simple formal problem should not only prove difficult, but should often arouse a rigid pattern of thought which is typically resistant to correction by the experimenter's intervention. Some people (not so much the subjects) seem to be worried about this. On the other hand, certain modifications may make the problem smoothly easy (almost a different problem), and hence can be said to elicit reasonable behaviour. In principle, this provides an opportunity to demarcate the conditions for rational thought, not of course that we have achieved this on any grand scale, but a map of the territory begins to become visible. That is the crux of the problem, and perhaps it is appropriate in this reappraisal to say first a few words about its origin.

Origins

The selection task was not devised as a technique for the investigation of propositional reasoning, nor was its formulation guided by any consideration for the psychological literature – indeed the literature at the time was almost entirely concerned with syllogistic reasoning. If it had any inspirational source at all it must have been my perplexity over the logical concept of material implication which I had encountered in Quine's (1952) *Methods of Logic*. I failed to understand how a two-valued logic could assimilate the use of conditional sentences in a natural language. But there was, as far as I can recall, no deliberation about the invention of the selection task. Like so much else in life, it just occurred as an amusing puzzle. Two friends to whom I showed it in late 1960 both solved it, conspicuously unlike the vast army of subjects who followed them. I think that this deflating experience, together with the scepticism of my research assistant, may have cooled my ardour for any serious experimental work. Who would want to work on such an easy problem? At any rate, the task was not mentioned in the literature until 1966 when I wrote my article on reasoning for *New Horizons in Psychology* (Wason, 1966), even though Athol Hughes (1966) had tried to develop it under my supervision in her PhD thesis.

Now that two decades have passed since its conception, it has acquired a measure of distinction (or notoriety), and I intend to reappraise some critical issues which have been generated by the research. In so doing I hope to remain consistent with my intellectual prejudices which, as a matter of fact, have been articulated during the process of writing. (This, *en passant*, is one of the good things about writing which ought to be recognized as a means of discovery.) Still, the reader should remember that what follows is a personal statement. A more comprehensive account of the research may be found in Evans (1982, Chapter 9).

The formal problem

The first published version (Wason, 1966) consisted of four cards displaying (respectively) a vowel (P), a consonant (P̄, i.e. not P), an even number (Q), and an odd number (Q̄, i.e. not Q), together with the sentence, 'If a card has a vowel on one side, then it has an even number on the other side.' The subject knows that this sentence refers to just these four cards and that each card has a letter on one of its sides and a number on its other side. The problem is to name those cards, and only those cards, which need to be turned over in order to determine decisively whether the sentence is true or false.

The solution is to select the vowel (P) and the odd number ($\bar{Q}$), but most subjects select the vowel (P) and the even number (Q), or just the vowel. Consistent results have been obtained under a wide variety of refinements in the task material, and in the linguistic form of the test sentence, e.g. (i) when all the information is potentially visible on the same side of the cards, part of it being initially concealed by a system of masks (Wason and Johnson-Laird, 1970), and (ii) when the test sentence lacks the surface structure of a conditional, e.g. 'A letter is above each number' (Wason and Golding, 1974). Thus the selection task is a deductive problem concerned with testing a conditional sentence in the general form, 'if P then Q'. Only instances of P and $\bar{Q}$ allow a valid inference because only the conjunction of these on the same card could *falsify* the sentence. Unlike most reasoning problems it is worth noting that this is a task of meta-inference: an inference has to be made about the conditions which would allow a valid inference.

The notation of the propositional calculus will be used to describe the problem without any commitment to explanatory force. When reference is made to a card, irrespective of the value associated with it, the appropriate letter will simply be cited. When both values are relevant, the disclosed value is mentioned first and the concealed value second, e.g. Q P.

Reactions to the experiments

The inability of the subjects to cope with the task in an adequate, or consistent, way has affronted a few academic critics. They have either argued that the problem is a conjuring trick which the subjects could quickly be brought to understand when the conjuror's magic has been dispelled, or else that the reasoning which is demanded is so complex that the subjects could not be expected to solve it. These opposite criticisms are wrong but plausible. For when individuals, who are by definition highly intelligent, perform like children on a reasoning task which is supposed to be simple, there must be something wrong somewhere. Hence the selection task has been deemed to portray a perverted picture of human reasoning powers, or even regarded as a weapon in a concerted campaign to denigrate the rationality of man.

When one is criticized the standard defence is to claim misunderstanding, and it is indeed true that not all the aims and assumptions of the research, which now seem fully apparent, were made explicit in the published papers. How could it be otherwise? But the reactions of my critics, even if they sometimes seem to lack penetration, are welcome because they tend to corroborate the experimental findings in a more general way. In their failure to understand the problem, the subjects have provided a performance which the critics, in turn, have failed to understand. I want to magnify their objections. For although they have made some interesting points the attack could have been launched on other fronts which seem potentially more vulnerable. In this way a spirit of concerted scepticism may delineate what is valuable in the selection task. But before considering (and amplifying) some criticisms I should like to discredit the most plausible gain we appear to have won because it has been radically over-simplified. It has been comfortable to suppose that there is an elegant distinction between irrational and rational behaviour, corresponding precisely to that between the 'abstract' and 'concrete' material used in the task, a distinction which has been presented in a large number of books on cognitive and educational psychology. An important, and hitherto unnoticed, exception to this neat package will be discussed in due course.

A few reactions have misinterpreted the *aim* of our research. Selection task work has been seen as part of a sinister trend in cognitive psychology. Thus Bryant (1978) supposes that we aim to demonstrate the stupidity of human beings. 'To read cognitive psychology these days,' writes Bryant, 'is to be filled with gloom at the apparent stupidity of one's fellow human beings.' Errors in reasoning are supposed to be regarded by cognitive psychologists as diagnostic of some cognitive deficit. Such an approach is contrasted with the program of those who do research on perception, and who regard the geometric illusions as aberrations from a highly efficient perceptual code. The contrast is a caricature, as Johnson-Laird pointed out in a reply (14 April 1978). There is a precise parallel between research on reasoning and on perception. In Wason and Johnson-Laird (1972) we suggested that the aberrant behaviour evoked in some experiments on reasoning, far from being a consequence of cognitive deficit, may merely reflect a lack of semantic support afforded by the conditions of everyday life. It is difficult to say more about a criticism of this kind because it is unclear what follows from it.

The most frequently voiced specific complaint about the selection task is that it is *deceptively simple* (not 'deceptively difficult' as some people write for reasons which escape me), with the corollary that it is really very difficult. Thus far, Cohen (1981), Finocchiaro (1980), and Vuyk (1981) are all in agreement. This verdict seems to imply that there is something which we could have done to alert the subjects to the true nature of the task, and that then they would no longer be deceived. My own opinion is that, without altering the material, there is nothing which could be done to induce the subjects to approach the task in a manner which befits its awesome difficulty. Certainly our experience suggests that a lecture on truth tables, an awareness of the possibilities which could occur on the other side of the cards, or exposure to conditional sentences in a more familiar form, would not be helpful. Cohen (1981) is wrong to claim that a particular kind of experimental situation has induced the subjects 'to indulge in a form of reasoning which on a few moments prompted reflection they would be willing to admit is invalid'. As we shall see later, erroneous reasoning in this task does not necessarily result in heedless responses which can readily be corrected. Its deceptive simplicity is not the kind of thing which can be altered by instruction, and this is one of the most interesting findings to come out of the research because it appears to be counter-intuitive.

On the other hand, it might be claimed that there is something *inherently* deceptive about abstract conditional sentences. In 1977 Finocchiaro (personal communication) sent me extensive comments about the selection task for inclusion in his book *Galileo and the Art of Reasoning* (Finocchiaro, 1980). He argues that the abstract hypothesis (the conditional rule) is simply 'a bad choice on the part of the experimenters'. This claim rests on his belief that the logical structure of the task is so complex that it takes pages of symbolic logic to elucidate it, a logic which is assumed to reflect the reasoning processes demanded by its solution. In contradistinction to Finocchiaro, I argue that it is *not* logical complexity which makes the problem difficult. As a matter of fact, Philip Johnson-Laird and I have tested the elicitation of the truth conditions of disjunctive sentences, and when these are made logically equivalent to material implication the reasoning was of a totally different kind from that which is typical of the selection task (Wason and Johnson-Laird, 1969). This was an early clue to the fact that underlying logical form is not a critical variable. But the crucial point in the 'deceptive simplicity' argument seems to be that the subject somehow has to overcome the deception and break through into a kind of Platonic realm of logical form. This I believe to be profoundly wrong. In our first theoretical paper (Johnson-Laird and Wason, 1970a), we proposed an algorithm with which a computer might be programmed to solve the problem in the most economical way. It is based on the instruction to select cards if, and only if, they could falsify the conditional. This algorithm, which can be tested intuitively, proves that the structure of the problem is simple. Hence it is of some interest that it has been called 'really very complicated' (Finocchiaro, 1980), a 'laboratory game' (Wetherick, 1970), a 'cognitive illusion' (Cohen, 1981), or quite simply 'irritating' (Vuyk, 1981). I suspect it is characterized in these terms because of a need to account for its difficulties despite the fact that this involves committing the fallacy of affirming the consequent – 'Such-and-such factors would cause difficulty; difficulty is observed; therefore such-and-such factors cause the difficulty.' In lecturing to philosophers, I find invariably they will say something like this: 'I am not surprised your problem is difficult. Material implication is a difficult concept to teach to students.' But the solution does not depend on a knowledge of material implication. There is considerable evidence to suggest (in accordance with common sense) that conditional sentences are evaluated in terms of a 'defective truth table', i.e. when the antecedent is false, the sentence is evaluated not as true, but as if it had never been made (Wason, 1966; Evans, 1972; Johnson-Laird and Tagart, 1969). The point, which is often forgotten, is that whether the conditional is interpreted in this way, or as material implication, or as a biconditional (a statement of equivalence), the common factor is the relevance of $\bar{Q}$. And this was always envisaged as the central interest of the problem (Wason, 1968).

This does not demolish the 'deceptive simplicity' argument, but it strongly suggests that the complexity of the structural factors in the task has been exaggerated in order to account for difficulty. If one were to look for more adequate scapegoats, a stronger argument might be built upon the nature of the experimental conditions. One might ask whether it is appropriate to test reasoning powers in the way in which they are tested by psychologists, and this argument, if it were tenable, would provide a source of comfort to all the critics.

The test conditions

Suppose an intelligent critic, a philosopher perhaps unacquainted with the psychological laboratory, but armed with a knowledge of his natural language, were to be presented with the raw data of our typical experiments. What might he conclude?

An initial reaction might well be to criticize the conditions of the test because of incredulity at the stupidity of the answers. How could the most intellectually endowed section of the community fail, in such a striking manner, to identify the truth conditions of a conditional sentence? There must be something wrong with the experiment which makes people respond in this way.

The subject in such an experiment is required (usually for a modest sum of money these days) to present himself to an experimenter whom he doesn't know in order to perform a task whose purpose he doesn't understand. And if that were not alienating enough, an element of reassurance is provided by the injunction, 'This is not an intelligence test, but you will have to *think*.' These efforts to make the subject relax, and dispel that crippling anxiety which experimenters seem to assume besets their subjects, may even be taken further by a touch of genius: 'I am not interested in your performance as an individual.'

Quite apart from what is told the subjects, the mere presence of the benign experimenter may prove unsettling. An unpublished study by Roger Goodwin (personal communication) showed that subjects were significantly better at solving the selection task when the experimenter was not present in the room. This experiment was replicated in an undergraduate project (Nicola Jamieson) conducted under my supervision. More dramatically (and painfully) I found myself unable to formulate the proof of my *own* THOG problem when an official came to my office to collect some problems for an exhibition. I had learned five minutes something which my friends had teased me about over the last 25 years.

But weren't some of the experiments conducted as group tests, and hence immune to this particular kind of stress? This rather neatly allows a complementary criticism. Such conditions might not encourage the subjects to care particularly what they do. How about paying the subjects for doing well? I tried this once many years ago, only to be reprimanded by a subject who considered it degrading. It would seem that, whichever way one turns, the experimental conditions may militate against the elicitation of logical competence.

There is obviously a lot of truth in this argument, and we should enlist the help of social psychologists to try to determine the best conditions for any kind of test. But, of course, this criticism does not nullify the value of the results already obtained, especially when the subjects act as their own controls. A persistent critic, however, is not so easily quietened, and may return to the attack again.

The question of sampling

Here is something curious: some experiments conducted around 1970 do not seem to have been replicated under identical instructions about 10 years later. Let us assume that the critic has written a report about the selection criteria for accepting students. He might conclude, with some justification, that the discrepancy is due to differences in intellectual calibre. Furthermore, he might argue, regardless of academic potential, that students in 1980 might be less interested in abstruse experiments because of the bleak future which confronts them. In the same critical vein, he might have noticed that some experiments were carried out in seat of learning X and some in seat of learning Y, institutions not comparable in terms of the intellectual quality of students. Now all this would not matter if the experiments were concerned with the discrimination of the two-point threshold, but since they were concerned with reasoning the homogeneity of the population from which the samples were drawn could be critical. The experiments may not be impervious to differences in time and place.

The experimentalist is likely to regard such observations as heretical; the philosopher (or linguist) may regard them as apt. Part of the critic's objection is based on the assumption that we have been trying to determine the difficulty of the problem in some more or less exact sense, and if that had been so we might as well have asked ourselves whether the task would be more difficult if the experiment had been conducted under water, as some investigators have done with other reasoning tasks. But this has never been our concern. However, it could still be maintained that extraneous factors may interact with the effect of experimental variables, such that variable x may exert an effect on sample s^1 at time t^1, but not on sample s^2 at time t^2. And so on.

This criticism is less devastating than it might sound because specific results in the human sciences are seldom decisive one way or another, and every finding is susceptible to new interpretations and checks etc., etc., etc. Indeed, the specific concrete case picked on by the critic, the non-replicability of certain experiments between 1970 and 1980, would seem to suggest, not trivial differences in sampling, but, as we shall see, a difference in the subjects' experience over time which is of considerable theoretical importance.

Still, it is fair to say that the problem of individual differences in research of this kind should give the experimentalist more cause for concern where questions of interpretation are involved. JOHNSON-LAIRD (this volume) quite rightly points out that mental tests have little value in the study of thinking because the data they yield are too gross. However, it does seem to me that the results of relevant standardized tests may be useful for validating comparisons between individuals and samples. They would then have a methodological use in the service of control.

The critic might now ask himself, 'What on earth were the subjects doing?'

The question of the responses

Suppose he were to ask (more precisely), if the subjects had not been reasoning, what cards would they have selected? The immediate answer would be that they would choose the cards at random, but even a cursory examination of the data shows this is wrong. The next plausible answer would be that they would tend to select the two cards named in the rule, and there is strong evidence to support this. Thus the thought arises that individuals, who are by definition highly intelligent, respond in a way which they would do if they were not thinking. The critic would not conclude, of course, that the subjects had not been thinking because such a conclusion would be a fallacious inference, but the thought could still occur and thoughts cannot be fallacious. This is the analogue to explain performance of the 'deceptive simplicity' claim which was directed against the structure of the task. At the theoretical level two more principled explanations of unenlightened performance have been proposed: 'verification' (Johnson-Laird and Wason, 1970a) and 'matching response' (Evans, 1972; see also EVANS, this volume).

It is often forgotten that between 4 and 10 per cent of the subjects do solve the problem. Of course, if they were random generators, then the occurrence of the correct solution could be attributed to a random process. Finocchiaro makes a similar claim although he argues that it is not the responses but the meaning of the test sentence (the hypothesis) which is governed by a random process: 'The few subjects whose response is labelled "correct" by Wason and Johnson-Laird are merely those who happened by accident to choose the meaning of the hypothesis intended by the experimenters and who then reasoned in accordance with formal logic. For one finds it simply incredible that the subjects could have actually been engaged in reasoning as complex as that outlined above. . . .' I think this is doubly wrong. First, I do not believe that the problem is multiply ambiguous such that it is capable of yielding a variety of interpretations although I concede that the relevant experiment to test this supposition has not been conducted. Second, it seems to me unlikely that, if the 'intended meaning' were to occur, the subject would then reason 'in accordance with formal logic'. I suggest, on the contrary, and this is again consistent with Johnson-Laird's idea of 'alternative mental models' (see JOHNSON-LAIRD, this volume), that such a subject appreciates the crucial importance of testing the counter-examples to the truth claim of the sentence. Hence, as we originally proposed, such a subject selects only those cards which could falsify.

The critic might accept this argument, but still retort that it is the failure of the masses which needs to be accounted for rather than the achievement of the elect. And no evidence has so far been produced to suggest that their lack of insight is anything but a consequence of superficial error governed (perhaps) by the 'deceptive simplicity' of the task. In order to examine this question the critic would have to go back to experiments conducted in 1969 and

1970 because nearly all subsequent studies do not allow the subjects to be confronted with the consequence of their choices. Indeed, at Plymouth Polytechnic, which has become a sort of centre of excellence for selection task research, Jonathan Evans tells me that the cards are glued down on the table.*

The question of irrationality

Many subjects do not follow the explanation of the task after they have tried to solve it. It is as if the computing space available for grasping the correct solution is already dominated by the effects of reaching the wrong solution. This is important. For if the subjects do not understand the problem when it is explained, then, *a fortiori*, they would hardly be expected to solve it unaided. One might begin to explain it by making reference to the possibilities (and their effects) on the other side of the cards. This technique revealed surprising asymmetries in the very first experiment (Wason, 1968), e.g. Q̄ hypothetically associated with P invariably elicited an inference, but P hypothetically associated with Q̄ tended not to do so. Even more startling, when the Q̄ P contingency is granted a falsifying status, the subsequent relevance of Q̄ to the solution of the problem is frequently denied. This latter error is not a chance observation; it permeated the results of three further experiments in which corrective feedback was given (Wason, 1969; Wason and Johnson-Laird, 1970; Wason and Golding, 1974).

This profound failure to come to grips with the meta-inferential nature of the task may be best illustrated by citing a concrete case. The following 'Mensa protocol' demonstrates how a highly articulate subject defends his initial decisions when these are shown to be incompatible with the facts. The technique used was to create a dialogue between experimenter and subject in which the latter is confronted with progressively strong contradictions between his initial neglect of Q̄ and the hypothetical (and then real) consequences of its falsifying status (Wason, 1969).

Four cards are displayed showing (respectively) face upwards: red triangle, blue circle, red circle, and blue triangle. The order in

---

* Editor's note: Our latest and most sophisticated technique involves presentation of computer-generated pictures of the cards. Even the computer does not know what is on the other sides.

which they are laid out is, of course, immaterial. This subject already knows from inspecting a larger set of cards, of which the displayed ones are a subset, that every card has a triangle (red or blue) on one side and a circle (red or blue) on the other side, i.e. shape is invariant and colour disjoint – the shape on the other side is determined, but its colour is one of two alternatives. The test sentence is, 'Every card which has a red triangle on one side has a blue circle on the other side.' The task is to name the necessary cards which would determine the truth value of the sentence. The solution is red triangle and *red circle*, but this subject makes the typical mistake of naming red triangle and *blue circle*.

E: 'Your task is to tell me which of the cards you need to turn over in order to find out whether the sentence is true or false.'

S: 'A red triangle on one side . . . although there were some in which both sides were red. . . . I don't know how many of them. At present we have two cards which could satisfy those conditions, so you only have two cards to choose from: the red triangle and the blue circle.'

E: 'What could be on the other side of the red triangle?'

S: 'A red circle or a blue circle.'

E: 'If there were a red circle on the other side, could you say anything about the truth or falsity of the sentence?'

S: 'It would be untrue.'

E: 'And if there were a blue circle on the other side, could you say anything about the truth or falsity of the sentence?'

S: 'It would be true.'

E: 'By the way, what was your choice of cards to turn over in order to find out whether the sentence in front of you is true or false?'

S: 'The red triangle and the blue circle.'

E: 'Are you quite happy about this choice?'

S: 'Quite happy as the other two do not agree with the statement made.'

E: 'What could be on the other side of the red circle?'

S: 'A red triangle or a blue triangle.'

E: 'If there were a red triangle on the other side, could you say anything about the truth or falsity of the sentence?'

S: 'The statement would be meaningless because it doesn't apply.'

E: 'In fact it would be false.'

S: 'It could be but you are not doing it that way round. The statement would be untrue in any case, no matter what is on the other side.'

E: 'If there were a blue triangle on the other side, could you say anything about the truth or falsity of the sentence?'

S: 'No.'

E: 'Are you quite happy about needing to turn over just the red triangle and the blue circle in order to find out whether the sentence is true or false?'

S: 'Yes.'

E: 'Please turn over the red triangle and the blue circle and tell me whether the sentence is true or false.' [There is a blue circle on the other side of the red triangle, and a red triangle on the other side of the blue circle.]

S: 'The sentence is true.'

E: 'I am now going to turn over the red circle, and I want you to tell me whether you still think the sentence is true.' [There is a red triangle on the other side.]

S: 'Wait a minute. When it's put like that the sentence is not true. Either the sentence is true, or it is not true. You have just proved one thing and then you have proved the other. You've proved a theorem and then its contrary, so you don't know where you are. Don't ask me about the blue triangle because that would be meaningless.'

E: 'Are you quite happy about needing to turn over just the red triangle and the blue circle in order to find out whether the sentence is true or false?'

S: 'There is only one card which needs to be turned over to prove the statement exactly: the red triangle. Strictly speaking, you don't need the blue circle. You must find every card with a red triangle on it and turn it over, but there is only one.'

E: 'But you just said when the red circle was turned over the sentence was false.'

S: 'That is doing it the other way round.'

E: 'The problem is very difficult. Very few people get it right. What we are interested in is why they don't get it right.'

S: 'I am a member of Mensa. I wasn't going to tell you that until afterwards.'

In my original paper I contrasted this performance with the following dialogue with a five-year-old boy. 'Do you have a brother?' 'Yes.' 'What's his name?' 'Jim.' 'Does Jim have a brother?' 'No.' It is supposed to demonstrate the irreversibility which characterizes preoperational thought in Piaget's theory. But is it any more irreversible than acknowledging that a red circle on the other side of the red triangle would falsify, and then denying that a red triangle on the other side of the red circle would do so? I ventured to suggest that this subject (and others in the same experiment) had regressed to an earlier mode of thinking in trying to get to grips with the problem. I received no thanks for this suggestion which might have encouraged the Piagetians by showing an enduring representation of much earlier stages. Both Piagetian and anti-Piagetian scholars were quick to repudiate the notion, but all is seldom lost in psychological research. A distinguished psychoanalyst (Joseph Sandler) wrote to say it was the evidence he had in mind to demonstrate how an individual, faced with a novel problem, may recapitulate earlier attempts to solve problems.

A performance of this kind represents a clear refutation of Piaget's classical theory of formal operational thought. According to Piaget, the thinking of the intelligent adolescent can be described in terms of formal logic. The variables of a problem will be isolated, and subjected to a combinatorial analysis which exhausts all the possibilities so that the real will be apprehended as an instance of the possible. More specifically, Piaget assumes that such an adolescent, confronted by a complex causal situation, will ask himself whether fact X implies fact Y, and frequently do this by formulating the proposition 'If P then Q.' In order to test this proposition he will search for the counter-example, X and non-Y, i.e. P and $\bar{Q}$ (Beth and Piaget, 1966). This is exactly what the subject in our protocol does not do, almost if he had been asked to provide a scenario of the preoperational child. It should be remembered, of course, that a radical dilution of the classical theory postulates that the content of a problem is (after all) crucial (Piaget, 1972).

More important than the criticism of Piaget is the question of rationality in the performance of the individual whose protocol I have presented. According to the moral philosopher, W. D. Hudson (1980), three possible criteria for rational thought are that it should not be self-contradictory, that it should be backed by relevant evidence, and that it should be open to correction by data. The 'Mensa protocol' fails to meet any of these criteria, but concerted efforts were made by friends to salvage the subject's rationality in accordance with the thesis that all mistakes in reasoning can be attributed to some kind of misinterpretation of the premises (Henle, 1962). This view is appealing because it implies that everybody is rational in the last resort if only we knew the way in which they saw the world. For instance, it is a thesis which is consistent with some schools of existential psychoanalysis, e.g. Laing (1966). But I believe it to be wrong in the present instance, and I shall try to substantiate this claim.

Somebody pointed out that if 'the other side' of the card had been interpreted as the side which is face downwards, then the subject's performance could be seen as rational and consistent. A similar proposal was made by Bracewell (1974) and by Finocchiaro (1980). The claim, more precisely, is that the test sentence is ambiguous; the 'other side' could be interpreted as either (a) the hidden or the showing side, or (b) just the hidden side. But against this, it is surely clear that in ordinary usage othersidedness is a symmetrical relation: 'X is on the other side of Y' entails, and is entailed by, 'Y is on the other side of X.' In concrete terms, 'There is a house on one side of the hill and a church on the other side,' would not seem to be falsified if the church is encountered first.

Moreover there is empirical evidence to back up this conceptual analysis. Three observations count against the claim that this subject, and others who make a similar error, has interpreted the premise of the problem in an idiosyncratic way. First, when the other side of the red circle is actually revealed to show a red triangle, any putative hidden side interpretation cannot be operative: the card is granted falsifying status. Second, the blue circle should not have been selected according to this interpretation because it is specified as being on the other side of the red triangle, i.e. relevant only when face downwards. Third, an experiment was conducted to make a direct test of the plausibility of this interpretation (Wason and Johnson-Laird, 1970). In one condition all the information was potentially visible on the same side of the cards, partially concealed by a system of masks. In a control condition the information was partitioned in the standard way on either side of the cards. There was no difference at all between these two conditions. As a bonus, this experiment provided the most dramatic evidence of the failure to use corrective feedback.

It is difficult to make any rational reconstruction of the reasoning processes elicited in the 'Mensa protocol'. For instance, the premise could not have been construed as a conjunction of red triangles and blue circles because then it would be already falsified by the presence of the other two cards in the array. Nor could it have been construed as a disjunction of red triangles and blue circles because then only the other two cards would have been relevant. No truth function is compatible with the initial selection of cards, and hence we can say that the behaviour elicited is irrational. This provides an affirmative answer to Jonathan Cohen's question: 'Can human irrationality be experimentally demonstrated?' (Cohen, 1981).

Cohen seems to me wrong in a trivial and in a profound sense. He is obviously wrong to claim that 'a few moments' prompted reflection' would enable the subjects to admit that their reasoning had been invalid. This is the image of a momentary aberration, a lapse from the sturdy advance of rational thought. As we have seen, in our task at least, the errors are often systematic and resistant to correction. A deeper claim is that the tasks devised by experimental psychologists are atypical of everyday life situations – they are cognitive illusions, or 'conjuring tricks'. This rests on the assumption that irrationality is a function of a contrived situation.

It seems to me that Cohen over-estimates the pervasiveness of rational thought in everyday life. And it could be argued that irrationality, rather than rationality, is the norm. People all too readily succumb to logical fallacies, especially when they are trying to be persuasive. Indeed, several books published in the 1930s and 1940s, e.g. Crashay-Williams (1947), Stebbing (1937), and Thouless (1936), all assume that we must be vigilant in the presence of a predominant tendency towards irrationality in argument.

The selection task reflects this tendency to the extent that the subjects get it *wrong*. (At a deep level this is what is irritating about it.) As we have clearly seen in the 'Mensa protocol', the subject's reasoning does not appear consistent with any concealed premises; it is self-contained and encapsulated. These are the hallmarks of irrational thought. And it is the achievement of the selection task to be able to elicit it when the subject matter is concerned, not with momentous or emotional issues, but with the distribution of coloured shapes on four cards.

What Cohen calls 'cognitive illusions', as I pointed out in my reply (Wason, 1981), far from being the unique prerogative of the

academic conjuror, may not be radically different from circumstances and contingencies, which are sometimes met in daily life,
and which are quite irrational, e.g. incorrigible convictions about
quite ordinary things, delusions of reference, and other transient
symptoms such as falling in love. Diaconis and Freedman (1981)
trace the influence of such effects in the understanding of probability: 'On our view, many of the illusions cannot be dispelled by "a
few moments prompted reflection", or several months of college
teaching; if dispelled, the illusions seem to return in full force the
next time a similar situation comes along. Such illusions seem to be
rooted very deeply in the human mind.' This contrasts with Cohen's
view that a 'cognitive illusion' would not exert its force if the subject
were to recognize the similarity between the task and those 'familar
issues' in which the same logical principle had been applied outside
the psychological laboratory. The paradigm cases of such illusions,
however, are not those embodied in driving cars, or finding faults
in machinery, but those which carry an ineffable and immediate
conviction of certitude. Moreover, the competence theory of rationality proposed by Cohen, and supported by psychologists such as
Henle (1962) and Smedslund (1970), is unfalsifiable. What it does
is to mark off a capacity supposed to be shared by 'normal human
beings' (whoever they may be), and its limitation is that it fails to
acknowledge the irrational motives which dominate much of our
thinking and behaviour.

A deeper discussion of the conflict between rational and irrational
thinking in the selection task, in which a single individual sometimes
begins to sound like two different people (Wason and Johnson-
Laird, 1972, Chapter 15), is not the concern of this essay. The idea
of two different types of thinking, which interact in the performance
of a difficult task (the so-called dual process theory), and which
may be connected with differential functioning of the cerebral hemispheres (Evans and Dennis, 1982; Golding, 1981a; Golding, Reich,
and Wason, 1974), is discussed in Evans (1982, Chapter 12).

Having persuaded the critic that the selection task may elicit
irrational behaviour, we should now try to persuade him that it
may elicit rational behaviour.

The question of rationality

Present-day psychologists have developed a phobia about abstract material in their experiments just as psychologists of a previous generation did for meaningful material. So great is the power of fashion in experimentation that it seems a weak defence to point out that it all depends upon what you are trying to do.

The mental manipulation of abstract material, it may be thought, is an unfair test of inferential powers. 'Perhaps the most characteristic use of the conditional by experimental psychologists is one in which the propositions involved are general and abstract, and the connection between them a completely arbitrary one. . . . This sort of procedure may be found even in Wason on hypothesis testing' (Fillenbaum, 1977). I thank him for the 'even', but I would argue that it is quite appropriate to test inferences about an abstract conditional, and that the arbitrariness of the connection expressed in it is no impediment. The proposition, 'If A is above D, then C is below E', may be arbitrary, but it is perfectly clear and unambiguous.

Perhaps it is not so much the use of abstract material, but the over-load imposed by four items of information (or eight, in effect, if all the contingencies are counted) which tends to create havoc in the selection task. To be quite fair to Finocchiaro, this idea is connected with his criticism. Consider an experiment by Johnson-Laird and Wason (1970b/Experiment 1) which involved successive choices between only the two values of the consequent: Q and Q̄. The elimination of the antecedent values, P and P̄, was sensibly motivated because the discrimination between them is trivial. This experiment seems to be theoretically very important. It has been totally ignored, perhaps because of an almost Jungian (archetypal) fascination exerted by the four cards in the standard task. Unlike the selection task, it has one significant feature: all the subjects at some stage have a very high probability of success. I shall bestow upon it the acronym RAST (Reduced Array Selection Task). Emilie Roth (1979) introduced a modification to the selection task, consisting of the elimination of P from the array, which she called RST (Reduced Selection Task), but those initials are unpronounceable. A similar modification was introduced by Eric Lunzer (Lunzer, Harrison, and Davey, 1972) to investigate the effects of a 'reduced presentation' of both abstract and realistic material.

In our experiment the subjects had to prove a sentence, like 'If they are triangles then they are black', either true or false, by requesting to examine either BLACK shapes, or WHITE shapes, provided by the experimenter. The subjects knew that there were 15 shapes of each colour, and that the only kinds of shape involved would be triangles and circles. They were instructed to perform the task in the most economical manner, by requesting the smallest number of shapes (WHITE or BLACK). Regardless of whether the sentence has to be proved true or false, the solution is to request only WHITE ($\bar{Q}$) shapes in order to ensure that none are TRIANGLE (P). Only the absence of a WHITE TRIANGLE ($\bar{Q}$ P) proves the sentence true, and only the presence of one proves it false. Hence the BLACK (Q) shapes are gratuitous: a BLACK TRIANGLE (Q P) is verifying, but a BLACK CIRCLE (Q $\bar{P}$) is not falsifying. It is evident that the RAST throws into sharp relief the salient feature of the selection task.

When the test sentence had to be proved false the problem was trivial, but even when it had to be proved true an average of only 4·29 BLACK shapes were inspected, and all the subjects inspected all 15 WHITE shapes. Furthermore, insight was gained (on average) spontaneously – before encountering pseudo-disconfirmatory feedback, i.e. a BLACK CIRCLE (Q $\bar{P}$).

David Green and I have replicated this experiment with certain modifications, e.g. presenting partially concealed stimuli in two arrays, each of eight items. This produced even more remarkable results. Nine out of 24 subjects (37·5 per cent) solved the problem immediately by saying (in effect): 'I would need to see all the white shapes.' On the very first trial, 66·67 per cent chose to inspect $\bar{Q}$ rather than Q, and 22 out of 24 solved the problem eventually.

Such findings are not only impressive, they are also paradoxical. For if the RAST is regarded as a miniaturized component of the selection task, then the subjects should *not* be able to solve it. The argument is simple: In the selection task (1) the choice between P and $\bar{P}$ is trivial and errors seldom occur; (2) the choice between Q and $\bar{Q}$ is difficult and errors usually do occur. But (3) when only Q and $\bar{Q}$ are presented $\bar{Q}$ is decisively chosen at least at some stage. It can be concluded (4) that in the selection task the presence of antecedent values (P and $\bar{P}$) in some unknown way inhibits the correct solution. The standard explanations postulated to account for performance in the selection task – 'verification', 'matching response', and 'availability of responses', hardly seem relevant to performance in the RAST. In concrete terms, why should exposure to black triangles make the subject appreciate in quite a decisive way that only the non-existence of a white triangle would establish the truth of the statement: 'If they are triangles, then they are black'?

There are at least three possible explanations. First, the problem may be simply one of attention. The reduction in the number of stimuli from four to two may increase the attention which can be paid to $\bar{Q}$. This is the explanation postulated by EVANS (this volume): '. . . if $\bar{Q}$ is attended subjects may perceive its relevance and select it.'

Second, since solution does not depend on a single decision it may free the subject from a compulsive, non-rational, response tendency. The subject knows, even before making the first choice, that any decision can be revoked.

Third, it may not be the reduction in the number of stimuli, but in the kind of stimuli, which is effective. Roth (1979) found facilitation in performance when P was omitted from the selection task, but the total number of cards was held constant by including two instances of $\bar{Q}$. Lunzer, Harrison and Davey (1972) were the first to suggest that the presence of P in the array exercises a potent effect because it is selected to verify, whereas (logically) it should be selected to falsify: 'The presence of this card combined with its logical necessity has the effect of reinforcing the incorrect auto-instruction.'

A fourth possible explanation, however, which may be more convincing, will be considered when the effects of 'realism' are discussed. Let me summarize the potential of the RAST as an investigatory technique:

(a) By utilizing a series of decisions it provides a fairer test of reasoning abilities, and one which subjects may find more congenial.

(b) The effect of two kinds of feedback can be examined after the erroneous responses, i.e. $Q\,P$ and $Q\bar{P}$.

(c) The absence of any 'floor effect' enables a wider population to be investigated.

(d) The task permits the use of a wide range of material and methods of presentation. For instance, it can be run mentally without any stimuli. The stimuli could be imagined in the brain of the subject (or experimenter).

(e) The presolution trials could be analysed by techniques developed in earlier studies of concept attainment.

The advantages are methodological, but the theoretical implications, to which we shall return, are more important. The results demonstrate high-level rational behaviour in a meta-inference task which shares the critical features of the selection task. Some people, however, are still likely to raise the problem of the 'representativeness' of the selection task, and we must say something about this.

Representativeness

It has been argued that the selection task lacks 'representativeness' with respect to how the scientist solves problems, and that consequently selection of $\bar{Q}$ is irrelevant as a model for hypothesis testing (Wetherick, 1970). I would have thought that the hypothetico-deductive structure of science (according to Popper, 1959) is based on the idea of falsifying the consequent of conditional sentences, and so it is unclear why a miniature instantiation of such a system should be suspect.

The selection task does, in fact, have an analogy to 'real life' behaviour, and a concrete example is given in Wason and Johnson-Laird (1972, p. 173), but the criticism is misplaced even if there were no such analogy. Many of the famous Gestalt problems are valuable, not because they are representative of ordinary life, but because they are not representative of it. The difficulty of Duncker's (1948) 'nine dot problem' is due to a failure to overcome the tacit assumption that, in joining up the 3 × 3 matrix of dots with four continuous straight lines, the lines must not extend outside the boundary of the matrix. 'Mere laboratory games' and 'conjuring tricks' can have serious purposes. Every experiment on problem solving depends on a trick; if everything were fully apparent, then there would be no problem. Indeed, it could be argued that it is through the discernment of nature's tricks that we make advances in knowledge, and in hindsight we may call them deceptively simple. The term 'deception' is loaded. Do we deceive our subjects by not warning them about the introduction of a novel stimulus in a series of trials? In the same way the application of the term 'representative' must be exercised with care.

An experiment can be assessed as representative of some situation to the extent that it purports to be representative of it.

Realism

It has been argued that the selection task is interesting regardless of whether it is representative of anything at all, but it can also be argued that it would be interesting in a different way (and perhaps even more interesting) if it were made to represent something familiar. For we could then see if (and how) a familiar setting affected performance.

In recent years the most prolific and controversial research has been concerned with the effects of casting the selection task into some kind of realistic guise. In my own view such studies constitute a dialectical progression over about a decade from thesis to antithesis to synthesis. At least such an interpretation integrates a number of independently conceived studies into some recent theorizing in cognitive psychology. The experiments have been well surveyed by GRIGGS (this volume) and by Evans (1982), so this allows me simply to cite them by name, or reference, and to present an interpretation which differs slightly from Griggs's. The work should be considered in three phases.

Thesis

This phase commenced with the apparent establishment of facilitatory effects through the use of realistic material. The first experiment to show such effects (Wason and Shapiro, 1971/Experiment 2), was based on a consideration of hypothetical journeys, an idea I had developed without success at Harvard in 1963. This was soon followed by the startling Johnson-Laird, Legrenzi and Sonino Legrenzi (1972) 'envelopes experiment' which has become so controversial. Subsequently the experiments of Petrus Van Duyne (1974; 1976), from our stable, fully supported these findings. And from elsewhere the experiments by Bracewell and Hidi (1974) and by

Gilhooly and Falconer (1974), although differing in their results from each other, corroborated the main effect. The facilitatory effect of realism would seem to have been consolidated.

Antithesis

During the second phase these early studies were both criticized and not replicated. And when facilitation was observed with other kinds of realistic material it was attributed to the subjects' direct experience with such material, i.e. to the memory of a real-life situation, rather than to inference. The memory-cueing hypothesis postulates that the counter-example to the rule in question, i.e. $\bar{Q}$, is cued in from long-term memory as a function of the subjects' experience (Griggs and Cox, 1982a). The complete failure of these investigators to replicate the Johnson-Laird *et al.* (1972) 'envelopes experiment' has become a sort of negative test case of the hypothesis. Their American subjects would not have experienced a postal regulation of this kind, and hence there is no counter-example to be cued in. The hypothesis would seem to have been corroborated in a highly original experiment by Evelyn Golding (1981b). With British subjects there was a significant difference on the 'postal task' as a function of age: 13 out of 22 subjects aged over 45 solved the problem compared with two out of 22 under 45 ($p<0.01$). Why? Those over 45, but not those under 45, would have actually experienced the postal regulation used in the task. In her paper, Golding (incidentally) makes the nice anecdotal observation that we all know people over 45 who still send their Christmas Cards without sealing the envelope, in spite of the fact that the regulation was annulled many years ago. It would seem that actual experience of a particular real-life situation, represented in the material of the selection task, is a necessary condition for success in solving the problem. But it does not follow that it is a sufficient condition. In its simplest form, the memory-cueing hypothesis is not a satisfactory explanation of enhancement (see GRIGGS, this volume).

The reasons for the original success of Johnson-Laird *et al.* (1972) have been discussed by Evans (1982, p. 182), and they provide a good illustration of the way in which the hypothesis was first used.

The experiment can be criticized on the grounds that it is *too* realistic. The British university students tested at that time would certainly have experienced a similar rule in their own real-life experience. They would then bring to the experiment the knowledge that one may not seal a letter with a *lower valued* stamp on it. . . . The point is that the subject can solve the problem without *reasoning* at all; he can transfer directly his learned response to an analogous real-life situation.

However, it could be argued that it is not the relevance of the counter-example ($\bar{Q}$) which is stored in long-term memory, but some representation of the positively expressed postal regulation, i.e. 'if sealed then higher value stamp.' Hence the *modus tollens* inference, 'if lower value stamp then unsealed', which sanctions the relevance of $\bar{Q}$, may be an original inference triggered by the task material in relation to the regulation. Such an inference, however, would not be the self-conscious procedure which would be involved in reasoning from a novel premise, but an implicit inference of the kind which pervades so much of everyday activities. Support for this argument, both empirical and theoretical, must be deferred until I have discussed one more criticism of this experiment.

According to Michael Doherty (personal communication), and to Yachanin and Tweney (see GRIGGS, this volume), the instructions used by Johnson-Laird *et al.* (1972), and those in all subsequent experiments which have shown facilitation, have changed the original nature of the selection task. The subjects are required, not to determine whether a hypothesis is true or false, but to choose stimuli which could infringe a given rule. The point is quite correct – the instructions are subtly different. But the modification is not consequential because in Johnson-Laird *et al.* (1972), at any rate, exactly the same type of instruction was given under the control conditions.

These remarks about Johnson-Laird *et al.* (1972) have been necessary, not only for the sake of the record, but to suggest that the antithesis to the facilitation by realism effect carries within it an element of over-simplification even though it has been invaluable as a corrective to the original claims of the thesis. We turn now to some research which suggests the possibility of a synthesis between opposing views.

Synthesis

The critical question is whether the solution of realistic versions of the selection task is a function of remembering specific information, or a function of inferences made about such information. If inference is implicated in arriving at the solution, then it is fair to say that these transformations of the task do elicit rational behaviour.

Facilitation of performance with realistic material, which is either only vicariously related to experience, or directly inconsistent with it, has now been observed in several different experiments, e.g. Cox and Griggs (1982); Griggs and Cox (1982b); D'Andrade (1980), reported in Rumelhart and Norman (1981). For an account of these experiments see GRIGGS (this volume). The D'Andrade (1980) problem involves supposing what it would be like to be a store manager concerned with authorization of purchases; the experiments by Cox and Griggs (1982) involved (among other variants) the converse of a familiar American law, and an incidental variable (colour of clothes) in relation to this law; and the experiment by Griggs and Cox (1982b) involved the systematic negations of the clauses within such laws and regulations. All of these experiments yielded some degree of facilitation, and this cannot be explained as a direct function of the cueing-in of counter-examples from memory because the specific stipulations used would have either *violated* actual experience, or been only *indirectly* related to it. But if the facilitation cannot be explained in this way, how can it be explained?

Schema theory The results are consistent with the hypothesis that the stimulus material evokes *schemata*, or cognitive structures, represented in long-term memory. According to Mandler (1981), such structures can be flexibly applied to varying content within a given area. This is obviously the kind of idea we need – it is related to Minsky's (1975) concept of a 'frame', i.e. 'a structured piece of knowledge about some typical entity or state of affairs', and to Bartlett's (1932) original definition, i.e. 'a mental framework into which new facts and ideas are incorporated'. The idea of schemata implies an intrinsic relation between reasoning and experience. As Rumelhart (1979) has put it in his comment on the very high success rate achieved consistently with the D'Andrade version of the problem, 'This is exactly the result we would expect if our knowledge of reasoning is embedded in task-specific procedures rather than in general rules of inference.'

All this is (perhaps necessarily) rather vague. The theory implies (1) that experience of specific classes of events is stored in terms of organized structures, (2) that the elicitation of such structures allows the elements within them to be mentally manipulated, and (3) that the structures are a necessary condition for the occurrence of inferential processes. Thus the theory fits very well the frequently reported total lack of transfer between realistic and abstract versions of the selection task which have the identical logical structure. Although the mechanisms of schema theory are still in a process of formulation the necessity for such a theory can be appreciated (almost by default) by considering cases in which a literal, or *ab initio*, processing of information, in which the processor contributes nothing, could hardly account for the phenomena. (1) A highly figurative prose passage, which defies comprehension, is illuminated by a knowledge of its title referring to a well-known historical event (Dooling and Lachman, 1971). (2) A negative sentence out of context is understood by means of self-conscious, algorithmic mental processes (Clark, 1974); the addition of an appropriate affirmative sentence enables it to be understood without such processing (Arroyo, 1982; Wason, 1965). (3) A chess master can reconstruct a position from a game of chess after inspecting it for only a few seconds, whereas an amateur does this with much greater difficulty over a series of trials (De Groot, 1965). In some unexplained way, it is assumed that schemata related (respectively) to knowledge of history, knowledge about the world, and knowledge about chess, short circuit the understanding of a situation without conscious computation.

The inferential processes which occur in these cases, and in realistic versions of the selection task, are not, as GRIGGS (this volume) rightly points out, instances of 'logical' reasoning. They reflect a kind of reasoning which does not usually pass as such because of its ubiquity, one which is directly related to Johnson-Laird's (1975) notion of 'implicit inference', and which is nicely captured by Rumelhart's (1980) remark: 'Thus, understanding the problem and solving it is nearly the same thing.' There is of course, nothing especially meritorious about such reasoning – it would not be characterized as 'clever'. Indeed, Perkins (1981) rightly points out that it may be an obstacle to creative achievement.

Analogous attempts at accounting for the phenomenon are 'reasoning-by-analogy' (GRIGGS, this volume), 'availability of cues' (Pollard, 1982), and the 'scenario hypothesis' (Pollard, 1981). The differences between these explanations and the idea of schema theory are terminological; it would seem that no tests could be carried out to decide between them. But one might corroborate the postulation of such a theory by supposing that facilitation would vary as a function of the extent to which the material had been over-learned, thus consolidating the relevant schemata. It is difficult to simulate this kind of depth of experience within the laboratory (e.g. Wason and Shapiro, 1971/Experiment 1) although an experiment by Paolo Legrenzi (1971) does seem to constitute an exception to this generalization. The idea could be tested, not by inducing experience experimentally, but by selecting subjects who have various *degrees* of specific experience, and then testing them on their understanding of conditional sentences which are inconsistent with propositions about the experience.

It would be a mistake, however, to assume that realism can be secured only by means of a standard paradigm in which the selection task is represented in terms of a scenario which fits the subject's experience of social life. In fact, to pursue that approach would run the risk of creating a new convention which, quite apart from methodological difficulties, might become stereotyped and lifeless. A simpler technique to investigate the problem is provided by the RAST.

The RAST revisited In spite of its use of 'abstract' or 'arbitrary' material, the RAST constitutes a claim to realism as much as any of the selection task experiments in thematic guise. As we pointed out in the original paper (Johnson-Laird and Wason, 1970b/Experiment 1), the antecedent and consequent terms were not spatially partitioned, as in the standard way on either side of cards, but cohered in a single stimulus (e.g. a black triangle). The difference may be critical: black triangles seem as real to me as any of our social conventions.

Recently, David Green and I have explored the effects of this 'coherence variable' by using two different test sentences which referred to physically identical stimuli. The *coherent* sentence was: 'Whenever they are triangles they are on black cards', and the *partitioned* sentence was: 'Whenever there are triangles below the line, there is black above the line'. Associated with each sentence was a linear array of eight (partially concealed) black cards, and eight (partially concealed) white cards. The subjects were instructed to inspect the minimum number of cards to prove the sentence true.

With the *coherent* sentence an average of 2·0 black cards were inspected, and an average of 0·17 before selecting any white cards. With the *partitioned* sentence, on the other hand, the corresponding figures were 3·8 and 1·5, the former figures between the two sentences being statistically significant.

It is plausible to suppose that the generalization in the *coherent* sentence, a statement about figures in relation to their ground, facilitates a search for counter-examples in the form of white triangles, and the testing of such a possibility is analogous to the construction of 'alternative mental models' (see JOHNSON-LAIRD, this volume). On the other hand, the generalization in the *partitioned* sentence seems less likely to elicit an 'alternative mental model' because a figure is never normally considered (seen, imagined, thought about) in isolation from its ground. Of course, the overall easiness of the RAST, relative to the selection task, is obviously connected with its binary nature. Its two inputs correspond to a sentence and its negation, and would thus be expected to facilitate the relevance of counter-examples, a relevance which is very difficult to grasp in the selection task.

Conclusion

It is apparent that any superficial dichotomy between 'abstract' and 'concrete' terms in the selection task may be seriously misleading. What matters is realism however it be achieved. It is not, as Piaget might have supposed, that realistic material enhances logical performance because it enables the individual to be guided by formal operations through matter into some superior world of logical structure. Understanding is related to content, an idea which we discerned but failed to formulate correctly (Wason and Johnson-Laird, 1972, p. 245). It has now been adequately corrected by Johnson-Laird in his criticism of the notion of 'mental logic' (see JOHNSON-LAIRD, this volume).

The critics, who have objected so strongly to the early research, have in a way been vindicated, even if their tolerance for the surprising has sometimes been surprisingly low. They may have understood the problem, but naturally failed to understand the significance of the results because they had no way of knowing how much their own reasoning powers are sustained by the material of the sensible world.

Our own early preoccupation with arbitrary sentences, which in retrospect can be seen to function as controls, may have seemed mildly shocking. But without the controls we could not speak about enhancement, or facilitation, by realism. In exactly the same way, we can only speak about the conditions for rational thinking in contrast to those for irrational thinking.

Acknowledgments

Grateful thanks are due to Jonathan Evans, David Green, Philip Johnson-Laird, and Joan Williams, all of whom read earlier versions of this paper, and suggested a number of invaluable improvements. If I have failed to meet their standards the fault is mine.

References

Arroyo, F. V. (1982), 'Negatives in context', *Journal of Verbal Learning and Verbal Behavior, 21*, pp. 118–26.

Bartlett, F. C. (1932), *Thinking: An Experimental and Social Study*, London, Allen & Unwin.

Beth, E. W. and Piaget, J. (1966), *Mathematical Epistemology and Psychology*, Dordrecht, Reidel.

Bracewell, R. J. (1974), 'Interpretation factors in the four card selection task', paper presented at the Selection Task Conference, Trento, Italy, April (unpublished).

Bracewell, R. J. and Hidi, S. E. (1974), 'The solution of an inferential problem as a function of the stimulus materials', *Quarterly Journal of Experimental Psychology, 26*, pp. 480–8.

Bryant, P. E. (1978), 'How stupid are we?', *Times Higher Education Supplement*, 3 March 1978.

Clark, H. H. (1974), 'Semantics and comprehension', in Sebeok, T. A. (ed.), *Current trends in Linguistics, XII, Linguistics and adjacent arts and sciences*, The Hague, Mouton.

Cohen, L. J. (1981), 'Can human irrationality be experimentally demonstrated?', *The Behavioral and Brain Sciences, 4*, pp. 317–70.

Cox, J. R. and Griggs, R. A. (1982), 'The effects of experience on performance in Wason's selection task', *Memory and Cognition, 10*, pp. 496–502.

Crashay-Williams, R. (1947), *The Comforts of Unreason*. London, Kegan Paul, Trench & Trubner.

D'Andrade, R. G. (1980), 'Reasoning and the Wason problem', unpublished manuscript, University of California, San Diego, 1980.

De Groot, A. D. (1965), *Thought and Choice in Chess*, The Hague, Mouton.

Diaconis, P. and Freedman, D. (1981), 'The persistence of cognitive illusions', *The Behavioral and Brain Sciences*, *4*, p. 333.

Dooling, D. J. and Lachman, R. (1971), 'Effects of comprehension on retention of prose', *Journal of Experimental Psychology*, *88*, pp. 216–22.

Duncker, K. (1948), 'On problem solving', Psychological Monographs, *58*, pp. 1–113.

Evans, J. St B. T. (1972), 'Interpretation and "matching bias" in a reasoning task', *Quarterly Journal of Experimental Psychology*, *24*, pp. 193–9.

Evans, J. St B. T. (1982), *The Psychology of Deductive Reasoning*. London, Routledge & Kegan Paul.

Evans, J. St B. T. and Dennis, I. (1982), 'Brain lesions and reasoning: a note on Golding', *Cortex*, *18*, pp. 317–18.

Fillenbaum, S. (1977), 'Mind your p's and q's: the role of content and context in some uses of *and*, *or* and *if*', *The Psychology of Learning and Motivation*, *11*, pp. 41–100.

Finocchiaro, M. A. (1980), *Galileo and the Art of Reasoning*. Dordrecht, Reidel.

Gilhooly, K. J. and Falconer, W. A. (1974), 'Concrete and abstract terms and relations in testing a rule', *Quarterly Journal of Experimental Psychology*, *26*, pp. 355–9.

Golding, E. (1981a), 'The effect of unilateral brain lesion on reasoning', *Cortex*, *17*, pp. 31–40.

Golding E. (1981b), 'The effect of past experience on problem solving', paper presented at the Annual Conference of the British Psychological Society, Surrey University, April.

Golding, E., Reich, S. S. and Wason, P. C. (1974), 'Inter-hemispheric differences in problem solving', *Perception*, *3*, pp. 231–5.

Griggs, R. A. and Cox, J. R. (1982a), 'The elusive thematic-materials effect in Wason's selection task', *British Journal of Psychology*, *73*, pp. 407–20.

Griggs, R. A. and Cox, J. R. (1982b), 'The effect of problem content on strategies in Wason's selection task', *Quarterly Journal of Experimental Psychology* (in press).

Henle, M. (1962), 'On the relation between logic and thinking', *Psychological Review*, *69*, pp. 366–78.

Hudson, W. D. (1980), 'The rational system of beliefs', in Martin, D., Orme Mills, J. and Pickering, W. S. F. (eds), *Sociology and Theology: alliance and conflict*, Hassocks, Harvester Press.

Hughes, M. A. M. (1966), 'The use of negative information in concept attainment', University of London unpublished PhD thesis.

Johnson-Laird, P. N. (1975), 'Models of deduction', in Falmagne, R. J. (ed.), *Reasoning: representation and process*, Hillsdale, New Jersey, Erlbaum.

Johnson-Laird, P. N and Tagart, J. (1969), 'How implication is understood', *American Journal of Psychology, 82*, pp. 367–73.

Johnson-Laird, P. N. and Wason, P. C. (1970a), 'A theoretical analysis of insight into a reasoning task', *Cognitive Psychology, 1*, pp. 134–48.

Johnson-Laird, P. N. and Wason, P. C. (1970b), 'Insight into a logical relation', *Quarterly Journal of Experimental Psychology, 22*, pp. 49–61.

Johnson-Laird, P. N., Legrenzi, P. and Sonino Legrenzi, M. (1972), 'Reasoning and sense of reality', *British Journal of Psychology, 63*, pp. 395–400.

Laing, R. D. (1966), *Interpersonal Perception*, London, Tavistock.

Legrenzi, P. (1971), 'Discovery as a means to understanding', *Quarterly Journal of Experimental Psychology, 23*, pp. 417–22.

Lunzer, E. A., Harrison, C., and Davey, M. (1972), 'The four card problem and the generality of formal reasoning', *Quarterly Journal of Experimental Psychology, 24*, pp. 326–39.

Mandler, J. M. (1981), 'Structural invariants in development', in Liben, L. S. (ed.), *Piaget and the Foundation of Knowledge*, Hillside, New Jersey, Erlbaum.

Minsky, M. (1975), 'Frame-system theory', in Schank, R. C. and Nash-Webber, B. L. (eds), Theoretical issues in natural language processing (unpublished, Massachusetts Institute of Technology), reprinted in Johnson-Laird, P. N. and Wason, P. C. (1977), *Thinking: Readings in Cognitive Science*, Cambridge, Cambridge University Press.

Perkins, D. N. (1981), *The Mind's Best Work*, Cambridge, Mass., Harvard University Press.

Piaget, J. (1972), 'Intellectual development from adolescence to adulthood', *Human Development, 15*, pp. 1–12.

Pollard, P. (1981), 'The effect of thematic content in the "Wason selection task"', *Current Psychological Research, 1*, pp. 21–9.

Pollard, P. (1982), 'Human reasoning: some possible effects of availability', *Cognition, 12*, pp. 65–96.

Popper, K. R. (1959), *The Logic of Scientific Discovery*, London, Hutchinson.

Quine, W. V. O. (1952), *Methods of Logic*, London, Routledge & Kegan Paul.

Roth, E. M. (1979), 'Facilitating insight into a reasoning task', *British Journal of Psychology, 70*, pp. 265–72.

Rumelhart, D. E. (1979), 'Analogical processes and procedural representation', Center for Human Information Technical Report no. 81, La Jolla, University of California, San Diego.

Rumelhart, D. E. (1980), 'Schemata: the building blocks of cognition', in Spiro, R. J., Bruce, B. C. and Brewer, W. F. (eds), *Theoretical Issues in Reading Comprehension*, Hillsdale, New Jersey, Erlbaum.

Rumelhart, D. E. and Norman, D. A. (1981), 'Analogical processes in learning', in Anderson, J. R. (ed.), *Cognitive Skills and their Acquisition*, Hillsdale, New Jersey, Erlbaum.

Smedslund, J. (1970), 'Circular relation between understanding and logic', *Scandinavian Journal of Psychology, 11*, pp. 217–19.

Stebbing, L. S. (1937), *Thinking to Some Purpose*, Harmondsworth, Penguin.

Thouless, R. H. (1936), *Straight and Crooked Thinking*, London, English Universities Press.

Van Duyne, P. C. (1974), 'Realism and linguistic complexity in reasoning', *British Journal of Psychology*, 65, pp. 59–67.

Van Duyne, P. C. (1976), 'Necessity and contingency in reasoning', *Acta Psychologica*, 40, pp. 85–101.

Vuyk, R. (1981), *Critique of Piaget's Genetic Epistemology 1965–1980*, II, London, Academic Press.

Wason, P. C. (1965), 'The contexts of plausible denial', *Journal of Verbal Learning and Verbal Behavior*, 4, pp. 7–11.

Wason, P. C. (1966), 'Reasoning', in Foss, B. (ed.), *New Horizons in Psychology*, I, Harmondsworth, Penguin.

Wason, P. C. (1968), 'Reasoning about a rule', *Quarterly Journal of Experimental Psychology*, 20, pp. 273–81.

Wason, P. C. (1969), 'Regression in reasoning?', *British Journal of Psychology*, 60, pp. 471–80.

Wason, P. C. (1981), 'The importance of cognitive illusions', *The Behavioral and Brain Sciences*, 4, p. 356.

Wason, P. C. and Golding, E. (1974), 'The language of inconsistency', *British Journal of Psychology*, 65, pp. 537–46.

Wason, P. C. and Johnson-Laird, P. N. (1969), 'Proving a disjunctive rule', *Quarterly Journal of Experimental Psychology*, 21, pp. 14–20.

Wason, P. C. and Johnson-Laird, P. N. (1970), 'A conflict between selecting and evaluating information in an inferential task', *British Journal of Psychology*, 61, pp. 509–15.

Wason, P. C. and Johnson-Laird, P. N. (1972), *Psychology of Reasoning: Structure and Content*, London, Batsford.

Wason, P. C. and Shapiro, D. (1971), 'Natural and contrived experience in a reasoning problem', *Quarterly Journal of Experimental Psychology*, 23, pp. 63–71.

Wetherick, N. E. (1970), 'On the representativeness of some experiments in cognition', *Bulletin of the British Psychological Society*, 23, pp. 213–14.

Yachanin, S. A. and Tweney, R. D. (1982), 'The effect of thematic content on cognitive strategies in the four-card selection task', *Bulletin of the Psychonomic Society*, 19, pp. 87–90.

3 The language and thought of disjunction

Stephen E. Newstead and Richard A. Griggs

In this chapter we examine how people understand and use disjunctive information. Disjunctives appear in a variety of different guises in the psychological literature, but there is surprisingly little cross-referencing between the different areas. In a review of work in logic, linguistics, concept formation and reasoning, we point out links between these areas and extract the main underlying themes. Our aim is to ascertain what it is that makes thinking with disjunctives difficult in some situations, and in particular what are the relative contributions of linguistic and conceptual factors to this difficulty.

The logic of disjunction

The standard way of defining disjunctives in logic is in terms of their truth tables. If there are two disjuncts, P and Q, the overall disjunction is true in the situation where P is true and Q is false, and also in the situation where P is false and Q is true; but it is false when both P and Q are false (see Table 3.1). However, there is an ambiguity in the situation where both P and Q are true; under inclusive disjunction this case would make the rule true, whereas under exclusive disjunction this case would be false.

Traditionally, logic has given precedence to inclusive disjunction, to the extent that it has its own logical operator assigned to it, usually symbolised *v*. It is interesting to examine just why there should be this preference for inclusive disjunction – a preference, incidentally, which is echoed in psychological studies of disjunction.

TABLE 3.1 *The truth tables for inclusive and exclusive disjunction*

P	Q	Inclusive disjunction	Exclusive disjunction
T	T	T	F
T	F	T	T
F	T	T	T
F	F	F	F

T = true   F = false

There are two plausible explanations for this preference, the first being on the grounds of parsimony. If an inclusive interpretation is adopted, then as Suppes (1957) has pointed out, all other logical operations can be defined in terms of this operator and negation. Developmental psychologists will be familiar with such an analysis, since Inhelder and Piaget (1958) define the formal operational stage of thinking in terms of sixteen binary operations which use just negation $(-)$, inclusive disjunction (v) and conjunction $(\cdot)$. Conjunction can be defined, albeit rather clumsily, in terms of negation and inclusive disjunction, since $P \cdot Q$ is the same as $- (\bar{P} \vee \bar{Q})$. A second plausible explanation concerns the relationship between symbolic logic and set theory. A basic relationship between two sets is that of union, expressed symbolically as U. The union of two sets, A U B, contains all the items which fall into either of the two sets – including any items that fall into both. This union can be translated into symbolic logic as A v B.

The truth-table definition of v determines the inferences that can be drawn. Valid inferences can only be drawn from premises that deny one of the disjuncts; no valid conclusion follows from the assertion of one of the disjuncts. Thus both the following arguments are valid:

P v Q,
not P,
Therefore, Q.

P v Q,
not Q,
Therefore, P.

An example of the first argument is: Either John is rich or he is foolish; he is not rich; therefore, he is foolish.

The following conclusions are not permitted:

P v Q,
P,
Therefore, not Q.

P v Q,
Q,
Therefore, not P.

The reason for this, obviously, is that P v Q can be true when both disjuncts are true.

It can be seen, then, that the use of the operator v leads to an economical and internally consistent system of symbolic logic. We shall see, however, that this logical analysis bears little resemblance to how disjunctives are normally used; in particular, many uses of disjunction in everyday language seem to suggest an exclusive interpretation.

Another problem that has attracted considerable attention in recent years arises from the idea of 'fuzzy logic'. Traditional logic adheres to the principle of the excluded middle, which claims that any proposition must be true or false – it cannot have an inter-mediate value like 'maybe true' or 'possibly false'. Following Zadeh (1965), a number of writers have questioned this assumption, sug-gesting that truth is in fact a continuous dimension. Clearly this undermines the whole logical analysis of disjunction just discussed, since logical operators such as v can no longer be defined in terms of their truth tables. It also means that any conclusions that can be drawn from disjunctive propositions will be probabilistic rather than all-or-none.

While a 'fuzzy' analysis of disjunction is much more complicated than the clear-cut analysis of two-valued logic, it has some attraction from the psychological point of view. We do talk about things being 'probably true' or 'almost certainly false' – something which is easily captured by fuzzy logic. Such statements may be made through ignorance of all the facts, or they may reflect a genuine belief that truth is a continuous dimension; whichever is the case, fuzzy logic will give a more accurate account of actual behaviour than will two-valued logic. It is, of course, an empirical question as to how well the two logical systems account for human behaviour. Unfortunately, however, most studies of disjunctive thinking have forced subjects to adopt a two-valued logic. We will argue in this chapter that this has led to some rather artificial results and a rather simplistic conception of human thought. It seems to us that not only is truth a fuzzy, continuous dimension, but also that the English language equivalent for disjunction – the word 'or' – is itself a fuzzy concept susceptible to a variety of interpretations.

Linguistic and psycholinguistic studies of disjunction

Linguistic considerations

In everyday language, disjunction is normally expressed using the word 'or', though this does not mean that there is an exact corres-pondence between this word and the logical operator *v*. Indeed, perhaps the hottest issue in linguistic studies of disjunction is that of whether the 'basic' meaning of 'or' is inclusive, exclusive, or whether there are in fact two quite distinct meanings. Intuitively, there do seem to be some contexts in which 'or' is inclusive, and others in which it is exclusive. If an advertisement for a lecturing position was phrased, 'Applicants must have either a PhD or teach-ing experience,' this would surely not be taken to exclude someone who had both a PhD and teaching experience; hence this would be an inclusive disjunction. On the other hand, if a mother said to her son, 'You can either have some candy or some cake,' her instruction would surely have been disobeyed if her son had both candy and cake; hence this is an exclusive disjunction.

Many linguists, perhaps following the lead of logicians, have claimed that the inclusive meaning of 'or' is the basic one. To quote just one example, Pelletier (1977) says, '*or* in English is always inclusive' (p. 63). At first sight this is surprising, since exclusive uses of 'or' seem quite common in English usage. However, Pelletier adopts a very stringent criterion for demonstrating the existence of exclusive 'or': 'The *only* way to demonstrate that a given sentence employs an exclusive *or* is to imagine both disjuncts true, and see if such a state of affairs would *logically imply* the falsity of the disjunctive sentence' (p. 64). The difficulty of achieving this cri-terion can be illustrated with Pelletier's own example, 'I'll either be with Arlene or Suzi tonight,' which at first sight seems to suggest exclusive disjunction. However, the events might have turned out thus: 'I went to the bar with Arlene and we met Suzi; we three then spent the rest of the night together' (p. 64). Pelletier claims that this would not prove the falsehood of the original statement, nor that I had lied in making the statement. While this is true, it is surely the case that the original statement would be called misleading, since it led to an expectation that was not fulfilled.

That Pelletier's criterion is too strict can be illustrated by considering what would happen if neither of the disjuncts had occurred. For example, I might have arranged to go out with Arlene, but since she was not sure whether she would be free, I had a tentative arrangement to go out with Suzi just in case Arlene could not come. In the event, however, I had a car accident and went out with neither of them. I would not have lied nor been deliberately misleading, since at the time I uttered the statement I genuinely believed it to be the truth. Hence, as with the case when both disjuncts turned out to be true, all one can say is that the original statement was misleading in that it led to an expectation which was not fulfilled. This is why Pelletier's criterion is too strong; it is generally agreed that a disjunction is not consistent with a state of affairs in which neither disjunct occurs; yet on Pelletier's criterion of logical implication, the disjunction seems to be consistent with this state of affairs. It seems sensible to conclude that there are situations in which 'or' is used with its exclusive sense.

While the extreme claim that 'or' is always inclusive can be rejected, it is still possible that the inclusive interpretation is the basic one. This point of view has been championed by, among others, Gazdar (1979), who claims that the exclusive use is a derived one based on 'conversational implicatures'. This can be illustrated with reference to the example already considered, 'I'll either be with Arlene or Suzi tonight.' According to Gazdar, this would be interpreted inclusively but for implicatures derived from Grice's (1975) maxim of quantity. This maxim states that speakers should be as informative as possible; hence if I intended going out with both Arlene and Suzi, I should have said so. The fact that I did not say this suggests to the listener that I intend going out with only one of them. Gazdar's position is a perfectly tenable one, but there is no direct evidence that this linguistic analysis is the correct one.

The claim that 'or' has two meanings, one inclusive and one exclusive, has been advocated by Hurford (1974). This is consistent with the linguistic evidence, since as we have seen there are examples in English of both uses. Once again, however, there is little direct evidence either for or against the position. One prediction that has been derived is that some languages should possess two distinct lexical items, one for inclusive 'or', the other for exclusive 'or'. One of the best examples of this is Latin, which has the words 'vel' and 'aut', the first of which is taken to be inclusive, the second exclusive. In fact, the logical operator v is a contraction of 'vel', supposedly to remind classicists that this operator is inclusive. However, this analysis has been challenged by both Gazdar (1979) and Pelletier (1977). These authors claim that the use of 'aut' by a speaker suggests that the speaker *expects* only one of the disjuncts to be true, but is not in fact inconsistent with the occurrence of both disjuncts. Given the dearth of native Latin speakers, it may prove impossible to resolve this issue. It has been claimed that words for both inclusive and exclusive disjunction exist in Cairene (Eid, 1973), in Finnish (Collinson, 1948), and in Kpelle (Gay and Cole, 1967). However, none of these accounts give adequate consideration of the possible pragmatic factors involved, and in the absence of such information it must be concluded that this issue is as yet undecided.

The final linguistic analysis to be considered is that of Lakoff (1971). Her position is quite explicit: 'except for a very few possible exceptions, *or* must be exclusive' (p. 142). In this claim, she has the backing of the Oxford English Dictionary: 'An *alternative* (or *or*) proposition contains two statements, the acceptance of one of which involves the rejection of the other . . . either may be agreed to, but not both.' Her evidence to support her claim is purely distributional; she collects together a variety of disjunctive sentences, and points out that most seem to indicate an exclusive interpretation. However, such evidence is not conclusive. We have already seen that inclusive disjunctives do occur in English; and the occurrence of exclusive disjunctives is readily explained in terms of either conversational implicatures or the dual-meaning theory of Hurford (1974).

The linguistic analyses considered so far are misguided if, as seems to be the case, 'or' is an ambiguous term, having a variety of different but related meanings. Looking for *the* meaning of 'or' is rather like Wittgenstein's (1953) attempt to find *the* meaning of the word 'game'; and, as Wittgenstein showed, such a search is futile. The various meanings of 'or' share certain 'family resemblances', but any two uses of the term may share little or nothing in common with each other. One of the meanings of 'or' may be its truth-functional use corresponding to the truth table for inclusive disjunction, another might be the use corresponding to the truth table for exclusive disjunction. But there are a number of other uses which have no truth-functional equivalent. The example cited earlier from Pelletier is a case in point: 'I'll either be with Arlene or Suzi tonight.' It seems rather absurd to apply a truth-functional analysis to this, since it expresses an intention rather than a logical relationship between two propositions. In fact, as we argued earlier, the intention can be 'true' in the sense of being genuinely held even in the event that neither of the events occurs.

Psychological studies of interpretation

Clearly we have reached the stage where we require direct evidence as to how subjects actually interpret disjunctive sentences. Unfortunately, there are relatively few psychological studies of this problem, and those that have been carried out have yielded inconsistent results. For example, Evans and Newstead (1980) carried out a study using abstract material in a neutral context. In the first experiment in this study, subjects were asked to construct verifying or falsifying instances of a disjunctive rule such as 'Either the letter is A or the number is 3.' In the second experiment, subjects were given a similar rule followed by a letter + number combination, and had to judge whether the rule was true or false with respect to the combination. Both of these techniques allow an investigation of whether subjects are adopting inclusive or exclusive interpretations, and in both cases there was a preference for the former. However, there are a number of problems with this study.

Firstly, although the majority (50–60 per cent) preferred the inclusive interpretation, this still leaves a fairly large number of subjects (over 20 per cent) who consistently adopted an exclusive interpretation (the remaining subjects were inconsistent). Secondly, while there was no linguistic context for the rules, they did occur in an experimental context which might have affected interpretation. It is well known that subjects will frequently adopt strategies of responding in experimental situations, and a reasonable strategy in Evans and Newstead's second experiment would be to call a rule true if the first element of the disjunct was true. Thus, given the rule, 'Either the letter is A or the number is 3,' the subject might look for an A and if one was found, respond true. If no A was found, the subject would look for a 3, and respond true if one was found, false if not. The point is that if an A is found, the subject looks no further, so it makes no difference whether the letter is 3 or some other number – the response will still be true. Thus the preference for inclusive interpretation could be due to the adoption of an experimental strategy rather than to purely interpretational factors. The third point to be borne in mind is that the results might not be replicable; Manktelow (1979), in what was almost an exact replication of the Evans and Newstead study, found that the majority of subjects favoured the exclusive interpretation. Thus while all these results are interesting in their own right, they tell us little about what is the 'natural' interpretation of disjunctives.

Other studies of how adult subjects understand disjunctives have been carried out in the context of developmental research. For example, Paris (1973) gave child and adult subjects sentences such as 'The bird is in the nest or the shoe is on the foot.' The subjects were then presented with pairs of slides, each slide either verifying or falsifying one of the disjuncts. On the critical case where both disjuncts were true, 71 per cent of adult subjects thought that this confirmed the original disjunctive sentence; in other words, they preferred an inclusive interpretation.

Other experiments, using slightly more realistic material, have found a preference for exclusive interpretations. Sternberg (1979) gave his subjects sentences describing the contents of a box, such as 'There is a circle in the box or there is a square in the box.' Subjects had to evaluate outcomes as to whether they rendered the sentence true, maybe true, or false. The interesting outcome, of course, is when both the disjuncts are true – in the above example when there is both a circle and a square in the box. On Sternberg's criterion, only 16 per cent of the college students were classified as having adopted an inclusive interpretation, while 82 per cent were classified as having an exclusive interpretation. In a study by Braine and Rumain (1981) subjects heard a puppet make a statement like 'Either there's a dog or there's a horse in the box.' The subjects could see the box, and were asked to indicate whether or not the puppet was right. With adult subjects, 32 per cent produced the truth table of inclusive disjunction, 41 per cent that of exclusive disjunction. Thus although there are variations between the different tasks used, in general adults seem to show a slight preference for exclusive interpretations.

However, none of the studies cited so far has investigated disjunctives in genuinely realistic contexts. The linguistic analyses reviewed earlier suggested that different contexts could bias interpretations in different ways, so we decided to put this to an experimental test. In the experiment, subjects were given short prose passages which set the context for a disjunctive sentence, for example:

> Frank and Jane had been dating regularly for several months when Jane found out that Frank had been seeing Mary on the side. Jane said to Frank: '*Either you stop seeing Mary or I will start dating someone else.*'

Following this passage, there appeared four sentences corresponding to the four possible combinations of affirmation and denial of each of the two disjuncts. Thus the double affirmative version of the above was, 'Frank did stop seeing Mary; Jane started dating someone else'; the version which negated the second disjunct was, 'Frank did stop seeing Mary; Jane didn't date someone else', and so on. Subjects had to indicate whether each of these outcomes was consistent or inconsistent with the underlined disjunctive sentence in the previous paragraph.

The passages were designed to produce five different contexts, those of threat, promise, choice, qualification and uncertainty; in addition two neutral contexts were used, one of which used concrete material, the other abstract. Type of context seemed to determine interpretation. When the context was that of a threat, as in the example given, there was almost universal agreement that the double affirmative case was inconsistent, and hence that the disjunction should be interpreted exclusively. In fact, there was a preference in most of the seven contexts used for an exclusive interpretation, though few preferences were as strong as that with threats. The only context which produced a preference for the inclusive interpretation was that of 'qualification', for example:

> An exclusive club is selective about its membership. The club rules say: '*A member must earn £20,000 a year or be distinguished in his field.*'

With contexts such as this, 53 per cent of the interpretations were inclusive. Thus this experiment provides strong evidence that the interpretation of disjunctions is determined by the contexts in which they occur. There was a suggestion that, in the contexts we used, the exclusive interpretation was the preferred one, but agreement on this interpretation was unanimous only in the case of threats. It seems better to view the difference between inclusive and exclusive interpretation as a continuum, with some contexts giving strong biases towards one end, but others producing no strong biases. The results from the abstract and concrete neutral contexts produced a preference for exclusive interpretations but by no means a universal one; this ties in nicely with most previous research (e.g. Sternberg, 1979; Braine and Rumain, 1981) which has found similar results with such contexts.

Developmental studies of interpretation

The interpretation of disjunctives has also been studied from a developmental perspective. Paris (1973) claimed that there was a gradual development over age from an overwhelming preference for inclusive interpretations at age 7 to an increased preference for exclusive interpretations in adults. There is a serious problem in this study, however, since children were classified solely on their responses to the case where both disjuncts were true. Throughout Paris's study, there seems to have been a strong tendency, at least with the younger children, to call the T-T case true and the F-F case false, regardless of the connective used. Performance in cases where just one of the components was true was more variable though there was a tendency to call these true as well. These results may indicate that the children were interpreting all connectives as conjunctions, or they may result from perceptual matching to the items given (cf. Evans, 1972). In either case it is clearly wrong to classify their responses as indicating inclusive interpretations.

The way round this problem is given by Sternberg (1979) and Braine and Rumain (1981): that of looking at individual truth tables. Thus subjects are classified as adopting an inclusive interpretation only if they call the T-T case true, the F-F case false *and* the T-F and F-T cases true. On this criterion, fewer than 20 per cent of Braine and Rumain's 5- to 6-year-olds were classified as adopting inclusive interpretations. Sternberg (1979), using a slightly stricter criterion, found fewer than 10 per cent. While there is no obvious change in inclusive interpretations over age in either of these studies, both found an increasing preference for exclusive interpretations. It seems reasonable to conclude that in tasks such as these young children do not clearly understand the connective 'or', but that they gradually learn its more frequent, exclusive interpretation.

A related line of research has examined children's understanding of class union, which as we have seen is logically equivalent to inclusive disjunction. Although most of these studies were not designed specifically to investigate the interpretation of 'or', they do provide some evidence on this. The work of Neimark and Slotnick (1970) is fairly representative of these studies. Children were given a test statement, for example, 'black or birds', and were asked to circle all the alternatives which were described by the statement. The alternatives for this instance were two black birds, two white birds, two black flowers and two white flowers. The logically correct class union response was to circle all the items except the white flowers, but the younger subjects gave relatively few such responses; in fact, this response was given reliably only by college students.

These results are a little surprising since they suggest that college students tend to give the class union response which corresponds to the inclusive interpretation of 'or'; previous research has suggested that adults prefer the exclusive interpretation. What is more, this preference for inclusive interpretation increases over age. There are a number of possible explanations for these results, but the most plausible is in terms of the linguistic form used. In general, it seems that what might be called the contracted form of the disjunction is more likely to lead to inclusive interpretations, at least with adults. For example, a non-contracted disjunction would be, 'Choose the caramels or choose the coffee creams'; this can be contracted to, 'Choose the caramels or (the) coffee creams.' The non-contracted version seems to preclude the possibility of selecting both, but the contracted version seems much less precise. An examination of the previous literature reveals that contracted versions are indeed more likely to be interpreted inclusively. Johansson (1977) found that adults given the contracted instruction, 'Encircle all figures that are blue or square', were equally divided between inclusive and exclusive interpretations. But subjects instructed to 'Encircle all figures that are blue or all that are square', adopted predominantly exclusive interpretations. Since Neimark and Slotnick's (1970) study used a contracted form, 'black or birds', this would explain why adults preferred inclusive interpretations.

The younger children in this study failed to give inclusive interpretations presumably because they were not sensitive to these subtle linguistic cues. If this is the case, it has important implications for research on children's understanding of logical connectives. For example, Suppes and Feldman (1971) found that children aged between 4 and 6 responded more accurately to a command which required an exclusive disjunction response than to one which required an inclusive disjunction response. However, the type of response required was cued by rather subtle linguistic means. For example, exclusive disjunction was cued by the instruction, 'Give me the green things, or, the round things', while inclusive disjunction was cued by several linguistic means, including a contracted version of the above, 'Give me the things that are green or round.' Poor performance on the latter command is readily understandable if these young children failed to realise that it suggested an inclusive interpretation. In fact, the evidence available seems to suggest that children given commands involving 'or' tend to interpret these as meaning 'choose one'. Many of the errors made by children in experiments such as that of Suppes and Feldman (1971) can be explained in this way. Further, Johansson and Sjolin (1975) found that children aged 5 or over typically gave just one of the items mentioned when instructed to 'Put up the car or the bicycle.' Similar findings are reported by Braine and Rumain (1981).

While individual experimental results can be explained in terms of linguistic factors or the type of demands that the particular task makes, it is difficult to provide a synthesis of research into the development of disjunctives. Young children given the task of judging whether truth-table outcomes are consistent or inconsistent with a disjunctive statement frequently adopt the truth table for conjunction, possibly because of perceptual matching to the elements mentioned in the statement. With increasing age, there is an increasing tendency to adopt the truth table for exclusive disjunction. However, when young children are given instructions to choose certain items from a set, they tend to interpret 'or' as meaning 'choose items containing one of the attributes.' Only gradually do they come to realise that some linguistic forms indicate exclusive interpretations, others inclusive ones. Since there are so many differences between the tasks and linguistic forms used in different experiments, general conclusions are premature.

Other interpretational considerations

There are other problems in the interpretation of 'or' quite apart from the ambiguity concerning inclusion-exclusion. In logic, the operator *v* can connect any two propositions, and the order of these has no effect on truth value. This appears not to be the case with 'or'. Lakoff (1971) has pointed out that in natural language, the two disjuncts must have a common topic. For example, it would be acceptable to say, 'Either this letter was written by John or it was written by his brother', but anomalous to say, 'Either this letter was written by John or the ball is round.' Fillenbaum (1974) showed that subjects were sensitive to such violations of common topic; subjects consistently rated them as strange, and also found considerable difficulty in remembering them.

Fillenbaum's research also investigated unordered and ordered uses of disjunctives. An unordered use would be, 'He will drive to Washington or fly to New York', where there is no indication of one action occurring before the other in time. In contrast, 'Do your job properly or you'll get fired' is ordered since it suggests the opportunity for doing the job properly before the threat is carried out. Subjects were again sensitive to such differences; altering the order of the disjuncts had little effect on unordered sentences, but it led to high ratings of strangeness and difficulties in memorisation with ordered items.

Fillenbaum's work confirms our earlier conclusion that 'or' has a variety of different meanings. In other words, as we have mentioned before, 'or' is a fuzzy concept. Like most fuzzy concepts, it probably has a prototypical meaning. We will stick our necks out and suggest that this is to indicate the existence of two alternatives, with the expectancy that only one will occur. (A similar suggestion has been made by Dik, 1968.) This seems to cover most of the major uses of 'or' that we have come across. It might seem to exclude inclusive interpretations, but this is not the case. Consider, for example, the inclusive disjunction cited earlier: 'Applicants must have either a PhD or teaching experience.' This suggests that the

applicant needs the minimum requirement of one of these qualifications and that the employers are expecting to appoint someone
with just one of the qualifications. It would be an additional bonus
for the employers if a candidate had both, but this is more than
they are expecting. (Indeed, if they had expected a number of
applicants with both qualifications, the advertisement would presumably have been phrased as a conjunction.)

Although the above 'prototypical' meaning of 'or' might well be
wrong, it does seem clear that 'or' will not be forced into a truth-
functional strait-jacket. This can be illustrated with reference to the
unpublished experiment we mentioned earlier on the interpretation
of disjunctives. According to truth-functional logic, the disjunctive
is always true when just one of the disjuncts is false; however, in
certain contexts some subjects did not give this interpretation. For
example, the sentence, 'In each pair, either the triangle is green or
the square is red', was presented as a child's description of the way
he had arranged his toy bricks. More than 10 per cent of the
responses to this classified the instance in which one disjunct was
denied as being inconsistent with the sentence; subjects giving this
response apparently treated the statement as a conjunction rather
than a disjunction. In addition, when the context involved choice,
e.g. 'You can either have ice cream or apple pie for dessert', 6 per
cent of subjects classified the double denial case as consistent with
the sentence. This is not as bizarre as it seems at first sight, since
the disjunctive sentence seems to specify that both desserts must
not be eaten, but does not preclude having nothing at all. Thus this
illustrates quite clearly the varied uses to which 'or' can be put.

Psychological research on non-truth-functional logic is sparse,
but Oden (1977) has shown one way in which such research might
be carried out. In this study, subjects first of all rated the truthfulness of single statements such as 'a sparrow is a bird' and 'a penguin
is a bird'. Then subjects rated the truthfulness of combinations of
such statements, in conjunctions and in disjunctions such as 'a
sparrow is a bird or a penguin is a bird'. Oden was interested in
the relationship between the initial ratings of truthfulness and those
given to such combinations, and found that for disjunctions the
relationship was best described by an inverted multiplying rule.
What this means is that the falsity of the disjunction is obtained by
multiplying together the falsity ratings of the two component statements. This is an interesting possibility, and clearly very different

from truth functional analyses. However, it is by no means clear that such results will generalise to other situations. Oden used only logically true statements, and these may combine in different ways to logically false statements. In addition, it could be argued that the experimental design forced subjects to adopt fuzzy interpretations, since they were obliged to rate logically true statements on a scale of truthfulness. Nevertheless, this is clearly a fruitful and interesting area of research.

Disjunctive concepts

The literature on concept formation is enormous, and a sizeable number of the studies carried out have used some form of disjunctive concept. It is generally found that inclusive disjunctive concepts are harder to acquire than conjunctive ones and that exclusive disjunctive concepts are harder than both of these (see, for example, Neisser and Weene, 1962). In this section we will consider possible explanations for the differential difficulty of these conceptual rules.

It is tempting to attribute the difficulty of disjunctive concepts to the interpretational ambiguity discussed in the previous section, but such an approach runs into problems. In most studies of concept formation there *is* no ambiguity, since the interpretation to be adopted is indicated very clearly. Furthermore, one would expect that exclusive disjunction should prove easier than inclusive, since the former is the preferred linguistic interpretation, at least with adults. However, the reverse order of difficulty is normally found. We will return later to studies of disjunctive concept formation in people whose language has separate words for inclusive and exclusive disjunction (e.g. Gay and Cole, 1967). In general, the influence of linguistic factors on concept formation is not great, which means that research in this area should provide insight into the logical difficulty of disjunction.

Bruner, Goodnow and Austin (1956) devote a whole chapter of their classic book to disjunctive concepts. They suggest that social factors may be important in determining the difficulty of disjunctive concepts, since there seems to be a general tendency in society to change disjunctive definitions into conjunctive ones. They give the example of the concept 'clinical psychologist', which initially referred to someone with appropriate academic training or to someone who, without training, had helped disturbed people in a clinical setting. Bruner *et al.* point out, quite rightly, that this disjunctive definition has been 'regularised' so that clinical psychologists are now defined in a single way – i.e. anybody having the appropriate qualification. But is this because of some inherent dislike of disjunctive concepts, or is it because there was some desire to get rid of possible charlatans? In any case, explaining the difficulty in terms of 'social factors' is no explanation at all: we do not know whether disjunctive concepts are abandoned (if they are) because disjunction is inherently complex; or if disjunction is difficult because it is shunned by society.

Bruner *et al.* also suggest that disjunctive concepts are difficult because they rely heavily on negative information, and this explanation seems more plausible. Two examples of a disjunctive concept may share no attributes at all: if the concept is red or square, one instance may be a red circle, the other a blue square. For this reason, positive instances are not very informative, but negative ones are. For example, the information that a blue circle is not an example of the concept means that both of these properties can be ruled out as relevant attributes. The best way of tackling disjunctive concepts, then, is by focusing on negative instances, but this is something that subjects seem to find difficult to do. Instead, subjects tend to concentrate on positive instances, and thus make errors such as the 'common element fallacy'. This involves 'collating all the features common to the positive instances one has encountered and proposing these common features as an hypothesis about the correct concept'. Occasionally, this fallacy will lead fortuitously to a correct answer, but more often it will not.

Bruner *et al.* found that subjects did markedly better on disjunctive concepts when the first instance they saw was a negative one. This seems to draw attention to the usefulness of such instances, and subjects then go on to use appropriate strategies. However, when the first instance was positive, inappropriate strategies were the norm. This tendency to rely on positive instances, thus treating disjunctions as conjunctions, seems to be a common error with disjunctives. Schroth and Tamayo (1972) have shown that disjunctive concepts are actually easier than conjunctive ones when only negative instances are given. Further, it is usually found that disjunctive concepts are harder than conjunctive ones only for initial trials; after practice, there is little difference between them (Bourne,

1970). It is tempting to argue that, with practice, subjects learn the importance of negative information. In general, then, there is good evidence that the difficulty of learning disjunctive concepts stems from the difficulty of handling negative information. (See EVANS, this volume, for further discussion on the difficulty of negative information.)

A popular experimental technique in recent years has been the study of how subjects *use* conceptual rules rather than how they learn them. In this technique, the subject is given a disjunctive rule followed by a number of instances; the task is to classify each instance as to whether it is true or false with respect to the rule given. This is, of course, very similar to the techniques used to investigate the interpretation of disjunctive statements (cf. Paris, 1973). The principal differences are that in studies of rule using, the interpretation is usually specified to the subject beforehand; and the dependent variable is reaction time rather than the responses given.

In perhaps the best-known study of this kind, Trabasso, Rollins and Shaughnessy (1971) gave their subjects rules such as 'large triangle or green circle'. There followed a picture of a triangle or circle which could be large or small, orange or green, and the subject had to indicate whether the picture was a positive or negative example of the rule. In most (though not all) experiments, conjunctive rules were easier than inclusive disjunctions, which were in turn easier than exclusive disjunctions – i.e. just the same order as in concept learning studies. However, the explanation for these relative difficulties is seemingly rather different, being due not to problems caused by negative instances but to the sorts of processing strategies that subjects use in this task. These can be envisaged as decision trees (Hunt, Marin and Stone, 1966), examples of which can be seen in Figure 3.1.

To illustrate what these decision trees involve, consider that given for inclusive disjunction. The subject first examines one of the attributes of the conceptual rule (A1). If this is present, then without looking any further, the subject knows this is a positive (True) instance. However, if the first attribute is not present, the subject must examine for the presence of the second attribute, responding True if it is present, False if it is not. The decision tree for conjunction is the mirror image of this, which would lead one to expect similar response times for the two rules; however, it is also possible

Conjunction   Inclusive disjunction   Exclusive disjunction

```
        A1                    A1                         A1
      /    \                /    \                     /    \
     Y      N              Y      N                   Y      N
     |      |              |      |                   |      |
     A2     |              |      A2                  A2     A2
    /  \    |              |     /  \                /  \   /  \
   Y    N   N              Y    Y    N              Y    N Y    F
   |    |   |              |    |    |              |    | |    |
   T    F   F              T    T    F              F    T T    F
```

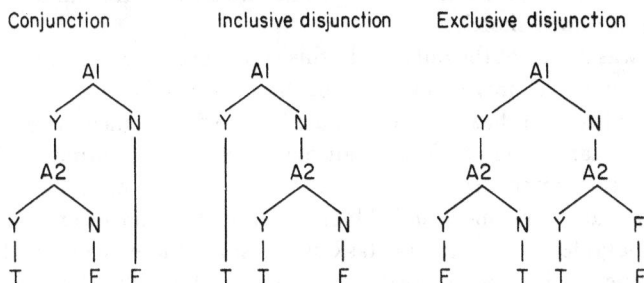

FIGURE 3.1 Decision trees for three conceptual rules

to carry out a parallel processing for conjunctive rules, looking for the joint presence of the two attributes, which might explain why conjunctive rules sometimes lead to faster responding. A further assumption of the model is that the choice of which attribute to search for first is randomly determined.

An additional but highly interesting determinant of performance in this task has been demonstrated recently by Ketchum and Bourne (1980). They gave subjects conjunctive and disjunctive rules relating different combinations of attributes: colour-shape (e.g. red hexagon); size-shape (e.g. small square); and number-shape (e.g. one square). The subjects' task was to classify various instances into positive and negative categories. There was a tendency for colour-shape combinations to lead to better performance on disjunctive rules and for the other combinations to lead to better performance on conjunctive rules. However, this effect held mainly for the T-F case. To illustrate what this means, consider the rule 'red or square'. The T-F case here is a red non-square (e.g. red triangle), and subjects have no difficulty assigning this instance to the positive category. However, if the rule had been 'red *and* square' subjects would have been reluctant to assign it to the negative category. It would appear that the colour dimension is highly salient in colour-shape combinations, and seems to dominate any instance in which it occurs to such an extent that there is a strong tendency to call it positive. This coincides with the rule in disjunctive concepts but not in conjunctive ones, hence the discrepancy. Here we have an instance of a perceptual strategy biasing logical performance –

something which is common in the reasoning literature and to which we will return shortly.

It was hoped at the outset that this research on concept formation and use would provide evidence on the logical difficulty of disjunction. This hope has been only partially fulfilled, since once again task demands seem to be a major determinant of performance. The fact that disjunctives involve negative instances does seem to contribute to their conceptual difficulty. Even this, however, may be attributable in part to the task used, since there seems to be a tendency to focus upon positive instances in this task. The difficulty of disjunctives in studies of rule using seems most easily explained in terms of the types of strategies subjects use. It is in fact possible to make disjunctive concepts easier than conjunctive ones by altering the task demands, for instance by increasing the relevance of negative instances in concept formation tasks. Once again, it is relatively easy to understand performance in particular situations, less easy to draw any general conclusions concerning the difficulty of disjunction.

Disjunctive reasoning

As we indicated in the first section of this chapter, only one type of inference is logically valid with all disjunctives: reasoning from the falsity of one component to the truth of the other. With exclusive disjunction it is valid to argue from the truth of one component to the falsity of the other, but this is not permissible with inclusive disjunction. In this section we examine how accurately subjects can draw such inferences, both with abstract and with realistic material.

A recurrent theme in work on disjunctive reasoning has been the effect of negatives. These can be systematically introduced into disjunctives by negating the first component (Either not P or Q), by negating the second component (Either P or not Q), or by negating both (Either not P or not Q). This research has been reviewed recently by Evans (1982) and for this reason we will pay little attention to those studies.

The main question we will consider in this section is that of whether subjects can draw the permitted logical inferences from disjunctives, and on this there is surprisingly little evidence. One problem, of course, is the ambiguity of disjunctives, since the permitted inferences depend upon whether the disjunctive is exclusive or inclusive. For this reason, several studies have specified the type of disjunction by adding 'or both' to indicate inclusive disjunction and 'but not both' to indicate exclusive disjunction. We will examine first whether subjects can infer the truth of one component from the falsity of the other – an inference that is valid under both kinds of disjunction. Intuitively, this kind of inference would seem quite straightforward. It underlies many 'detective' or 'fault finding' activities. To take a simple example, if the doorbell rings, you might conclude that either there is somebody at the front door or there is somebody at the back door. If you investigate the front door and there is no one there, it would seem reasonable to infer that there is somebody at the back door.

However, an examination of the research in this area would suggest that many subjects – including university undergraduates and postgraduates – have some difficulty with this kind of reasoning. For example, Roberge (1976a) gave graduate students a paper-and-pencil test including exclusive and inclusive disjunctions phrased in abstract terms – letters of the alphabet. When both disjuncts were affirmative, subjects made 16 per cent errors on exclusive disjunctions and 31 per cent on inclusive disjunctions! Almost identical results were obtained by Roberge and Flexer (1979) using adolescent (eighth grade) boys and girls, though Roberge (1978) found slightly better performance – 6 per cent errors on exclusive disjunctions and 14 per cent on inclusive disjunctions.

Why should subjects make errors with such simple-looking problems? It is tempting to attribute the errors to the abstract nature of the material, but using more realistic material seems to have little effect. Roberge (1977; 1978) found almost identical error rates with concrete and abstract material for both inclusive and exclusive disjunctives. Furthermore, Roberge and Antonak (1979) actually found better performance with abstract material than with concrete. However, it might be maintained that the concrete material used in these studies was far from realistic. Consider a concrete item from Roberge (1978): 'Either Joan is athletic or she is rich (but not both).' This is unnatural in a number of ways. Firstly, it seems to break Lakoff's (1971) principle of common topic, since there seems to be no link between the two disjuncts. It is difficult to imagine any context in which such a sentence might be uttered. Secondly, the 'but not both' at the end of the sentence makes the whole thing jar. Except in reasoning experiments, it is the context rather than the inclusion of words in parentheses that determines interpretation.

For this reason, we decided to look at disjunctive reasoning in a more naturalistic context. We used the same contexts we had used in our earlier interpretational experiment and put them into disjunctive syllogisms, for example:

Tom was in debt to his brother. He told him, '*I will either pay you back next week or mow the lawn for you.*' Tom didn't pay his brother back. Therefore, Tom mowed the lawn for his brother.

The subject's task was to indicate whether or not the conclusion followed from the italicised sentence and the second premise. The results were surprisingly clear-cut. When the first disjunct was denied subjects had no difficulty in inferring that the second must therefore be true, regardless of the context used. In fact, there were fewer than 5 per cent errors on such inferences. This proportion of errors is much lower than that found in previous studies, though Roberge (1978) obtained results which approached this level of performance. The second type of inference we will consider involves concluding the falsity of one component from the truth of the other – an inference that is valid only with exclusive disjunction. Although a number of studies have manipulated this variable only a small number break down the data in such a way as to permit an analysis of such inferences. Roberge (1977) analysed whether subjects drew such (invalid) inferences with disjunctives explicitly marked as inclusive. He found that subjects made just over 20 per cent errors, regardless of whether the material was abstract or concrete (what Roberge termed 'compatible' material). Roberge (1976b) has investigated subjects' ability to draw this inference with exclusive disjunctions and found approximately 8 per cent errors when all the items were affirmative. To the best of our knowledge no one has investigated this type of reasoning using genuinely realistic material. Hence the results of our syllogism experiment mentioned previously provide interesting evidence.

The overwhelming majority of responses (87 per cent) were ones in which subjects assumed that the truth of the first component implied the falsity of the second. This is perhaps not surprising since in our earlier study we had found an overall preference for exclusive interpretations with these contexts, and such conclusions are valid with exclusive disjunctives. Interestingly there were differences between contexts in the willingness of subjects to draw this conclusion. Specifically, in the qualification context, there was an almost equal division between subjects who said the conclusion followed and those who said it did not; this is precisely the context that we found in our earlier study to lead to an almost equal number of inclusive and exclusive interpretations. It seems reasonable to conclude from this study that subjects have little difficulty in drawing valid conclusions from disjunctive syllogisms, though the conclusions that are valid depend on the interpretation given to the disjunctive statement.

Throughout the studies we have cited, reasoning performance was better on exclusive disjunctives than on inclusive ones. This is in marked contrast to the concept formation literature, when the reverse order is usually found (e.g. Neisser and Weene, 1962). This is probably due to the strategies that subjects can adopt in the different types of tasks. In a concept formation experiment, inclusive disjunction lends itself to a relatively simple strategy, since a positive response is given whenever one or both of two attributes is present. With exclusive disjunction, the strategy must be more complex, since the presence of both attributes leads to a negative response. In reasoning experiments exclusive disjunctives are the more straightforward, since the inferences are symmetrical: the truth of one component implies the falsity of the other, and vice versa.

A final point concerns the way in which these studies of reasoning assume a two-valued logic. In order to draw any conclusions at all, this assumption must be made, but as we have seen earlier, there have been recent trends towards a 'fuzzy logic' which rejects this assumption. To our knowledge, no studies of disjunctive reasoning have taken account of fuzzy logic, but this may explain some of the errors made in disjunctive reasoning tasks. For example, Roberge (1978) found that a sizeable number of errors – especially with inclusive disjunction – involved saying that a conclusion was maybe true rather than definitely true. Such a response is consistent with an interpretation in terms of fuzzy logic, but of course we have no way of knowing if this was why this response was given. Once again it seems that psychological research has imposed the logical interpretation on disjunctives and in so doing has masked the variety of ways in which 'or' can be interpreted.

THOG: a disjunctive reasoning problem

There has recently been considerable interest in a reasoning problem which involves a disjunctive rule – the THOG problem described by Wason (1977). Since this research has been reviewed by
GRIGGS (this volume), we will not attempt a review here. Nevertheless, there are some interesting parallels between research on the
THOG problem and the other work on disjunction that we have
reviewed in this chapter, and it is worth drawing attention to these.

The THOG problem involves a disjunctive concept, since a
THOG must contain either one of two properties; hence the most
obvious parallel is with the concept formation literature. In our
review of work on disjunctive concepts, we saw that subjects were
prone to the 'common element fallacy' (Bruner *et al.*, 1956), that is,
they tended to assume that the properties occurring most frequently
were the ones that defined the concept. Subjects attempting to solve
the THOG problem seem prone to a similar fallacy, since they seem
to assume that the designated positive instance (the design that *is*
a THOG) contains both of the properties written down. Such an
assumption leads to what Wason and Brooks (1979) call intuitive
errors, a pattern of responding which is very common with the
THOG problem. Bruner *et al.* demonstrated that disjunctive concepts were easier when the first instance given was a negative one;
this seemed to draw subjects' attention to the importance of negative
instances. Our own research on the THOG problem reveals an
analogous finding; if subjects are told that one of the designs is *not*
a THOG, then this leads to a significant improvement in performance (Griggs and Newstead, in press). This raises the interesting
possibility that at least part of the difficulty of the THOG problem
arises from the fact that, as with disjunctive concepts, subjects are
required to handle negative information (see GRIGGS, this
volume).

A further parallel between the THOG problem and the concept
formation literature can be derived from the study of Ketchum and
Bourne (1980). It will be remembered that these authors found that
combinations of properties of colour and shape seemed particularly
conducive to the learning of inclusive disjunctive concepts. The
THOG problem uses such a combination (black and diamond), yet
requires subjects to use an *exclusive* disjunctive rule. It is conceivable

that the exact choice of properties for the THOG problem is one factor that contributes to its difficulty.

Wason (1977) suggested that one possible reason for the difficulty of the THOG problem was that it involved the complex logical relation of exclusive disjunction. The work we have reviewed in this chapter suggested that subjects are quite capable of understanding and reasoning with this logical relation. Indeed, our review of the language of disjunction suggested that this was the preferred interpretation of the linguistic connective 'or'. Wason and Brooks (1979) have produced evidence consistent with our claim that the logical relationship itself is easily understood. In two of their experiments, they checked whether subjects had understood the exclusive disjunction relationship, and over 80 per cent had. Thus while the use of a disjunctive rule might contribute to the difficulty of the THOG problem, it is not the major source of difficulty.

Although we can draw no firm conclusions concerning the difficulty of the THOG problem, it is clear that there are interesting connections with the other areas reviewed in this chapter. Furthermore, at least part of the difficulty stems from the fact that a disjunctive concept is used.

General conclusions

In this chapter we have reviewed studies in linguistics, concept formation, reasoning and developmental psychology, all of which are linked by the fact that they have examined the interpretation and use of disjunctives. It is now time to draw some general conclusions about this work. We will concentrate particularly on the links between linguistic usage and psychological complexity, in other words on the relationship between language and thought.

Our review of research on the interpretation of disjunctives led us to the conclusion that 'or' has a wide variety of related uses. The exact interpretation given is determined by a variety of different factors: the linguistic and extralinguistic context in which it occurs; the exact form of words used; and, in many cases, the task that is used to assess interpretation. Thus 'or' is a fuzzy concept whose meaning sometimes corresponds to inclusive disjunction, sometimes to exclusive disjunction and frequently to neither of these, since it can be used to express intentions, or alternative ways of phrasing

something. Nevertheless, it does seem to have a prototypical meaning, to indicate the existence of two alternatives, with the expectancy
that only one will occur.

It is tempting to attribute the difficulty of disjunctive concepts to
the fact that the word 'or' is so ambiguous in the English language.
There are, however, inconsistencies in such a claim, not least of
which is the finding that concepts involving exclusive disjunction,
which is the more frequent usage of the word 'or', are generally
more difficult than concepts involving inclusive disjunction. However, this greater difficulty might be attributed to other factors,
since inclusive disjunction lends itself to fairly straightforward strategies in concept formation tasks while exclusive disjunction does
not. The crucial test of the hypothesis is to compare concept formation across different languages. One would expect that in
languages where the word for disjunction is less ambiguous, performance on disjunctive concepts should be better. From this point
of view, the work of Cole, Gay and their colleagues is of great
importance, since they studied concept formation among the Kpelle,
whose language contains one word for inclusive and one for exclusive disjunction. In their original studies (Gay and Cole, 1967; Cole,
Gay and Glick, 1968), there was a clear interaction between culture
(Kpelle or American) and type of concept used (conjunctive or
disjunctive), with the Kpelle showing little difference in performance between the two types of concept. However, Ciborowski and
Cole (1972) criticise this work on the grounds that the stimulus
attributes all involved the same dimension, colour. While in our
opinion this is not a serious criticism, it is clearly of interest to know
if the interaction will be found with other types of stimulus attributes. Ciborowski and Cole's results are difficult to interpret in this
respect. In one experiment they found no evidence of an interaction,
and in fact there was a slight suggestion that it went in the opposite
direction. However, in a second study in which the procedure was
varied slightly, the predicted interaction occurred.

Although the data are not entirely consistent, there does appear
to be some evidence that the Kpelle find disjunctive concepts relatively easier than do American subjects. This finding is arguably
the best cross-cultural evidence we have for the Whorf-Sapir hypothesis (Whorf, 1956) that language determines or at least predis-
poses thought. Inevitably, however, there are problems of
interpretation. Perhaps the most serious of these is that many of the

Kpelle people would, according to Ciborowski and Cole (1972), be bilingual in Kpelle and English. The national language of Liberia (where the Kpelle live) is English, and instruction in English is given in all schools. It is impossible to assess what confounding effect this would have on the results obtained.

The difficulty of disjunctive reasoning which has been found in previous research might well be due, at least in part, to linguistic ambiguity. Much research has specified the exact interpretation to be adopted, but this has been achieved only at the expense of making the phraseology rather artificial – and it is possibly this artificiality which leads to difficulty, rather than the disjunction itself. Certainly our own research has shown that when interpretation is indicated by the context in which the sentence occurs, reasoning performance is at a high level. However the great difficulty of the THOG problem can be attributed only in small part – if at all – to linguistic ambiguity.

The developmental literature should, hopefully, provide invaluable information on the relationship between linguistic and cognitive development. Such a hope remains unfulfilled, however, primarily because there is insufficient data on when children acquire the correct linguistic usage. Children as young as 5 years old understand 'or' quite adequately in its sense of 'choose one', but it is only later that they acquire the full range of usage. Unfortunately there is insufficient data to be more specific than this. Nevertheless, this leads to a clear-cut prediction: since the early use of 'or' is exclusive, young children should be relatively poor at acquiring inclusive disjunctive concepts. The available literature, however, indicates that this is not the case. One would expect an interaction between age and the kind of rule used (conjunctive or disjunctive); neither King (1966) nor Bourne and O'Banion (1971) found such an interaction.

Furth and his colleagues (e.g. Furth, Youniss and Ross, 1970) have also made an important contribution to this debate in their studies of children's ability to use logical operators. Children were presented with an arbitrary symbol pattern which represented the logical relation between two attributes. Following this, pictures combining two attributes were presented, and the children had to say whether or not the picture matched the symbolic description. Children aged 6 or 7 years old had considerable difficulty with disjunctive concepts, though this was part of a general difficulty with *all* the connectives used. Just as in other studies we have considered, the younger children had a tendency to 'match' their responses to the attributes mentioned in the rule. They classified instances containing both attributes as positive and instances containing neither as negative, irrespective of the logical relationship used. It was only by the age of 11 or 12 that children performed at all well on this task, which led Furth to conclude that it is beyond the capabilities of children who have not reached Piaget's formal operational stage. Furthermore, deaf children were not greatly impaired in this task by their lack of language (Youniss, Furth and Ross, 1971), suggesting that linguistic factors play a relatively minor role.

The task used by Furth and his colleagues can be criticised on the grounds that it is a highly artificial one, involving as it does the learning of an arbitrary symbol to designate a logical relationship. While research on class union lends general support to Furth's claims (e.g. Neimark and Slotnick, 1970), research using more normal disjunctive concepts suggests that young children *are* capable of acquiring these (e.g. Bourne and O'Banion, 1971; King, 1966). Nevertheless, there do seem to be parallels between linguistic and cognitive development: young children have a very simplistic understanding of the word 'or' and also have difficulty with a variety of cognitive tasks involving disjunction. However, by the time they have reached the formal operational stage, children have acquired both the linguistic and cognitive aspects of disjunction. We can, however, draw no conclusions as to whether linguistic factors influence cognitive development or vice versa, or whether, as seems most likely, there is a complex interaction between the two.

We have been searching for evidence of an effect of linguistic usage on thinking, and while there are some suggestive indications, no firm conclusions are possible. It is likely, in fact, that there are influences working in the opposite direction, where cognitive considerations determine linguistic usage. We saw earlier that one reason for the conceptual difficulties of disjunction was that it involved an implicit negation. This might well be the reason why it is so unusual to negate disjunctions in everyday language: adding an explicit negation to an implicit one is bound to cause processing difficulties.

One wide-ranging conclusion that can be drawn from this review is the importance of task variables in determining performance.

Time and again we have found it possible to provide clear, persuasive explanations of performance in a particular task. The problem is that a quite different explanation can be provided for another, ostensibly similar task. Thus we have ended up with a whole range of different explanations of performance in individual experiments, but relatively few overall generalisations. This does, of course, illustrate the dangers of generalising from the results of just one experimental paradigm.

While it is somewhat disappointing not to be able to reach more positive conclusions, the usefulness of attempting such an integration is clearly illustrated. It is all too easy for experimenters to explore their own favourite paradigm and to ignore the results of other research paradigms. This is nicely demonstrated by the different uses of the technique of asking subjects to evaluate instances with respect to a disjunctive rule. This has been used in studies of children's and adults' comprehension of disjunctive statements (e.g. Paris, 1973); in developmental studies of class inclusion (e.g. Neimark and Slotnick, 1970); and in studies of conceptual rule use (e.g. Trabasso *et al.* 1971). Many of these studies have been conducted in seeming oblivion of research in related areas. Only by comparing performance across such tasks can we hope to gain real insights into the main determinants of performance.

Acknowledgment

The authors would like to thank Jay Chrostowski for his assistance in running some of the experiments discussed in this chapter.

References

Bourne, L. E. (1970), 'Knowing and using concepts', *Psychological Review*, 77, pp. 546–56.

Bourne, L. E. and O'Banion, K. (1971), 'Conceptual rule learning and chronological age', *Developmental Psychology*, 5, pp. 525–34.

Braine, M. D. and Rumain, B. (1981), 'Development of comprehension of "or": Evidence for a series of competencies', *Journal of Experimental Child Psychology*, 31, pp. 46–70.

Bruner, J. S., Goodnow, J. J. and Austin, G. A. (1956), *A Study of Thinking*, New York, Wiley.

Ciborowski, T. and Cole, M. (1972), 'A cross-cultural study of conjunctive and disjunctive concept learning', *Child Development, 43*, pp. 774–89.

Cole, M., Gay, J. and Glick, J. (1968), 'Some studies in Kpelle quantitative behaviour', *Psychonomic Monographs, 2* (whole no. 26), pp. 173–90.

Collinson, W. E. (1948), 'Some recent trends in linguistic theory with special reference to syntactics', *Lingua, 1*, pp. 306–32.

Dik, S. C. (1968), *Coordination: Its Implication for the Theory of General Linguistics*, Amsterdam, North-Holland.

Eid, M. (1973), 'Disjunction and alternative questions in Arabic', mimeograph, Indiana University Linguistics Club, cited in G. Gazdar (1979), op. cit.

Evans, J. St B. T. (1972), 'Interpretation and matching bias in a reasoning task', *Quarterly Journal of Experimental Psychology, 24*, pp. 193–9.

Evans, J. St B. T. (1982), *The Psychology of Deductive Reasoning*, London, Routledge & Kegan Paul.

Evans, J. St B. T. and Newstead, S. E. (1980), 'A study of disjunctive reasoning', *Psychological Research, 41*, pp. 373–88.

Fillenbaum, S. (1974), 'Or: Some uses', *Journal of Experimental Psychology, 103*, pp. 913–21.

Furth, H. G., Youniss, J. and Ross, B. M. (1970), 'Children's utilization of logical symbols', *Developmental Psychology, 3*, pp. 36–57.

Gay, J. and Cole, M. (1967), *The New Mathematics in an Old Culture*, New York, Holt, Rinehart & Winston.

Gazdar, G. (1979), *Pragmatics: Implications, Presupposition and Logical form*, New York, Academic Press.

Grice, H. P. (1975), 'Logic and conversation', in P. Cole and J. L. Morgan (eds) *Syntax and Semantics* (vol. 3), *Speech Acts*, New York, Academic Press.

Griggs, R. A. and Newstead, S. E. (in press), 'The source of intuitive errors in Wason's THOG problem', *British Journal of Psychology*.

Hunt, E., Marin, J. and Stone, P. (1966), *Experiments in Induction*, New York, Academic Press.

Hurford, J. R. (1974), 'Exclusive or inclusive disjunction', *Foundations of Language, 11*, pp. 409–11.

Inhelder, B. and Piaget, J. (1958), *The growth of logical thinking from childhood to adolescence*, New York, Basic Books.

Johansson, B. S. (1977), 'Levels of mastery of competence of the co-ordinators *and* and *or* and logical test performance', *British Journal of Psychology, 68*, pp. 311–20.

Johansson, B. S. and Sjolin, B. (1975), 'Preschool children's understanding of the co-ordinators "and" and "or" ', *Journal of Experimental Child Psychology, 19*, pp. 233–40.

Ketchum, R. D. and Bourne L. E. (1980), 'Stimulus-rule interactions in concept verification', *American Journal of Psychology, 93*, pp. 5–23.

King, W. L. (1966), 'Learning and utilization of conjunctive and disjunctive classification rules: a developmental study', *Journal of Experimental Child Psychology*, 4, pp. 217–31.

Lakoff, R. (1971), 'If's and's and but's about conjunction', in C. J. Fillmore and D. T. Langendoen (eds), *Studies in Linguistic Semantics*, New York, Holt, Rinehart & Winston.

Manktelow, K. I. (1979), *The Role of Content in Reasoning*. unpublished PhD thesis, Plymouth Polytechnic.

Neimark, E. D. and Slotnick, N. S. (1970), 'Development of the understanding of logical connections', *Journal of Educational Psychology*, 61, pp. 451–60.

Neisser, U. and Weene, P. (1962), 'Hierarchies in concept attainment', *Journal of Experimental Psychology*, 64, pp. 640–5.

Oden G. C. (1977), 'Integration of fuzzy logical information', *Journal of Experimental Psychology: Human Perception and Performance*, 3, pp. 565–75.

Paris, S. G. (1973), 'Comprehension of language connectives and propositional logical relationships', *Journal of Experimental Child Psychology*, 16, pp. 278–91.

Pelletier, F. J. (1977), 'Or', *Theoretical Linguistics*, 4, pp. 61–74.

Roberge, J. J. (1976a), 'Effects of negation on adults' disjunctive reasoning abilities', *The Journal of General Psychology*, 94, pp. 23–8.

Roberge, J. J. (1976b), 'Reasoning with exclusive disjunction arguments', *Quarterly Journal of Experimental Psychology*, 28, pp. 419–27.

Roberge, J. J. (1977), 'Effects of content on inclusive disjunction reasoning', *Quarterly Journal of Experimental Psychology*, 29, pp. 669–76.

Roberge, J. J. (1978), 'Linguistic and psychometric factors in propositional reasoning', *Quarterly Journal of Experimental Psychology*, 30, pp. 705–16.

Roberge, J. J. and Antonak, R. F. (1979), 'Effects of familiarity with content on propositional reasoning', *The Journal of General Psychology*, 100, pp. 35–41.

Roberge, J. J. and Flexer, B. K. (1979), 'Propositional reasoning in adolescence', *The Journal of General Psychology*, 100, pp. 85–91.

Schroth, M. L. and Tamayo, F. M. V. (1972), 'Disjunctive concept formation under different information conditions', *The Journal of General Psychology*, 86, pp. 273–8.

Sternberg, R. J. (1979), 'Developmental patterns in the encoding and combination of logical connectives', *Journal of Experimental Child Psychology*, 28, pp. 469–98.

Suppes, P. (1957), *Introduction to Logic*. New York, Van Nostrand.

Suppes, P. and Feldman, S. (1971), 'Young children's comprehension of logical connectives', *Journal of Experimental Child Psychology*, 12, pp. 304–17.

Trabasso, T., Rollins, A. and Shaughnessy, E. (1971), 'Storage and verification stages in processing concepts', *Cognitive Psychology*, 2, pp. 239–89.

Wason, P. C. (1977), 'Self-contradictions', in P. N. Johnson-Laird and P. C. Wason (eds), *Thinking: Readings in Cognitive Science*, Cambridge, Cambridge University Press.

Wason, P. C. and Brooks, P. G. (1979), 'THOG: The anatomy of a problem', *Psychological Research, 41*, pp. 79–90.

Whorf, B. L. (1956), *Language, Thought and Reality* (edited and with introduction by J. B. Carroll), Cambridge, Mass., MIT Press.

Wittgenstein, L. (1953), *Philosophical Investigations*, Oxford, Blackwell.

Youniss, J., Furth, H. G. and Ross, B. M. (1971), 'Logical symbol use in deaf and hearing children and adolescents', *Developmental Psychology, 5*, pp. 511–17.

Zadeh, L. A. (1965), 'Fuzzy sets', *Information and Control, 8*, pp. 338–53.

4 The role of 'representativeness' in statistical inference: a critical appraisal

Paul Pollard and Jonathan St B. T. Evans

In this chapter we will look at research into people's intuitive abilities to make judgments and inferences about statistical information. In some tasks subjects are required to estimate likelihoods of certain data, given hypotheses about populations – termed a P(D/H) judgment. In other tasks subjects must make inferences about hypotheses on the basis of sample evidence – P(H/D) judgments. According to Bayes's theorem, the latter should be influenced by the prior probability of the hypothesis – P(H).

Like the logical reasoning tasks with which several chapters of this book are concerned, there is a normative system (probability theory) against which performance may be assessed. Until comparatively recently, the main interest in the field was the assessment of man's ability to perform as an 'intuitive statistician' in the absence of formal instruction, statistical tables and the like (see Peterson and Beach, 1967). However, Evans (1982, and this volume) has argued that psychological research into reasoning has been hampered by too much search for 'competence' and insufficient attention to what actually causes people to perform as they do.

For this reason, we feel that the statistical decision literature has gained enormous benefit from the writings of Amos Tversky and Daniel Kahneman. They proposed that people's judgments are mediated by use of several 'heuristics' which, while appropriate in some contexts, lead to systematic error in others. These heuristics are termed 'availability' (Tversky and Kahneman, 1973), 'representativeness' (Kahneman and Tversky, 1972) and 'anchoring' (Tversky, 1974; see also Tversky and Kahneman, 1974). In this chapter we will focus on the representativeness heuristic and ask (a) what psychological information has been gained from the research it has stimulated, and (b) how has the construct stood up to empirical evaluation?

In the original paper, Kahneman and Tversky (1972) present representativeness as a heuristic for making P(D/H) judgments:

> A person who follows this heuristic evaluates the probability of an uncertain event, or a sample, by the degree to which it is (i) similar in essential properties to its parent population; and (ii) reflects the salient features of the process by which it is generated. Our thesis is that, in many situations, an event A is judged more probable than an event B whenever A appears more representative than B. In other words, the ordering of events by their subjective probabilities coincides with their ordering by representativeness.

An empirical illustration of the first part of this definition is provided by their findings that 75 out of 92 subjects rated the birth sequence (of boys and girls in six-children families) GBGBBG as more likely than BGBBBB, despite their objective equiprobability. The latter sequence 'fails to reflect' the population proportion and is rated unlikely under the definition that a sample should be 'similar in essential properties to its parent population'. The second part of the definition is illustrated by another experiment in which 36 out of 52 subjects reported a 4/4/5/4/3 (random) distribution of 20 marbles among five children to be more probable than the objectively more probable even split. The slight deviation of the former sample reflects 'the salient features' of the process by which it was generated.

Kahneman and Tversky explain certain previous findings reported in the literature in terms of representativeness. For instance, subjects viewed the birth order BBBGGG as less likely than GBBGBG and, in general, Kahneman and Tversky explain the typical finding that subjects' judgments of randomness are biased against prolonged runs of either outcome (i.e. show a negative recency bias – e.g. Wagenaar, 1972) as due to long runs not being *locally* representative. Subjects are held to prefer sequences that are locally representative of the population in terms of relative frequency. (Wagenaar, 1972, mentions that a German psychologist, Mittenecker, had proposed a similar explanation of negative recency in 1953.)

The basis of the theory is essentially that outcomes are judged more likely, the more they 'look like' or are *similar* to the source distribution. This has been most directly tested by Bar-Hillel (1974). She showed subjects three bar graphs (said, in Groups 2 and 3, to represent a trinomial population) and asked either:

(1) Which of the two outer graphs (L or R) was more similar to the middle one (M); or

(2) Given that M was the sample of 20 beads from one of the 'outside' populations, from which of these (L or R) was it more likely to have been derived; or

(3) Given that M was a population, which 'sample' of 20 beads (L or R) was more likely to emerge from it.

The graphs, which all had three bars, were carefully constructed so that certain similarity features favoured the mathematically less likely alternative. Subjects in Groups 2 and 3 were first shown a large jar filled with red, yellow and green beads, were shown 'how the jar composition can be described by an appropriate bar graph' and a sample of 20 beads was randomly drawn in their presence. The responses of all three groups were highly correlated across problems and the correlation between Groups 2 and 3 was no higher than those between 1 and 2 or 1 and 3. Bar-Hillel concludes that the results support representativeness and that the latter result, in particular, 'suggests that there are no systematic differences between judgements of likelihood and judgements of similarity.'

The results of Bar-Hillel's experiment provide some indication that P(D/H) judgments are based on perceived similarity, although the task was complex and there were no immediately available cues other than similarity. Kahneman and Tversky (1973) do, in fact, extend the representativeness construct to explain P(H/D) judgments, by proposing that subjects ignore base rate information. In other words P(H/D) inferences are based solely on information about P(D/H) without regard for P(H). This work has stimulated a large and interesting literature which will be reviewed later in the chapter.

Firstly, however, we will examine the other main line of research to have arisen, based on a prediction made in the original 1972 paper, namely, that people will overlook the importance of sample size in probability judgments. In a final section we will examine the current theoretical status of the representativeness construct itself.

The influence of sample size

The 'law of large numbers' is that sample parameters estimate population parameters with high accuracy, when the sample size is large. With small samples, deviation of sample from population parameters becomes relatively likely. This is why statistical significance tests are more powerful when based on large numbers. For a given size of an effect observed in the sample, the effect is less likely to have occurred by chance (i.e. the data provides better evidence for a real effect), the larger the sample size.

Tversky and Kahneman (1971) claimed that subjects have a fallacious 'law of small numbers'. They show that professional psychologists grossly overestimate the power of small-sample experiments in several tasks involving assessment of hypothetical research findings. Kahneman and Tversky (1972) provide a theoretical account of this apparent insensitivity to sample size by use of the 'representativeness' heuristic. Since sample size is a feature of samples but not of populations, it cannot be one of the 'essential features' by which their similarity can be assessed. The use of the representativeness heuristic thus leads people to assess the likelihood of a sample by its similarity to the population in a measure such as proportion or mean, without regard to sample size.

Kahneman and Tversky (1972) present several experiments which provide apparent support for this hypothesis. In one of these, subjects had to produce subjective sampling distributions by estimating the relative frequency of different sample outcomes. They did this for three sample sizes (N = 10, 100, 1000) and for the following three populations:

(1)   Sex of babies born in a certain region. Subjects were told that approximately N babies were born per day and asked to assess the percentage of days on which different numbers of boys were born. Subjects distributed percentages across 11 categories (up to 50, 50–150 etc.; up to 5, 5–15, etc.; or 0, 1, 2 etc., depending on N) and were told that their answers should add up 'to about 100%'.
(2)   Percentages of days on which different amounts of babies with heartbeat type α (base rate = 80%) were born.
(3)   Percentages of the heights of males in a sample size N, distributed across seven categories.

In all three cases, sample size had *no* effect. The distributions produced by the different groups were indistinguishable for different sample sizes of the same problem. Fischhoff, Slovic and Lichtenstein (1979) report comparable results for Problem 1 using a within-subject design. Kahneman and Tversky argue that subjects generate a distribution that is representative of their idea of the population, in terms of *proportion*. A proportion judgment is not affected by sample sizes and thus sample size is ignored.

However, the results observed by Tiegen (1974a, 1974b), suggest that this subjective distribution task is at least very difficult, if not impossible, for most subjects, as they do not appear to 'possess' any consistent statistical distribution. In line with this, Evans and Du-soir (1975) report that, although they replicated Kahneman and Tversky's results, there were such great differences across subjects (and, apparently, so many bizarre distributions) that averaging across subjects was meaningless. Vlek (1973) has suggested that Kahneman and Tversky's results 'could be explained by the fact that most people just have no daily experience with probabilities of large sample statistics.' These points bring into question whether subjects do have a 'representative' idea of the population in terms of proportion which they translate into their estimates of sample distributions.

Olson (1976) asked subjects to produce frequency distributions of male babies for samples of 100 and 1000. Like Kahneman and Tversky, he gave subjects 11 response categories and similarly ob-served no significant effect of sample size. However, he varied the category labels – the middle nine categories spanning 5–95 (as did Kahneman and Tversky's), 41–59 and 46–54 (for $N = 100$) and 50–950, 455–545 and 487–513 (for $N = 1000$). Although there were small differences at the extremes, the spread across the 11 categories was more or less the same across the six groups of subjects (i.e. responses were not determined by proportion). These results cast further doubt upon the assumption that subjects 'possess' subjective sampling distributions, and certainly show that performance may be mediated by normatively irrelevant features of task content. The only sort of 'representativeness' which might influence subjects is one based on the *shape* of the distribution. Subjects may simply be imitating pictures they have seen of normal distributions and the like.

One of Kahneman and Tversky's other problems involved comparison of the likelihood of unusual distributions of male and female births in two maternity hospitals, one large and one small. The problem is described in detail by EVANS (this volume). In Kahneman and Tversky's experiment subjects showed no sensitivity to sample size, but subsequent research has shown that this, too, is a function of presentation factors. When the linguistic complexity of the problem is simplified, subjects do show significant preference for the correct answer (Evans and Dusoir, 1977; Bar-Hillel, 1979).

Evans and Dusoir (1977) also report an experiment to investigate the relative weight given to sample size and proportionality in making inferences about binomial samples. In this experiment subjects were presented with all 132 possible paired comparisons between 12 samples varying in sample size (10, 100, 1000) and proportionality (6:4, 7:3, 8:2, 9:1). The task was to decide which of the two samples gave better evidence of bias in the underlying population. In effect, the subject must estimate the direction of the likelihood ratio under the null hypothesis. The method of presentation would seem to make both sample size and proportionality information equally salient. Two types of problems allowed a crucial test of representativeness:

(a)   On 24 problems, proportionality was constant but sample size varied. These allowed a test of the bias as each sample is equally 'representative'. Most subjects behaved accordingly, either indicating that the samples gave equal evidence or indicating inconsistent preferences across problems. However, 15 of the 48 subjects 'decided in favour of the larger sample for more than 20 of the 24 problems.'
(b)   On 36 problems, the two factors varied in opposite directions. On 35 of these the normative response favoured sample size and was thus in direct opposition to representativeness. 34 subjects did give the majority of their responses in favour of proportion. However, of the remaining 14, 11 were members of the group of 15 who favoured sample size on the problems at (a).

This experiment provides important evidence of individual differences, which are often ignored in this literature. While a majority subset conformed to the representativeness predictions, a sizeable minority did not, and produced consistently normative responses.

This led the authors to question whether the majority were truly incapable of normative judgments or whether problem complexity had induced a reliance on proportionality cues to the exclusion of sample size.

Evans and Dusoir (1975) investigated the sensitivity to sample size in a very simple problem. When asked which procedure would lead to more accurate assessment of the average number of crisps in a packet, 154 out of 160 subjects correctly said counting the contents of 1000 rather than 10 packets. Thus virtually *all* subjects can attach appropriate weight to the evidence of larger samples, when no other cues are provided by the problem presentation.

Bar-Hillel (1979), however, has suggested that when subjects do take account of sample size, they may do so for the wrong reasons. Subjects may simply feel that a larger sample contains more of the population and is thus more representative. She tested this hypothesis by contrasting absolute sample size with sample to population ratio.

In Experiment 3, Bar-Hillel found that most subjects stated that they would be more confident in a sample of 1000 drawn from a population of 50,000, than from one drawn from a population of one million. The percentage of the population sampled thus appears important. However, when this was held constant (a 1 per cent sample drawn from the two populations), half the subjects did indicate that they would have more confidence in the larger sample. In the second part of this study, the (same) subjects were presented with nine different surveys simultaneously, 'described in terms of the sample size and the population size only.' Subjects were asked 'to rate each survey as to where its results were likely to be on a scale from 1 (highly inaccurate) to 10 (highly accurate).' Accuracy was not defined. These accuracy ratings were used to determine, for each subject, a ranking for the nine surveys. Collapsed across subjects, these rankings correlated only ·14 with the surveys ranked by sample size but correlated ·82 with the surveys ranked by sample to population ratio. When these correlations were performed for each subject, the rankings of 39 of the 57 subjects were correlated more highly with sample to population ratio than with sample size. (The mean difference in correlations was ·24.) A final experiment demonstrated that subjects would 'trade' sample size for an increase in sample to population ratio.

A number of other studies do show that subjects are sensitive to sample size, but not always in a normative manner. For instance, Levin (1974) found that subjects reported shopping preferences for (hypothetical) shops for which large samples of favourable, or small samples of unfavourable, price rises were given. Kassin (1979a) has shown that unrepresentative results may be attributed to low sample size. Subjects express greater confidence in their estimates of population means (Irwin, Smith and Mayfield, 1956; Little and Lintz, 1965) and population proportions (Du Charme and Peterson, 1969; Beach, Beach, Carter and Barclay, 1974), the larger the sample size on which their estimate is based. However, Pitz (1967) has reported a negative relationship between confidence and sample size on a task in which sample size was a normatively *irrelevant* variable.

In conclusion to this section, we must recognise that there are several questions arising from the research on sample size. Firstly, do subjects have an underlying *competence* to perceive the role of sample size, which is often suppressed by *performance* factors such as complexity of problem presentation? This view might account for the Evans and Dusoir (1975; 1977) results but is hard to reconcile with the normatively inappropriate use of sample size reported in some studies. Secondly, when systematic biases are shown, are these best accounted for by the representativeness heuristic, or in other ways? Clearly, only some of the biases reviewed can be accounted for by the representativeness hypothesis, at least in the form presented by Kahneman and Tversky (1972).

It seems that subjects' performance is little influenced by general *a priori* methods of reasoning, whether normative or otherwise. Responses appear to be highly specific to the task content. An important determinant of whether subjects will take account of a task feature appears to be its *salience* in the problem presentation. This is demonstrated clearly in a recent study by Evans and Pollard, which is described by EVANS (this volume).

If subjects' strategies are determined by specific features of task content, then it means that 'demand characteristics' may pose a particular problem. Consider, for example, Bar-Hillel's demonstration that subjects base judgments on sample to population ratios. The problem is that these ratios are made highly salient in problem presentation. Furthermore, the subject is entitled to wonder why information about population size has been presented if it is irrelevant to the problem. (A similar problem arises when sample size information is presented alone.) In real life, of course, irrelevant information is normally present when making judgments, but in an experiment the subject knows that the experimenter has constructed the materials. Consequently, the ecological validity of these kinds of experiments is questionable. It is not easy to see how this problem may be entirely overcome. However, it is worth noting that, when sample size is contrasted with proportion, although the possibility of demand characteristics can explain attention to the latter, it can hardly explain inattention to the former.

In conclusion, then, the influence of sample size on probability judgments is consistent with neither an underlying normative competence, nor performance biases based solely on representativeness. Behaviour appears to be highly dependent upon the manner in which problem information is presented, and the way in which the question is asked. Bearing these points in mind, we now turn to an examination of the base rate literature.

Base rates

If A is similar to B then B is similar to A. So when probability judgments are mediated by representativeness, i.e. similarity, then we must expect $P(H/D)$ judgments to be psychologically equivalent to $P(D/H)$ judgments. They are not, however, formally equivalent. The former should be weighted according to prior probabilities or base rate information – $P(H)$. Thus Kahneman and Tversky (1973) predict that use of the representativeness heuristic will lead subjects to ignore the effects of basic rate on $P(H/D)$ judgments. Their experiments will be considered in due course, but first we will use another problem to explain the importance of base rates:

> 85 per cent of the cabs in a particular city are green and the remainder blue. A witness identifies a cab involved in an accident as blue. Under tests, the witness correctly identifies both blue and green cabs on 80 per cent of occasions. What is the probability that the cab was, in fact, blue?

The above is a shortened form of a problem that first appeared in an Oregon Research Institute Research Bulletin, published by Kahneman and Tversky in 1972. The problem presents three pieces of information: (i) the *base rate* probability that any given cab is blue

(0·15), (ii) a specific statement that the cab has been identified as blue, and (iii) the probability of the witness's ability to discriminate blue and green cabs (0·8). P(H), the *prior probability* that the cab is blue, is low, whereas P(D/H), the probability yielded by the data (i.e. the witness's testimony), is high. How are these two to be combined?

Bayes's rule allows us to compute an exact probability that the cab was blue. In its more simple, *odds*, form the odds in favour of the cab being blue on the basis of the witness's testimony (80 to 20) are multiplied by the *prior* odds of the cab being blue (15 to 85), to provide an estimate of the posterior odds in favour of the cab being blue. In this case, these are 1200 to 1700, or 12 to 17. That is, 12 chances in favour and 17 against, or 12 chances in 29. This converts to a posterior probability, P(H/D) of about ·41. This leads to what is perhaps a surprising conclusion – the highest likelihood is that the cab was green, even though we have a reasonably reliable witness who identifies it as blue. As we shall see, most people do not reach this conclusion as they are generally prone to make a decision primarily, or entirely, on the basis of the specific information and tend to ignore the base rate information. For instance, the modal answer on the cab problem is 0·8, the probability on the basis of the witness's testimony alone (e.g. Lyon and Slovic, 1976; Bar-Hillel, 1980a).

For those readers whose original impressions accorded with this modal response, there is an easier method of solution than that provided by the Bayesian formulation. Suppose that there are 100 accidents in the town. Mathematically, we would 'expect' 85 to involve green, and 15 to involve blue cabs. The witness would be expected to identify incorrectly 20 per cent of the former (17), and to identify correctly 80 per cent of the latter (12), as blue. The witness would thus report blue on 29 occasions, but on only 12 of these would he be correct. As for the Bayesian solution, a probability of about 0·41 is derived, although this analysis possibly brings out more clearly *why* the witness is so likely to be wrong.

Various workers (e.g. Hammerton, 1973; Liu, 1975; Lyon and Slovic, 1976; Bar-Hillel, 1980a) have presented many versions of the cab and other isomorphic problems to large numbers of subjects and the results are almost invariably the same. The modal (although not the majority) response, and usually the median response, is the probability provided by the specific information and very few subjects yield a probability near to the normative answer. This typical finding has held up to various manipulations such as whether or not the base rate goes against the specific evidence, the order in which these are presented and the size of the discrepancy. The lack of attention to base rates is further underlined by findings that no notable difference in response profiles is observed when no base rates are given (Hammerton) or when the specific information is diagnostically worthless (Bar-Hillel). In fact, on a slightly different task, Doherty, Mynatt, Tweney and Schiavo's (1979) subjects actually chose to acquire worthless information and subsequently ignored base rates when making a decision on the basis of this.

It may appear that one possible explanation for the above results is that subjects have difficulty in performing what is a rather difficult mathematical computation. However, Bar-Hillel has shown computational inaccuracy to be an unlikely possibility. She gave subjects a problem concerning two witnesses who disagreed, with no base rates. All but one subject gave estimates between 50 and 60 per cent in favour of the colour identified by the witness said to have 80 per cent, rather than 70 per cent, reliability. These subjects were quite capable of combining two pieces of conflicting probabilistic information. Perhaps an even greater problem for a 'computational inaccuracy' explanation is that an 85 per cent probability should be fairly obviously *stronger* evidence than an 80 per cent probability. However, on problems such as that shown earlier in which the base rate suggests the opposite conclusion to that supported by the specific information, underestimation (of the 41 per cent probability) is very rarely observed and very few estimates fall below 50 per cent. Thus, if nominal responses (i.e. a simple, non-quantified statement of which is more likely, 'green' or 'blue') were inferred from the probabilities, most subjects would be wrong.

Another possible explanation is that the statement about the witnesses' reliability may be interpreted by subjects as meaning that (as Bar-Hillel, 1980a, phrases it), '80% of each of the witnesses' colour identifications turn out to be correct', although she points out that 'a very bizarre perceptual mechanism would have to be assumed' to produce this relationship. In fact, given the base rates in the cab problem, such a relationship is mathematically impossible. (It can be shown algebraically that, for the success rate to be the same when naming either cab colour, the success rate or failure rate, whichever is the higher, must be at least as high as the base rate of the more frequent cab colour. In this case, the success rate would have to be either at least 85 per cent or no greater than 15 per cent.) In any case, as Bar-Hillel points out, this implausible possibility cannot explain lack of attention to base rates when no probability is quoted for the specific information, such as in the Kahneman and Tversky (1973) studies.

In one set of experiments, Kahneman and Tversky showed subjects a description and asked them to rank the similarity of the description to the 'typical graduate student' in each of nine specialisation areas. These rankings provided a measure of the specific evidence value of the description. Another group of subjects estimated the percentage of students in the nine areas (i.e. the base rates). The crucial third group was given the description and asked to predict which area the person was in by ranking the likelihood of all nine areas (i.e. to make P(H/D) judgments). There was a very high correlation (·97) between these predictions and the similarity judgments but a *negative* correlation (−·65) between predictions and base rates. The predictions were thus apparently solely made on the basis of the evidence value (or, as Kahneman and Tversky referred to it, the *representativeness*) of the descriptions, with no attention to base rates. (The negative, rather than zero, correlation between prediction and base rates was due to the description tending to be rated as more similar to low base rate specialisation areas.)

The second problem studied by Kahneman and Tversky may be referred to as the 'engineers and lawyers' problem. In this study, subjects were told that descriptions had been prepared of 30 (70) engineers and 70 (30) lawyers. Subjects were shown a description and asked to predict whether it referred to an engineer or lawyer. The prime determinant of these predictions were the (five) descriptions, not the base rates. Average estimated probabilities of engineer (lawyer) were 50 per cent in the 30/70 condition and 55 per cent in the 70/30 condition. The base rates thus had a small, significant effect, but this was very minimal. Interestingly, one description, which was constructed to be non-diagnostic, yielded approximately 50 per cent estimates in both groups. Although the description was apparently of little or no use, the base rate still had no effect.

There is, then, much evidence that subjects underutilise, or fail to utilise base rates when specific evidence is available. It is not, however, the case that subjects do not use base rates appropriately in the *absence* of specific information. For example, in Kahneman and Tversky's first problem, subjects told that a description would not be given for 'Don' yielded predictive rankings that correlated (·74) with the base rates of the nine specialisation fields. In the engineers/lawyers problem, predictions about an individual chosen at random, with no information given, were 30 per cent or 70 per cent, dependent on base rates. Similarly, on the cab and similar problems, the base rate probability is given if the witness is not referred to in the scenario. Subjects thus know how base rates can be used as predictors and, as Bar-Hillel has shown, can combine two predictor cues. However, they fail to use them, or to use them adequately, when specific information is present, even if the specific information has no predictive value.

Base rates in the form of consensus information

Nisbett and Borgida (1975) propose that subjects' tendency to ignore base rates is comparable to a tendency to ignore consensus information when making causal attributions. They told subjects the results of two experiments, one concerning shock taking (Nisbett and Schachter, 1966) and one concerning helping behaviour, in a situation where one (stooge) participant in a group conversation by intercom feigned a seizure (Darley and Latané, 1968). These studies produced counterintuitive results in that many subjects accepted a very high level of shock in the former and failed to help in the latter. Nisbett and Borgida found that (consensus) knowledge of the results had no effect on predictions about the behaviour of target cases in the original studies (presented via either a videotaped interview or a 150-word description), or on subjects' estimates of how they themselves would have behaved, and only a very minimal effect on trait ratings of subjects described as having behaved counterintuitively. The response distribution recalled (at the end of the experiment) was very different to the response distribution estimated by subjects not given consensus information. The consensus information thus should have affected predictions, and that it did not could not have been due to subjects failing to remember it.

The Nisbett and Borgida contention that consensus information does not affect causal attribution may be thought too extreme. For instance, consensus information of the almost everyone/hardly anyone, else variety has been reported as having a reasonably strong effect on situation/person attributions when presented in the absence of other information (Orvis, Cunningham and Kelley, 1975) or as the last piece of information (Ruble and Feldman, 1976). However, such studies concern fairly simple inferences. For instance, there is little complexity in inferring from 'Sue (and "almost everyone else") is afraid of the dog' (Ruble and Feldman) that it is more reasonable to ascribe the fear to the dog's ferociousness than to conclude that Sue has a dog phobia. More importantly, when the consensus information is made very salient it may simply produce a demand characteristic.

Wells and Harvey (1977) replicated the Nisbett and Borgida study but used only brief (name and age) descriptions of targets and told some of their subjects that the subjects in the original experiments had been *randomly selected*. This condition did produce an effect of base rates on subjects' estimates of overall response distributions, predictions about a target's helping or shock-taking behaviour and dispositional/situational attributions of targets said to have behaved in the typical (but counterintuitive) manner. Wells and Harvey argue that counterintuitive consensus information is perceived as unrepresentative, and thus ignored, if it is not explicitly said to be based on a random sample. This hypothesis is supported by the results of Kassin (1979a), who found that subjects estimated that counterintuitive results from helping studies had been derived from smaller samples than had (subjectively) expected results, and, to some extent, by Zuckerman (1978). Zuckerman replicated Nesbitt and Borgida's findings regarding veridical consensus information but found that a group of subjects given 'socially desirable' consensus information (the opposite to Darley and Latané's results) predicted faster helping times. Subjects enter the laboratory with *a priori* ideas about the world. Given an expectation that people are usually helpful, subjects are apparently willing to accept information that shows people to be *very* helpful but resistant to information that shows people to be generally unhelpful.

However, although there has been some argument as to whether assuming counterintuitive results to be unrepresentative is (Wells and Harvey, 1978) or is not (Borgida, 1978) a reasonable way for subjects to behave, it is clearly not at all reasonable only to credit the results of experiments that accord with one's *a priori* opinions (although some converging evidence that subjects do behave in this way is provided by Lord, Ross and Lepper, 1979). In one sense, of course, subjects may be viewed as applying subjective prior odds to the assessment of the base rate information. In fact, subjects clearly do use priors when these concern opinions or expectations and rigidly held priors of this type may wholly dominate counterintuitive specific information (which is equally as suboptimal as base rate non-utilisation).

However, there are two reasons why the Wells and Harvey finding yields little explanation for subjects' failure to utilise base rates. Firstly, the effect of 'randomly sampled' consensus information reported by Wells and Harvey (1977) is very small. Further, in the helping evaluation studies referred to above, if the original sample may be perceived as unrepresentative, this can be used to explain a lack of effect of consensus on trait ratings and on subjects' estimates of how they themselves would have behaved, but it *cannot* be used to explain a lack of consensus effect on predictions about the behaviour of target persons in the original study, as the sample is obviously not unrepresentative of itself. More importantly, the idea that subjects generally apply subjective, rather than counterintuitive experimentally given, base rates cannot be applied to most of the studies discussed earlier. There is nothing counterintuitive about the base rates used in the cab problem and its isomorphs or in the problems studied by Kahneman and Tversky (1973). In fact, in the latter authors' study concerning graduate specialisation areas, it was specifically the *subjective* base rates that subjects ignored.

Situations in which greater base rate utilisation is observed

More recent studies have all investigated conditions under which base rate utilisation may be increased. Carroll and Siegler (1977) argued that base rate non-utilisation in the engineers/lawyers study is due to subjects' inability to 'translate' a 70/30 base rate on to a small sample of five (i.e. they are unable to 'probability match'), and attempted to demonstrate this by asking only for nominal responses. In some conditions in which base rates were 'translatable' (e.g. a 70/30 split and a sample of 10), half the subjects did probability match (i.e. they predicted seven profiles to be the majority occupation). However, this only occurred when translatable base rates were used in conjunction with high sample to population ratio (i.e. samples of 10 or 20 from a population of 20) and *non-*

individuating (i.e. non-diagnostic) profiles. This changes the nature of the task considerably and, given a situation in which the experimenter essentially asks 'here are 20 profiles, 14 of which are engineers (lawyers), guess which are which', it is perhaps more surprising that half the subjects *ignored* the base rates, especially as the profiles were non-informative and the base rates were strongly cued by the experimental presentation. Fischhoff *et al.* (1979) report findings that indicate that when base rates or consensus information are experimentally cued (by varying only this dimension in a within-subject design), highly significant, although not necessarily optimal, effects are obtained.

The basis of current work on the presence or absence of base rate effects was laid by Ajzen (1977). He pointed out that the 70/30 split doesn't cause a particular person to be an engineer or lawyer and proposed that base rate information will only be attended to properly when it has some *causal* relation to the event that the subject must predict. In two experiments he investigated isomorphs of the engineers/lawyers problem, one involving students who had passed or failed an exam and the other involving students who had chosen a history or economics option. Subjects had to predict whether given targets had passed/failed or, in the second experiment, chosen history or economics, on the basis of a base rate and a profile (which, for instance, in the first experiment, described intelligence and motivation level). In one condition of each experiment, base rates were quoted as being actual pass, or choice of option, rates. These would be expected to influence perceived difficulty of the examination (e.g. Fontaine, 1975; Frieze and Weiner, 1971) or perceived popularity of the options (manipulation checks confirmed this) and thus have a causal relevance to the prediction. Even a highly intelligent, hard-working student may fail a very difficult examination. In accordance with predictions, a very strong (although not entirely optimal) effect of base rates was observed. This was not the case when 'non-causal' base rates were given as stemming from a sample of 100 students drawn by someone primarily interested in pass/failure or in a particular option.

Tversky and Kahneman (1980) report an effect of base rates on the cab problem, rephrased to state that 'although the two companies are roughly equal in size', 85 per cent of cab accidents involve green cabs. They report responses to be 'radically different' to those observed on the standard problem and that the median answer was that the probability of the cab being blue (as the witness reported) was ·55. (It is interesting to note, firstly, that this median implies that most subjects would still be wrong if asked for a nominal response but, secondly, that the result provides further disconfirmation of the possibility that subjects misinterpret the statement about the witness's reliability.) Tversky and Kahneman argue that the recklessness and incompetence of green cab drivers, the 'causal' explanation inferred from the base rates, increases the perceived likelihood that a green cab was involved in the accident, and, citing Ajzen's results as further support, conclude that base rates will be effective when they 'induce a causal model' that explains the base rate and can be applied to the individual case being predicted. They point out, however, that, even in this case, base rates may be ignored 'if they conflict with an established prior conception or causal schema', as in the Nisbett and Borgida study.

Bar-Hillel (1980a) criticises Tversky and Kahneman for arguing that causal base rates will affect judgment whereas 'base rate information which cannot be interpreted in this manner is given little or no weight', on the grounds that the statement is too narrow. She argues that base rate use is determined by its perceived *relevance* and that causality is only one way in which a base rate may be made to appear as relevant as the specific information. However, both Ajzen, and Tversky and Kahneman had previously pointed out that 'causal' base rates are utilised because their relevance to the specific instance is highlighted. Thus the contribution value of her theory is solely a function of the extent to which she fulfils the promise in her introduction to 'show that under some conditions, even noncausal base rate information will affect judgments.' In fact, she reports only two studies in which base rates appear to have been substantially attended to and one of these involved causal base rates. Empirical support for the relevance theory is thus provided by one experiment.

This (cab) problem involved the usual statement of base rates (85 per cent blue) and description of an accident (adding 'in which a pedestrian was run down') and continued: 'The wounded pedestrian later testified that though he did not see the colour of the cab due to the bad visibility . . . he remembers hearing the sound of an intercom coming through the cab window. The police investigation discovered that intercoms are installed in 80 per cent of the Green cabs, and in 20 per cent of the Blue cabs.' Although a strong effect of base rates was observed, this provides no evidence for the relevance theory as, on this problem, it is impossible to take account of the specific information without taking account of the base rates. In natural usage, 'of' is equivalent to 'multiplied by'. On the standard problem, '80 per cent of the time' merely indicates multiplication by unity and the subject can 'solve' this equation without reference to the base rates (which are, in fact, subtly 'buried' in the word 'time'). However, on the intercom problem, initial attention to the specific information leads automatically to base rate utilisation. The subject is forced to consider the base rates in order to solve the equation '80 per cent of the green cabs', which must lead to some form of frequentist solution of the type given at the beginning of this section. The problem thus confounds the specific information with the base rate in such a way that the subject cannot attend to the former alone.

Even if this problem was not subject to this criticism, it could provide at best only weak support for Bar-Hillel's argument. She presents it as a problem in which the relevance of the specific information is reduced, which is not the crucial test of the argument. She makes no attempt to demonstrate that non-causal base rates may, in certain circumstances, be made more relevant and thus be utilised, in the presence of strong specific information. The crucial test would require a controlled experiment in which a 'relevant' non-causal base rate was shown to be effective when paired with specific information that (in another condition) wholly dominated a 'non-relevant' base rate.

Conclusions

To summarise all the results discussed here, although the great variability in subjects' responses, reported by most authors, makes the drawing of any general conclusions difficult, it is clear that many (possibly most) subjects generally ignore base rates completely whereas a minority, but usually sizeable, proportion of subjects do pay some attention to them. They are, however, very rarely properly utilised and if subjects' probability estimates were translated into nominal judgments, almost all of them would be wrong. Although Kassin (1979b) has proposed a variety of situations in which base rates or consensus information may be effective, in most cases these effects (e.g. of translatability or base rate extremity) are superficial. A strong effect of base rates is observed when a causal relation between the base rate and the predicted event may be inferred. The effectiveness of this has been well demonstrated by Ajzen and by Tversky and Kahneman, and the same principle may account for the findings of those studies which have found an effect of consensus information on causal attributions. Such consensus information (e.g. 'almost everyone compliments Barry's work' – Orvis *et al.*, 1975) clearly has causal implications. In situations where subjects may infer from a base rate that, for instance, 85 per cent of green cabs are involved in accidents *because* green cab drivers are reckless, or everybody praises Barry's work *because* Barry's work is good, or 75 per cent of the sample failed an examination *because* the examination was difficult, the relevance of the base rate information is cued in such a way that most subjects take account of it.

GRIGGS (this volume) has shown how deductive reasoning performance may be influenced by the meaning of the content of the problems, which has no bearing on their logical structure. The notion that realistic content seems to 'facilitate' performance has proved to be oversimplified in that area of study (see also Evans, 1982; Pollard, 1982). Similarly, we would not wish to describe the effect of perceived causality on base rate utilisation as facilitation, but rather as an effect of prior associations upon performance. In statistical judgments, as in deductive reasoning (e.g. Pollard and Evans, 1981) such associations need not improve performance. An example where they 'inhibit' is provided by the phenomenon of illusory correlation (see Nisbett and Ross, 1980, for a review).

The literature stimulated by Kahneman and Tversky's (1973) paper, whilst proving a rich psychological field, has moved well beyond the original theory of representativeness. For one thing, it has never been claimed that when base rates are ignored this is always because subjects base judgments on representativeness. Similarly, no attempt has been made to argue that increases in base rate usage due to 'causal' manipulations can be explained in terms of representativeness (e.g. Tversky and Kahneman, 1980). In fact, Tversky and Kahneman state that 'the neglect of base rate information appears to be a more general phenomenon, which occurs even when considerations of representativeness or similarity are not involved. We now believe that, regardless of whether or not probability is judged by representativeness, base rate information will be dominated by case data, except when given a causal interpretation.'

Theoretical implications of representativeness research

Kahneman and Tversky's (1972; 1973) theoretical formulations of 'representativeness' theory were, strictly speaking, never testable in the Popperian sense. The problem is that their predictions were based on what could happen *when* subjects based their judgments on representativeness, but the circumstances in which they would do so were not clearly specified. This means that the observation that, in a given situation, subjects take account of sample size or base rates does not falsify the theory. It could be argued that subjects were simply not using the heuristic on this occasion.

For this reason, a number of studies have focused on the question of whether representativeness can explain performance on the *particular* tasks which Kahneman and Tversky use in their own experiments. We have already seen, in the section on sample size, that some of their results have proved to be task specific. Another example is provided by what will be referred to as the 'majority problem' (Kahneman and Tversky, 1972). On this task, subjects were told that half the classes in a school (Program A) contained 65 per cent boys and half (Program B) contained 45 per cent boys and were asked, on the basis of observing 55 per cent boys in a class entered at random, whether the class belonged to Program A or B. Out of 89 subjects, 67 said A, although B is (very) marginally more likely. Kahneman and Tversky argue that the sample is more representative of A, as both sample and population have a *majority* of boys. However, Olson (1976) has shown responses to be independent of this distinction. His problems concerned two towns in Quebec, Anglophiles being 65 per cent of the voters in one and 45 per cent in the other. The Kahneman and Tversky results were replicated when subjects were asked which town an electoral list having 55 per cent Anglophiles had been sampled from, but when the population percentages were changed to 55 per cent and 35 per cent, most subjects judged that a list having 45 per cent Anglophiles had been sampled from the 55 per cent town. Representativeness must predict that, in the latter problem, the town with a *minority* of Anglophiles would be favoured.

Olson proposes that subjects have a bias towards treating the percentages as absolute numbers; 55 can be a subset of 65 but not of 45. This bias appeared to be very strong. For 100 per cent, 40 per cent towns and samples having 70 per cent Anglophiles, more than half the subjects estimated that the sample was derived from the town having 100 per cent Anglophiles. They thus behaved as though a town of all Anglophiles could generate a mixed sample. The bias was only removed by telling subjects that 70 per cent were Anglophiles *and that 30 per cent were not Anglophiles*. A more reasonable explanation than Olson's would appear to be that subjects respond to the sample percentage as though the words 'at least' had been inserted.

The 'majority' problem is thus one problem which, although revealing a non-normative bias, appears to have no relation to representativeness. It also seems to be unlikely that negative recency bias in the judgment or production of random binary sequences and lack of attention to sample size can both be mediated by representativeness. Evans and Pollard (1982) asked subjects to adjust a displayed sequence of H's and T's (heads and tails) on a VDU, until it seemed random, and also asked subjects to make comparative judgments about the evidence value of two samples, varying proportionality and sample size in a manner similar to that employed by Evans and Dusoir (1977). This procedure allowed a measure of each subject's negative recency bias and of his or her lack of respect for sample size. If these are both mediated by representativeness then it would be expected that individual differences would reflect differential susceptibility to the bias and thus that a correlation would obtain between the two measures. Although significant evidence of each bias was observed, there was no evidence of a correlation between the extent of each. Similarly, although no relevant experimental work has been performed, there is no evidence to show that errors associated with sample size and base rates, discussed above, have any common substrate.

In fact, there is little point in arguing at length that the representativeness heuristic is not as generalisable as it originally appeared, as this view would attract few opponents. Admittedly, Bar-Hillel (1980b) has recently presented a detailed and interesting account of 'what features make samples seem representative'. These features, however, could equally well be referred to simply as features determining $P(D/H)$ judgments. Subjects' forced choice decisions indicated that the subjective likelihood of a given height of an individual is a function of its distance from the mean and that the subjective likelihood of a sample (of the height of three people) is a function of non-repetition (i.e. most subjects viewed a sample of three equal heights as more unlikely than any other sample), symmetry, and the range and mean of the sample (these relations did not always lead to optimal judgments). These results are interesting but clearly have no status as a validation of the representativeness theory. Kahneman and Tversky themselves apparently accept that the theory cannot be regarded as a general theory of statistical judgment. It is noticeable in their paper on corrective procedures for judgmental biases (Kahneman and Tversky, 1979a), that the focus is upon biases observed in the various tasks rather than any common substrate. Also, as the quotation at the end of the last section shows, they do not regard it as a general explanation of base rate neglect.

Whilst 'representativeness' may not be a general heuristic underlying subjects' performances, the theory has been very valuable in stimulating important psychological research. The change of emphasis from seeking evidence of subjects' competence to appreciate normative factors towards a greater understanding of how non-normative factors influence performance, is wholly approved by the present authors. There are those who object to the 'irrational' portrait of man which appears to emerge, a point of view which is discussed below. Firstly, though, we should try to draw some specific conclusions from the research reviewed.

Clearly, subjects' judgments ought to be influenced by sample size and base rate, and it is important that attention has been drawn to the fact that they frequently are not. There are clear parallels in the literature on these two features. In general, evidence about sample and population proportions or means does tend to *dominate* information about sample size, at least for most subjects. Similarly, specific evidence tends to dominate base rate evidence. When the dominating cue is absent, however, subjects generally make normative judgments to the effect that larger samples are more reliable, and events with higher prior probabilities are more likely to occur.

However, in both cases the weight attached to the dominated cue may be increased, despite the presence of the dominating one. The principal factors responsible appear to be the salience of the cue in the problem presentation (see Pollard, 1982, for an explanation of cue salience effects in terms of differential availability; and EVANS, this volume, for an explanation in terms of selective attention), and the influence of semantic factors relating to subjects' prior experience of the problem content. It is most encouraging that these are also two major classes of performance factor to have emerged in the quite separate literatures on deductive reasoning (see Evans, 1982 and this volume; Pollard, 1982; and GRIGGS, this volume). The convergence upon such classes of performance factors has led inevitably to an emphasis on non-rational factors in human inference, rather than on people's logical and statistical abilities.

It is perhaps, then, not surprising that there has been a rationalist reaction in recent years, which in the case of Cohen (1981) is applied to both the deductive and statistical reasoning literatures. For discussion of this issue in deductive reasoning see WASON (this volume). We will look briefly at the arguments in relation to statistical inference. Fhaner (1977) suggests that the research is of little relevance, in that subjects do not make probability judgments in real life. This argument is presented on two levels – firstly that judgments under uncertainty are infrequent, and secondly that such judgments are not made numerically. Although mentioning decisions such as those concerning house purchase and employment, Fhaner underestimates the amount of uncertain decisions made – many everyday purchasing decisions and person judgments involve uncertainty as well as more major decisions, not to mention a wide range of judgments about moral, political and social questions concerned in voting and jury behaviour and child rearing. The second level of the argument seems valid, as it is unlikely that these judgments are made in terms of numerical probabilities. However, many statistical inference tasks involve nominal, rather than numerical, decisions and when probabilistic decisions have been asked for these often indicate that even a nominal decision would have been incorrect. Fhaner's argument thus seems to support, rather than oppose, Kahneman and Tversky's point of view. Subjects' frequent inattention to relevant numerical considerations when making judgments under uncertainty is not a matter of contention, the point is that this will often lead to non-optimal (nominal) decisions.

Cohen (1979) has attempted to argue that Kahneman and Tversky's subjects have not made incorrect decisions, on the grounds that two problems (not discussed above) are misleading and, more generally, that subjects' answers to many of the problems are correct when the problem is analysed in terms of 'Baconian probability'. Kahneman and Tversky (1979b) have accepted that one of the two problems mentioned was misphrased and probably should also have conceded the point about the importance of assumed temporal order in the other (conditional probabilities) problem criticised by Cohen. However, the main thrust of Cohen's criticism, the Baconian argument, has far less validity. Cohen describes the Baconian system and shows how it may lead to the typical answers observed on the engineers/lawyers and hospital problems and how it explains greater attention to 'causal' base rates on problems such as the cab problem. Any critical analysis of this system would involve an unwarranted amount of space and no description will be included here. As Kahneman and Tversky (1979b) remark, 'Cohen's system has little normative or descriptive appeal, and . . . his interpretation of our findings is hardly compelling.'

In fact, as Tversky (1981) points out, Cohen (1981) has made several important changes in his position, not least of which is the abandonment of his Baconian system. Cohen (1981) invokes a competence/performance distinction to argue that human irrationality cannot be experimentally demonstrated. This argument is long and detailed and is not entirely relevant to this chapter. However, two central points are worthy of attention. Cohen (1981) defends the base rate fallacy, not on the basis of Baconian logic as before, but on the basis of an argument that is essentially the same as the 'specific information only' argument with which 50 per cent of Lyon and Slovic's subjects agreed. This argument is invalid (see e.g. Kahneman, 1981; Evans and Pollard, 1981) and, together with arguments in favour of other fallacies (e.g. the gamblers fallacy) seriously undermines the credibility of his paper. The second argument of importance is that studies showing subjects' deviations from a normative model are essentially tests of education or intelligence (not rationality). Similarly, Cohen has earlier argued that only if the subject knows that sample size or base rates are relevant can his ignoring them be regarded as irrational (Cohen, 1979) and that it is rational to apply a (Baconian) probability system that one believes to be valid, even if this belief is erroneous (Cohen, 1980). Thus Cohen argues essentially that a subject's response is rational if it is the response he believes to be correct. This argument pinpoints the crux of Cohen's objections to Tversky and Kahneman's conclusions and also the crux of his misunderstanding of the purposes of the research. As has been pointed out (e.g. Evans and Pollard, 1981; Griggs, 1981; Tversky, 1981), the purpose of the research is to investigate actual human behaviour in judgmental situations. The research indicates that behaviour is often irrational, but it is not concerned with an evaluation of competence. As Evans and Pollard (1981) conclude, 'performance factors are not a theoretical complication to be removed in a search for rational competence. Understanding performance is the very essence of the scientific study of human inference.'

Acknowledgment

The writing of this chapter was supported by a research grant from the Social Science Research Council.

References

Ajzen, I. (1977), 'Intuitive theories of events and the effects of base-rate information on prediction', *Journal of Personality and Social Psychology, 35,* pp. 303–14.

Bar-Hillel, M. (1974), 'Similarity and probability', *Organisational Behaviour and Human Performance, 11,* pp. 277–82.

Bar-Hillel, M. (1979), 'The role of sample size in sample evaluation', *Organisational Behaviour and Human Performance, 24,* pp.245–57.

Bar-Hillel, M. (1980a), 'The base-rate fallacy in probability judgements', *Acta Psychologica, 44,* pp. 211–33.

Bar-Hillel, M. (1980b), 'What features make samples seem representative?', *Journal of Experimental Psychology: Human Perception and Performance, 6,* pp. 578–89.

Beach, L. R., Beach, B. H., Carter, W. B. and Barclay, S. (1974), 'Five studies of subjective equivalence', *Organisational Behaviour and Human Performance, 12,* pp. 351–71.

Borgida, E. (1978), 'Scientific deduction – evidence is not necessarily informative – reply to Wells & Harvey', *Journal of Personality and Social Psychology, 36,* pp. 477–82.

Carroll, J. S. and Siegler, R. S. (1977), 'Strategies for the use of base-rate information', *Organisational Behaviour and Human Performance, 19,* pp. 392–402.

Cohen, L. J. (1979), 'On the psychology of prediction: Whose is the fallacy?', *Cognition, 7,* pp. 385–407.

Cohen, L. J. (1980), 'Whose is the fallacy? A rejoinder to Daniel Kahneman and Amos Tversky', *Cognition, 8,* pp. 89–92.

Cohen, L. J. (1981), 'Can human irrationality be experimentally demonstrated? *The Behavioral and Brain Sciences, 4*, pp. 317–31.

Darley, J. M. and Latané, B. (1968), 'Bystander intervention in emergencies: Diffusion of responsibility', *Journal of Personality and Social Psychology, 8*, pp. 377–83.

Doherty, M. E., Mynatt, C. R., Tweney, R. D. and Schiavo, M. D. (1979), 'Pseudo-diagnosticity', *Acta Psychologica, 43*, pp. 111–21.

Du Charme, W. M. and Peterson, C. R. (1969), 'Proportion estimation as a function of proportion and sample size', *Journal of Experimental Psychology, 81*, pp. 536–41.

Evans, J. St B. T. (1982), *The Psychology of Deductive Reasoning*, London, Routledge & Kegan Paul.

Evans, J. St B. T. and Dusoir, A. E. (1975), 'Sample size and subjective probability judgements: a test of Kahneman & Tversky's hypothesis', paper read to the Experimental Psychology Society, Oxford University.

Evans, J. St B. T. and Dusoir, A. E. (1977), 'Proportionality and sample size as factors in intuitive statistical judgement', *Acta Psychologica, 41*, pp. 129–37.

Evans, J. St B. T. and Pollard, P. (1981), 'On defining rationality unreasonably', *The Behavioral and Brain Sciences, 4*, pp. 35–6.

Evans, J. St B. T. and Pollard, P. (1982), 'Statistical judgment: A further test of the representativeness construct', *Acta Psychologica, 51*, pp. 91–103.

Fhaner, S. (1977), 'Subjective probability and everyday life', *Scandinavian Journal of Psychology, 18*, pp. 81–4.

Fischhoff, B., Slovic, P. and Lichtenstein, S. (1979), 'Subjective sensitivity analysis', *Organisational Behaviour and Human Performance, 23*, pp. 339–59.

Fontaine, G. (1975), 'Causal attribution in simulated versus real situations: When are people logical, when are they not?', *Journal of Personality and Social Psychology, 32*, pp. 1021–9.

Frieze, I. and Weiner, B. (1971), 'Cue utilization and the attributional judgments for success and failure', *Journal of Personality, 39*, pp. 591–605.

Griggs, R. A. (1981), 'Human Reasoning: Can we judge before we understand?', *The Behavioral and Brain Sciences, 4*, pp. 38–9.

Hammerton, M. (1973), 'A case of radical probability estimation', *Journal of Experimental Psychology, 101*, pp. 252–4.

Irwin, F. W., Smith, W. A. S., and Mayfield, J. F. (1956), 'Tests of two theories of decision in an "expanded judgment" situation', *Journal of Experimental Psychology, 51*, pp. 261–8.

Kahneman, D. (1981), 'Who shall be the arbiter of our intuitions?', *The Behavioral and Brain Sciences, 4*, pp. 39–40.

Kahneman, D. and Tversky, A. (1972), 'Subjective probability: A judgment of representativeness', *Cognitive Psychology, 3*, pp. 430–54.

Kahneman, D. and Tversky, A. (1973), 'On the psychology of prediction', *Psychological Review, 80*, pp. 237–51.

Kahneman, D. and Tversky, A. (1979a), 'Intuitive prediction: Biases and corrective procedures', *Management Science*, *12*, pp. 313–27.

Kahneman, D. and Tversky, A. (1979b), 'On the interpretation of intuitive probability: A reply to Jonathan Cohen', *Cognition*, *7*, pp. 409–11.

Kassin, S. M. (1979a), 'Base rates and prediction: The role of sample size', *Personality and Social Psychology Bulletin*, *5*, pp. 210–13.

Kassin, S. M. (1979b), 'Consensus information, prediction and causal attribution: A review of the literature and issues', *Journal of Personality and Social Psychology*, *37*, pp. 1966–81.

Levin, I. P. (1974), 'Averaging processes in ratings and choices based on numerical information', *Memory and Cognition*, *2*, pp. 786–90.

Little, K. B. and Lintz, L. M. (1965), 'Information and certainty', *Journal of Experimental Psychology*, *70*, pp. 428–32.

Liu, A. Y. (1975), 'Specific information effect in probability estimation', *Perceptual and Motor Skills*, *41*, pp. 475–8.

Lord, C. J., Ross, L. and Lepper, M. R. (1979), 'Biased assimilation and attitude polarization – effects of prior theories on subsequently considered evidence', *Journal of Personality and Social Psychology*, *37*, pp. 2098–109.

Lyon, D. and Slovic, P. (1976), 'Dominance of accuracy information and neglect of base rates in probability estimation', *Acta Psychologica*, *40*, pp. 287–98.

Nisbett, R. E. and Borgida, E. (1975), 'Attribution and the psychology of prediction', *Journal of Personality and Social Psychology*, *32*, pp. 932–43.

Nisbett, R. E. and Ross, L. (1980), *Human Inference: Strategies and Shortcomings of Social Judgment*, Englewood Cliffs, New Jersey, Prentice-Hall.

Nisbett, R. E. and Schachter, S. (1966), 'Cognitive manipulation of pain', *Journal of Experimental Social Psychology*, *2*, pp. 227–36.

Olson, C. L. (1976), 'Some apparent violations of the representativeness heuristic in human judgment', *Journal of Experimental Psychology: Human Perception and Performance*, *2*, pp. 599–608.

Orvis, B. R., Cunningham, J. D. and Kelley, H. H. (1975), 'A closer examination of causal inference: The roles of consensus, distinctiveness, and consistency information', *Journal of Personality and Social Psychology*, *32*, pp. 605–16.

Peterson, C. R. and Beach, L. R. (1967), 'Man as an intuitive statistician', *Psychological Bulletin*, *68*, pp. 29–46.

Pitz, G. F. (1967), 'Sample size, likelihood, and confidence in a decision', *Psychonomic Science*, *8*, pp. 257–8.

Pollard, P. (1982), 'Human Reasoning: Some possible effects of availability', *Cognition*, *10*, pp. 65–96.

Pollard, P. and Evans, J. St B. T. (1981), 'The effects of prior beliefs in reasoning: An associational interpretation', *British Journal of Psychology*, *72*, pp. 73–81.

Ruble, D. N. and Feldman, N. S. (1976), 'Order of consensus, distinctiveness and consistency of information and causal attributions', *Journal of Personality and Social Psychology, 34*, pp. 930–7.

Tiegen, K. H. (1974a), 'Subjective sampling distributions and the additivity of estimates', *Scandinavian Journal of Psychology, 15*, pp. 50–5.

Tiegen, K. H. (1974b), 'Overestimation of subjective probabilities', *Scandinavian Journal of Psychology, 15*, pp. 56–62.

Tversky, A. (1974), 'Assessing uncertainty', paper read to the Royal Statistical Society, London, *Journal of the Royal Statistical Society* (B), *36*, pp. 148–59.

Tversky, A. (1981), 'L. J. Cohen, again: On the evaluation of inductive intuitions', *The Behavioral and Brain Sciences, 4*, pp. 54–6.

Tversky, A. and Kahneman, D. (1971), 'The belief in the law of small numbers', *Psychological Bulletin, 76*, pp. 105–10.

Tversky, A. and Kahneman, D. (1973), 'Availability: a heuristic for judging frequency and probability', *Cognitive Psychology, 5*, pp. 207–32.

Tversky, A. and Kahneman, D. (1974), 'Judgment under uncertainty: Heuristics and biases', *Science, 185*, pp. 1124–31.

Tversky, A. and Kahneman, D. (1980), 'Causal schemata in judgments under uncertainty', in M. Fishbein (ed.), *Progress in Social Psychology*, Hillsdale, New Jersey, Erlbaum.

Vlek, C. J. A. (1973), 'Coherence of human judgment in a limited probabilistic environment', *Organisational Behaviour and Human Performance, 9*, pp. 460–81.

Wagenaar, W. A. (1972), 'Generation of random sequences by human subjects: A critical survey of literature', *Psychological Bulletin, 77*, pp. 65–72.

Wells, G. L. and Harvey, J. H. (1977), 'Do people use consensus information in making causal attributions?', *Journal of Personality and Social Psychology, 35*, pp. 279–93.

Wells, G. L. and Harvey, J. H. (1978), 'Naive attributors, attributions and predictions – what is informative and when is an effect an effect?' *Journal of Personality and Social Psychology, 36*, pp. 483–90.

Zuckerman, M. (1978), 'Use of consensus information in prediction of behaviour', *Journal of Experimental Social Psychology, 14*, pp. 163–71.

5 Selective processes in reasoning

Jonathan St B. T. Evans

Experimental studies of inductive and deductive reasoning consistently find high error rates (see for example Nisbett and Ross, 1980; Evans, 1982). There are several types of theoretical argument proposed to explain this. Henle (1962) maintained that subjects reason according to the laws of formal logic and that errors often reflect misinterpretation of the premises of the argument. Others argue that reasoning should not be judged as irrational with reference to standard normative systems (Cohen, 1981) and that alternative 'natural' logics might obtain (e.g. Braine, 1978).

I have argued (e.g. Evans, 1982) that such approaches cannot account for many of the data observed in reasoning experiments. This is because many errors reflect systematic biases which can be linked to the specific form or content of the particular reasoning task, rather than to its underlying logical structure. To put it another way, 'performance' factors contribute much more than any underlying 'competence'. It is the purpose of this chapter to illustrate some specific ways in which performance is subject to cognitive limitations.

It will be argued here that an important source of reasoning errors lies in selective processing of task information. If attention is given to the wrong features or not given to the right features, then errors will result. In the parlance of problem-solving theory (cf. Newell and Simon, 1972), these would be regarded as *representational* errors. That is, the subject encodes the problem information in an inappropriate manner to start with. There will also be some discussion of selective processing of the problem information which is attended.

There is nothing new in the proposal that thinking is subject to attentional limitations and selective processing. As mentioned in the Introduction, Gestalt research on problem solving led to the conclusion that 'direction' or 'mental set' was a major influence on thinking (for a review see Woodworth and Schlosberg, 1954). In these studies a 'set' method of approaching a problem was often induced by reinforcement on problems where it was appropriate. When subsequently applied to a problem where it was inappropriate this led to an interference with performance.

The phenomenon of mental set is consequently often regarded as a 'bad thing', responsible for failures to solve problems or think 'creatively' (e.g. Luchins and Luchins, 1950). In fact, the ability to think in a highly selective manner is a remarkable achievement without which we could not hope to function. We select from the vast amount of information available from sensory input and memory storage, the relevant information needed to solve a problem. We formulate and choose a few of a vast number of possible operations that could be applied. It is in our ability to select successfully that we are vastly superior in intelligence to any computer that has yet been built. For example, a strong human chess player looks at a chess board and immediately 'sees' just a few moves that need be considered. In analysing the moves the player again need consider only a few alternative replies from his opponent and so on at each stage. It is precisely this 'heuristic' aspect of human thought that has been so difficult to mimic in artificial intelligence programs.

A remarkable aspect of the 'perception' of chess moves is the *ease* with which the human players make their selection. The process is entirely intuitive, pre-attentive and immediately 'given'. In general, the automatic selection of ideas, even where very complex information processing is required, is a dominant feature of human thought. Inevitably, however, there is a price to be paid for this enormous processing power. Sometimes important details will be selected out, irrelevant details selected in. It is these sorts of failures that will be emphasised in the present discussion of inferential errors.

In this chapter, several distinct groups of phenomena will be considered. Each will be shown to involve selective attention or direction of thought. General conclusions will be considered at the end.

Feature matching tendencies

There is various evidence to show that subjects tend to 'match' problem features when generating their solutions to the problems. One of the clearest examples occurs when people are asked to verify or check the truth of conditional sentences in which the presence or absence of negative components is manipulated, a phenomenon labelled 'matching bias' by Evans (1972).

The phenomenon is most easily illustrated with reference to the Wason selection task (see also the chapters by WASON and by GRIGGS for discussion of this task). In a typical selection task experiment, the subject is shown four cards lying on a table. He knows that each has a letter on one side, and a number on the other; the visible symbols are 'G', 'M', '2' and '6'. He is then asked to test the truth of the following rule:

'If there is a G on one side of the card then there is a 2 on the other side of the card.'

The subject must decide which cards need necessarily be turned over, in order to discover whether the rule is true or false. The correct answer is the 'G' and the '6' since only a card with a G on one side and a number that is *not* 2 on the other could disprove the rule. Typically, subjects choose either 'G' alone or 'G' and '2', which was originally attributed to a motivation to verify, rather than falsify, the rule (see Wason and Johnson-Laird, 1972). 'Matching bias', however, refers to a tendency to match one's responses to the stimuli named in the rules. That subjects are choosing the cards 'G' and '2' because they match, rather than for their logical status, is demonstrated by manipulating the presence of negatives in either component of the rule (Evans and Lynch, 1973; Manktelow and Evans, 1979). For example, when the rule has a negative consequent, e.g. 'If there is a G on one side of the card then there is not a 2 on the other side of the card', the matching choices (G and 2) are also logically correct. Far more subjects give the correct solution on this rule than in its normal affirmative phrasing.

How robust and general is this phenomenon? It occurs on truth table tasks where subjects are asked to construct cases which could verify or falsify conditional rules (e.g. Evans, 1972). They construct significantly more instances whose features match values named in the rules, regardless of the presence of negative components. Curiously, the phenomenon is still manifest when all logical truth-table cases are presented in turn to the subject to evaluate (e.g. Evans, 1975; Evans and Newstead, 1977). What happens here is that cases containing mismatching values (not named in the rules) are significantly more often rejected as 'irrelevant' to the rule, rather than classified as verifying or falsifying it. The effect is equally marked for rules phrased in the form 'If . . . then . . .' or '. . . only if . . .'.

Where the generality of the effect appears to break down is when disjunctive rules are substituted for conditionals. Disjunctive selection tasks do not show the effect (Wason and Johnson-Laird, 1969; Van Duyne, 1976), and a fully controlled truth table study by Evans and Newstead (1980) found no evidence of matching. However, Evans and Newstead also found evidence that the introduction of negatives disrupts subjects' comprehension of a disjunctive rule in a manner which confuses the test for matching.

Let us now consider possible explanations of the phenomenon. In previous publications I have referred to it as a 'response bias', but this description is now considered to be rather misleading. If the phenomenon were restricted to selection and truth table *construction* tasks, it might arise from some kind of response priming effect. However, the fact that subjects are also more likely to consider matching instances as relevant when they are presented for evaluation requires a more subtle explanation.

A second possibility is that matching reflects associational biases induced by the linguistic structure of the rule. Thus a conditional, 'If P then Q', induces an expectation of positive association between P and Q. The associational hypothesis put forward by Pollard and Evans (1981) has the advantage that it can explain the discrepant findings with disjunctives (see Evans and Newstead, 1980). However, it does require one to suppose that the associational biases claimed for affirmative rules are carried over when negatives are introduced. In other words, subjects must act as if the negatives were not actually there. Such an unconscious bias is possible, despite the fact that subjects clearly are aware of the presence of negatives when making retrospective reports (see Wason and Evans, 1975).

A third possibility, which conforms to the theme of this chapter, is that matching bias is the result of selective processing. In this approach it is supposed that the subject is more likely to *attend* to matching values and consider their logical significance (cf. Evans, 1975). It is as though the subject thinks that the problem is about the named cards only. One form of evidence that supports this interpretation is the protocols produced by subjects asked to justify their choices. For example, Wason and Evans (1975) gave subjects two selection tasks, one using an affirmative rule, of the logical form 'If P then Q', and the other a negative rule, 'If P then not Q'. In line with matching bias subjects tended to select P and Q and were consequently far more often correct on the negative rule, where these correspond to the logically correct choices. When subjects wrote justifications for their choices they tended to refer to the matching value on *the other side* of the card. Suppose, for example, subjects were explaining their reasons for choosing the P card. On the affirmative rule they tended to say that a Q on the other side would make the rule true, but on the negative rule to say that a Q on the other side would make the rule false. It would seem that subjects' attention is directed towards the matching values and that they are aware of the logical consequences associated with them. They also *lack* awareness of the logical significance of non-matching cards. Thus, they do *not* point to the fact that turning P on the affirmative rule would falsify the statement if a value which was not a Q was found on the other side.

Now, a 'set' effect is, by definition, *pre-attentive*, and the subject's report reflects the consequence of the matching, i.e. what the subject is aware of. This means that the 'reasons' that the subjects give for their choices are highly misleading if taken to be 'strategy reports'. Wason and Evans (1975) argued that previous investigators had mistakenly imputed verification and falsification strategies to their subjects for this very reason.

The argument is, then, that subjects fail to select $\bar{Q}$ because they do not *think* about this card. In problem solving jargon, this is equivalent to proposing a representational error, since subjects do not search a full problem space including the mismatching cards (see Evans, 1982). What other evidence supports this view? If subjects' choices are restricted to Q and $\bar{Q}$ only, performance improves (Johnson-Laird and Wason, 1970; Lunzer, Harrison and Davey, 1972). Roth (1979) has shown that replacing the P card by a second $\bar{Q}$ will produce facilitation with four cards present and produce transfer to a subsequent standard selection task. Taken together, these results suggest that P competes strongly for attention with other cards, but that if $\bar{Q}$ *is* attended subjects may perceive its relevance and select it.

A recent experiment run by P. G. Brooks also lends support to the attentional explanation of matching. In this experiment the selection task was presented by an on-line computer. The four cards were displayed on a VDU, with a separate yes/no choice key under each one. The subjects could press the keys in any order they wished to register the decision made on each card as to whether or not it should be turned over. The computer recorded the *order* in which decisions were made – a methodological innovation. Obviously enough, the left to right order of presentation of the cards was randomised independently for each trial. The mean rank order of decision for both affirmative and negative rules is shown in Table 5.1.

TABLE 5.1 *Mean rank decision order for selections on two rules in an experiment by P. G. Brooks (N = 42)*

Rule	P	$\bar{P}$	Q	$\bar{Q}$
If P then Q	2·15	2·80	2·38	2·66
If P then not Q	2·08	2·81	2·41	2·69

Note how similar the rank orderings are for each rule despite the fact that the logical status of the Q and $\bar{Q}$ cards is opposite for the two rules. The difference across the four cards (combining rules) is statistically significant. On both antecedent and consequent there is a tendency to make the decision about the matching card before the mismatching card (P before $\bar{P}$, Q before $\bar{Q}$), in line with the attentional hypothesis. The fact that the effect is more strongly marked on the antecedent points to the influence of a second factor, which will be discussed in a later section.

What, then, if one specifically directs subjects' attention to the $\bar{Q}$ card and asks them what would happen if it was turned over? All subjects then say, with a little prompting, that a P on the back would falsify the rule (e.g. Wason, 1969; Wason and Johnson-Laird, 1970). This shows that subjects do understand the logical significance of turning $\bar{Q}$ if they are forced to think about it. These experiments were designed as 'therapies' so this procedure was introduced only after an initial erroneous response to the normal selection task had been made. The procedure did tend to induce subjects to modify their subsequent selections to include the Q̄ card, but a number were highly reluctant to do so (see especially Wason and Johnson-Laird, 1970). This suggests a rather deeper fixation on the original choices than a simple attentional bias would predict. Wason and Evans (1975) actually suggest that separate types of thought must underlie card selections and verbal evaluations (for detailed discussion of the 'dual process' theory, see Evans, 1982).

If we assume that matching bias does nevertheless reflect selective attention to named cards, then we must ask *why* this should occur. In my view it reflects a *bias to positivity* which is a very general feature of human thought (see also GRIGGS's discussion of the THOG problem in this volume). There has been a considerable literature concerned with people's ability to comprehend affirmative and negative statements, in which the latter are almost universally observed to cause extra difficulty (see Clark and Clark, 1977; Wason, 1980; and Evans, 1982, for recent reviews). Also, various authors have stressed the fact that a negative is a statement *about* the affirmative it denies. Use of a negative *presupposes* a reason to believe the affirmative, and a negative out of context is anomalous (cf. Wason, 1972, 1980). There are thus two aspects to this positivity bias in the matching phenomenon. The rule, 'If B then 3', induced attention to 'B' and '3', because subjects will not spontaneously think about negative possibilities – 'not B' and 'not 3'. On the other hand, when a negative is actually used in the rule, 'If B then not 3', this does *not* direct subjects' attention to the negative possibility 'not 3' either. Linguistically, negatives make statements about affirmatives, so attention is still directed towards '3'. Thus a bias to think in terms of positive information, coupled with linguistic presupposition effects, ensures attention to only a selected number of logical possibilities. Accuracy of performance is then a consequence of whether subjects' attention is directed to the logically important, rather than psychologically salient, aspects of the problem.

The discussion in this section has focused on 'matching bias' in conditional reasoning, but there is evidence of feature matching on other reasoning tasks. For example, people tend to choose conclusions to syllogisms which share syntactic features with the premises, although there is considerable controversy as to why this occurs (see Evans, 1982). Inferential errors with disjunctive statements have also been attributed to the fallacious belief that instances conforming to a rule must share common features with one another (cf. Bruner, Goodnow and Austin, 1956; Wason and Brooks, 1979; NEWSTEAD AND GRIGGS, this volume). We will now consider some evidence for a similar positivity bias in inductive reasoning.

The failure to eliminate hypotheses

In an inductive reasoning task one has to try to discover a general rule by inspecting samples of evidence. Such tasks are especially interesting in that they constitute an analogue of research in the natural sciences, where natural laws must be discovered by controlled experiments. The best way to achieve this is by forming and testing *hypotheses* about a general rule. However, as Popper (1959) has pointed out, it is scientifically necessary to do this in a way which enables incorrect hypotheses to be falsified and rejected.

A number of studies have suggested that people are not very good at eliminating hypotheses in experimental tasks. The task environments range from learning artificial languages (Miller, 1967) to theory testing in artificial environments created by computer graphics (Mynatt, Doherty and Tweney, 1977). Probably the best-known example, however, is the '2 4 6' problem devised by Wason (1960; see also Wason, 1968).

The subject is told that the experimenter has a rule in mind concerning sets of three numbers, and that an example which conformed to the rule was 2 4 6. Subjects then had to discover the rule by stating other number triples which would be classified as conforming or not conforming by the experimenter. Subjects were asked to announce the rule only when they were very sure that they had solved the problem. The experimenter's rule is actually any ascending sequence. Subjects have great difficulty learning this rule since they tend to adopt a hypothesis that is a subset of the rule, e.g. ascending with equal intervals, and then test only *positive* examples such as 10 20 30, 1 2 3 or 100 104 108 etc. Such examples will always be positive examples of the experimenter's rule as well, so they cannot lead to falsification of the hypothesis. Very few subjects test negative examples such as 1 3 4 for the above example, which would lead to refutation of their hypothesis since they *do* conform to the experimenter's rule.

Wason (1960) proposed that subjects were motivated to verify rather than falsify their hypotheses. This hypothesis is still favoured in the literature (cf. Tweney *et al.*, 1980). However, there is a striking parallel between research on the 2 4 6 problem and early work on the selection task, employing only affirmative rules. In both cases the *logical consequence* of subjects' behaviour is that they will find confirmatory rather than disconfirmatory evidence. In both cases Wason suggested that this was due to a verification bias. In the case of the selection task, however, Wason and others have now recognised this hypothesis to be mistaken and attribute card selections to 'matching bias' (see previous section). Could the factors responsible for matching also provide an alternative explanation for the 2 4 6 results? I would argue that they can (see also Pollard, 1982).

Let us consider the nature of the 2 4 6 problem. One 'set' effect that no one disputes is a tendency to adopt an initial hypothesis which is part of the correct rule, due to the obviously biased example 2 4 6. Wason (1968) argues that the point is to see how subjects react when their hypotheses are confirmed. The misunderstanding which has remained in the literature is that the subjects' tendency to test *positive* examples of their hypotheses is due to a search for confirming evidence. For example, Tweney *et al.* (1980) classify positive tests as 'confirmatory' and negative tests as 'disconfirmatory'. This relationship is correct from the experimenter's but *not from the subject's* point of view (cf. Wetherick, 1962). If a subject makes a positive prediction, then he might expect to be told that it is in fact positive (confirmation) or in fact negative (disconfirmation). He does not know that the latter cannot occur, because he does not know that his hypothesis is a subset of the rule. Similarly, negative tests cannot be interpreted as seeking disconfirmation, since they can *confirm* the hypothesis if the experimenter says they are negative examples of the rule.

The argument is, then, that errors on the 2 4 6 problem reflect the same set for positivity, rather than verification, that underlies matching bias on the selection task. In both cases, I am arguing for a cognitive limitation as opposed to a motivational bias. It is not that subjects do not wish to falsify, it is simply that they cannot think of the way to do it. In concept identification tasks where subjects invariably encounter falsifying evidence of incorrect hypotheses, they normally reject the hypothesis concerned without difficulty (see, for example, Bourne, Dominowski and Loftus, 1979).

Similarly, on an inductive reasoning task which produces similar effects to the 2 4 6, Mynatt *et al.* (1977) observed subjects to make good use of falsifying evidence, although this was not true on a more complex task of the same type (Mynatt, Doherty and Tweney, 1978).

However, it must be pointed out that once established, the 2 4 6 error does become highly fixated in the same way as the selection task error (see Wason, 1968). This provides further evidence of 'dual processes' since simply telling subjects that they have the wrong rule may not force them to change their hypotheses – often they continue to generate the same kind of triples and simply re-formulate the same rule in other words. However, I do not dispute that successive reinforcements may convince subjects of the correctness of their hypotheses. My argument concerns the reason why they come to receive such reinforcements in the first place.

There is a further, recent finding to be explained. In the final experiment reported by Tweney *et al.* (1980), subjects were told that some triples were MEDs and others DAXs. The feedback was thus MED and DAX, rather than 'right' and 'wrong'. There was a dramatic improvement in performance with many subjects announcing the correct rule at their first attempt. This might indicate that subjects find it reinforcing to be told that they are right rather than wrong (cf. Miller, 1967). However, Tweney *et al.* state that their subjects were testing alternative hypotheses. In other words, if subjects are told that 2 4 6 was a MED, they would generate a negative version of their MED hypothesis as a DAX hypothesis and test both. Thus it seems that subjects are still testing their hypotheses in a positive manner; the negative instances of MED are *to the subject* positive instances of DAX. Why, though, should MED and DAX induce testing of alternative hypotheses whereas 'right' and 'wrong' do not? This is again a bias to positivity, a 'wrong' hypothesis is semantically negative and thus overlooked, whereas DAX is a positive alternative.

As stated earlier the 2 4 6 and related problems are often regarded as analogues of scientific theory testing. I would like to comment on this aspect before moving on. Wason (personal communication) expresses his views thus: 'Suppose a scientist were to elicit a phenomenon by varying X, is he still entitled to attribute the cause of the phenomenon to X if it is elicited when X is not varied? The subjects in my experiments are required to demonstrate this inference, where

X is their hypothesis and the phenomenon is a positive instance.' I would argue, in fact, that subjects *are* entitled to regard X as a *sufficient* cause for the phenomenon. Likewise, their hypothesis will always produce a positive instance. Their failure lies in the assumption that X, or their hypothesis, is a *necessary* condition for the phenomenon or positive instance. They have a partially correct theory which makes unnecessarily restrictive assumptions.

Since in science it is the convention to formulate one's theories as *generally* as possible, there may not be a great problem in practice. The 2 4 6 error would be equivalent to a scientist observing that an iron bar expands linearly with increases in temperature and never then checking whether other materials possessed the same property. One final point is that even if scientists *do* have a bias to verify their own theories, science is a collective exercise. There is always someone else all too ready to show one's theories to be false!

Directionality of reasoning

In the previous sections it has been argued that subjects selectively attend to positive rather than negative possibilities. This causes logical errors in that subjects in consequence overlook or fail to obtain evidence which is logically relevant to the task. In this section we shall look at various evidence of another form of selective processing, namely *directionality* of reasoning. Inferences may be facilitated or inhibited according to whether or not they result from processing in the favoured direction.

A clear example of directional reasoning is the 'figure bias' observed on syllogistic reasoning tasks. These tasks use the classical syllogisms of Aristotelean logic, in which two premises may or may not validly imply a conclusion. The premises and conclusions are all *quantified*, i.e. concern class relationships. There are four types of proposition each known by a capital letter (see Table 5.2(a)). The *figure* of the syllogism refers to the order of the three terms involved in the syllogism: the subject (S) and predicate (P) of the conclusion, and the middle term (M) to which each is linked in the premises. The four classical figures are shown in Table 5.2(b). The *mood* of the syllogism is determined by the type of statement in each premise and the conclusion. For example, a Figure III syllogism in mood AEI would be:

All M are P
No M are S
Some S are P

TABLE 5.2 (a) *The four forms of quantified propositions used in syllogisms*

Universal affirmative	A	All A are B
Universal negative	E	No A are B
Particular affirmative	I	Some A are B
Particular negative	O	Some A are not B

(b) *The four classical syllogistic figures*

I	II	III	IV
M – P	P – M	M – P	P – M
S – M	S – M	M – S	M – S
S – P	S – P	S – P	S – P

Thus there are 256 logically distinct syllogisms (64 moods × 4 figures), most of which are invalid, i.e. the premises do not logically determine the conclusion. Validity can be determined when one knows both mood *and* figure. There is, however, evidence of non-logical biases for subjects to base judgment on one of these, disregarding the other. The figural bias is best illustrated by an example. Consider the following two versions of an EIO syllogism, the first in Figure I and the second in Figure IV:

(i) No artist is colour blind.
Some mathematicians are artists.
Therefore, some mathematicians are not colour blind.

(ii) No one who is colour blind is an artist.
Some artists are mathematicians.
Therefore, some mathematicians are not colour blind.

The premises of each syllogism are logically equivalent since E and I statements imply their converse forms. In each case the conclusion is valid. The effect of figural bias is, however, to make the argument easier to perceive in the first case (Figure I) than in the second (Figure IV). Figures II and III would produce intermediate difficulty. This order of difficulty has been established in various papers (see Evans, 1982, for a review).

Clearly the key factor in figural bias is whether or not the subject and predicate terms of the conclusion occupy the corresponding first and second order positions in the premises. That this is a *directionality* effect is suggested by the major theoretical accounts proposed to explain the effect. Frase (1966) explained the effect with reference to mediated associations, drawing on the fact that 'forward chaining' is easier than 'backward chaining' in learning experiments. More recent cognitive models by Dickstein (1978) and Johnson-Laird and Steedman (1978) also stress directional limitations on processing.

Dickstein's model is devised to account for performance on the 'standard' paradigm, in which subjects have to choose one of several alternative conclusions – all in S – P order, or else to say that 'none of these' follows. He argues that Figure IV produces 'backward processing' which is a slightly confusing term. Subjects still process the premises in a forward (left to right) manner, but since they are searching for a conclusion from P to S it is backwards with regard to the choice alternatives. Having found a P – S conclusion the model stipulates that it is then converted to an S – P form. The syllogisms given above can be used to illustrate the effects of the model. On problem (1) subjects seek and find a valid S – P conclusion. On problem (2) they seek a P – S conclusion – relating colour blind people to mathematicians – but none can be logically deduced. They have no conclusion to convert and so declare the syllogism invalid. Dickstein provides evidence for this model by showing that the figural bias is not manifest on problems where 'backward' processing would not lead to a logical error.

Johnson-Laird and Steedman (1978) depart from standard methodology by presenting only premises and asking subjects to draw their own conclusions. Premise pairs which would be Figure IV for an S – P conclusion are now Figure I for a P – S conclusion. On Figure I/IV problems subjects tend to draw conclusions in a direction determined by the premises. On Figures II and III, when the direction of premises is in conflict, subjects generate conclusions in either direction. Johnson-Laird and Steedman present a complex but interesting model in which subjects' directional bias is explained within a heuristic representational stage (see JOHNSON-LAIRD, this volume), in contrast with Dickstein's hypothesis of a processing error.

Either way, figural bias appears to reflect a 'set' induced by the order of terms in the premises. Subjects fail to generate or fail to endorse conclusions with reversed terms. Directionality effects in *conditional* inference are a little more subtly cued by linguistic factors. Several authors have proposed that the sentence, 'If P then Q', (IT) encourages inferences in a forward direction (from P to Q) whereas its logical equivalent, 'P only if Q', (OI) encourages *backward* (Q to P) reasoning (Rips and Marcus, 1977; Evans, 1977; Braine, 1978). This does *not* mean that people simply convert (illicitly) 'P only if Q' to read as 'If Q then P'. Table 5.3 shows four possible inferences which can be made about conditional relationships, together with their frequency of endorsement in two separate studies (Evans, 1977; Evans and Beck, 1981).

TABLE 5.3 % *frequencies with which conditional inferences are endorsed in two studies*

Inference	Affirmative example (IT form)	Study			
		Evans (1977)		Evans and Beck (1981)	
		IT	OI	IT	OI
Modus Ponens (MP)	If P then Q, P, therefore Q	100	76	78	63
Denial of the antecedent (DA)	If P then Q, Not P, therefore not Q	38	38	54	41
Affirmation of the consequent (AC)	If P then Q, Q, therefore P	67	84	53	80
Modus Tollens (MT)	If P then Q, Not Q, therefore not P	42	59	42	66

The data shown are averaged over the four rules which can be produced by varying the presence of a negative in either component. This gives a more accurate estimate of the true inference rates than looking only at affirmative rules (as in the examples) owing to a response bias to prefer negative conclusions (see Evans, 1977). In both studies MP is made more often with the IT rule and AC more often with the OI rule, which could be due simply to conversion. However, the significantly higher MT rate with OI rules shows that subjects prefer a 'backward' inference with OI which is only valid if P is taken to imply Q rather than vice versa. In one study there is also evidence of an increase in invalid but *forward* DA inferences in the IT group.

The frequency data of Table 5.3 are supported in parts by the studies of Roberge (1978) and Rips and Marcus (1977). Further evidence accrues from an interaction of IT and OI rules with directionality induced by a semantic context. Both Evans and Newstead (1977) and Evans and Beck (1981) have shown that the direction of a temporal order of the events designated by P and Q interacts with the form of rule in response *latency* analysis. Comprehension of the 'If P then Q' form is relatively facilitated when P precedes Q in time, and comprehension of 'P only if Q' facilitated when Q precedes P in time. Times are fastest when the linguistic directionality of the rule form is congruent with the semantic directionality in the given context.

Why do these directionality effects occur? It would seem that subjects' attention is directed to the component modified by the word 'if' whether or not accompanied by an 'only' which alters its logical significance. Evans (1977) suggested that 'If P then Q' is used in natural language to focus attention on *one* logical property of an implication, that P is *sufficient* for Q. On the other hand, 'P only if Q' seems to direct one towards the other property, that Q is *necessary* for P. These properties determine the MP and MT inferences respectively. Consider the following examples:

E1   If it is a dog then it has four legs.
E2   It is a dog only if it has four legs.

These two sentences are logically equivalent in that only a dog without four legs could disprove either rule. The suggestion is that with E1 one thinks primarily about MP or the fact that being a dog is a sufficient reason to have four legs. In E2 one thinks about the four legs realising that they are a necessary condition for being a dog, i.e. if you haven't got four legs you can't be a dog (MT). It is reasonable to suppose that different linguistic forms serve to emphasise different aspects of a logical relationship. As with the negation effects discussed earlier, linguistic cues may be responsible for the selective direction of thinking observed. Negatives direct one's attention to the propositions they deny, 'ifs' to the propositions which they modify.

In the earlier discussion of the Wason selection task the role of matching bias was emphasised. However, when matching bias is averaged out there is also a reliable preference to choose the true antecedent (G in the example given) much more often than the false antecedent (M). This is obviously related to the high MP rate observed with IT rules on conditional inference tasks. Subjects focus on the supposition that the antecedent will be true rather than false (cf. Rips and Marcus, 1977). This also explains why the attentional bias to true over false antecedent shown in Table 5.1 is larger than results from matching bias alone, as on the consequent cards.

Selection task protocols also reveal some clear directionality effects which Wason (1977) has used as evidence against Piaget's theory of formal operations. He argues in essence that some subjects show marked lack of reversibility. In several experiments (e.g. Wason, 1969; Wason and Johnson-Laird, 1970; Wason and Golding, 1974) subjects have been observed to argue that a P with a Q̄ on the back falsifies the rule while a Q̄ with a P on the back does not. This is how some subjects justify a refusal to select Q̄ even *after* revealing that it is, in fact, linked to a P.

The phenomenon is especially striking in Wason and Golding's (1974) study. Symbols appeared on top and bottom halves of the same face of a card. At the start of the experiment either the top or the bottom half of each card was masked. The rule might be:

'Whenever there is a number below the line there is a letter above the line.'

If the mask above a number was taken away to reveal a blank then it was clearly seen to contradict the rule. If a mask was removed from below a blank to reveal the same number, a few subjects denied its relevance despite the fact that *two identical cards* had been revealed. The authors interpret these results in terms of a perceptual set effect induced by the initial appearance of the cards. It is an extreme example of the perseveration of initial responding in the face of contradictory evidence (for a general discussion of self-contradiction, see Wason, 1977).

Statistical inference

A large field of research is concerned with how people make statistical inferences, some aspects of which are discussed by POLLARD AND EVANS (this volume). In this section I will discuss a few examples from this literature which suggest the operation of attentional factors.

Clearly relevant is the argument that subjects may assess subjective probabilities by use of an 'availability' heuristic (Tversky and Kahneman, 1973). The hypothesis is that the frequency of an event will be judged by the ease with which examples 'come to mind'. While in some situations this may be a useful guide, it may also lead subjects into systematic biases. For example, one's memory is organised in such a way that some sorts of information are more easily retrieved than others. An example is when subjects are asked to compare the frequency of words with a specified initial or third-placed letter (Kahneman and Tversky, 1973). The former are easier to retrieve and hence judged more probable even for letters where the latter are objectively more common. Alternatively, subjects' retrieval may accurately reflect their experience, but that experience be subject to biased samples of evidence. This could explain subjects' tendency to overestimate the risk of spectacular forms of death such as natural disasters, relative to mundane ones such as heart attacks (see Lichtenstein *et al.*, 1978). This could be due to the disproportionate media coverage given to the former type of event.

Pollard (1982) has made a detailed attempt to apply the availability heuristic to the explanation of deductive reasoning phenomena. The similarities and differences between his approach and mine will be discussed later. For the moment, I wish to concentrate on features of problem presentation (as opposed to memorial availability) which influence attention and performance in statistical inference. One of the clearest examples of a presentation factor involves a problem devised by Kahneman and Tversky (1972):

A certain town is served by two hospitals. In the larger hospital about 45 babies are born each day. As you know, about 50% of all babies born are boys. The exact percentage of baby boys, however, varies from day to day. Sometimes it may be higher than 50%, sometimes lower.

For a period of one year, the hospitals recorded the days on which more than 60% of the babies born were boys. Which hospital do you think recorded more such days?

In this paper, Kahneman and Tversky were concerned with the 'representativeness heuristic' discussed in detail by POLLARD AND EVANS (this volume). This asserts that judgments of likelihood of samples are based on the similarity of essential features to those of the population. They claimed that mean, proportion etc., were the dominant features for comparison and that the statistically critical feature of sample size would be overlooked. In the above problem the event referred to, 'most days on which more than 60% are boys', deviates from the population value – 50 per cent – and is thus objectively more likely to occur with the smaller hospital. In line with their prediction, however, Kahneman and Tversky found subjects to be indifferent between the two choices.

The authors take this as evidence that subjects do not understand the role of sample size. Could this be due to a failure in problem representation, however? Certainly the sample size feature itself is clearly enough communicated in the problem information. But what of the nature of the *event* itself? An event which deviates from the population expectation can be much more simply expressed. Evans and Dusoir (1977) substituted the following second paragraph:

Which hospital do you think is more likely to find on one day that all the babies born were boys?

Using a forced choice procedure, Evans and Dusoir found that in the original problem 11/20 chose the correct answer (chance level is 50 per cent), but in the simplified version 17/20 chose correctly. In fact just simplifying the problem by substituting 'one a day' for 'most days in the year' was sufficient to produce significant facilitation of performance. Bar-Hillel (1979) also reported significant facilitation by simplification of the same problem.

This example suggests that linguistic complexity may lead to a failure to encode a crucial piece of information. This, in turn, may be *misinterpreted* as inability to make an inference – in this case to appreciate the role of sample size. However, inferential errors may arise not only from failures to attend to the relevant information, but also by giving attention to the *wrong* information. An example of this arises from the same Kahneman and Tversky (1972) study of 'representativeness', which is discussed in detail by POLLARD AND EVANS (this volume).

In this experiment, subjects had to generate subjective sampling distributions by estimating the frequency with which sample outcomes would fall into a number of different categories. The categories were defined by proportion and fixed in number (11) for each sample size tested. Consequently, the fact that subjects distributed their estimates over categories without regard to sample size is perhaps not surprising. Kahneman and Tversky seem to have loaded the odds in favour of their prediction by using a fixed number of categories which make the proportionality cue more salient than sample size. The real explanation is even more basic. Olson (1976) varied the range of each category drastically so that they no longer conformed to the same proportions. Subjects continued to distribute their percentages over the 11 categories in precisely the same way, disregarding both the sample size and proportion represented by the categories. Only the number and order of the categories were heeded by the subjects – their *content* was ignored altogether. Recently, Kahneman and Tversky (1982) have conceded that subjects have some understanding of the effects of sample size and that their ability to express it is task-dependent.

There are many examples in the statistical inference literature which could be discussed in this way. I will, however, conclude this section by reference to some recent experiments which I designed in collaboration with Paul Pollard. This study suggests strongly that attention, and thus performance, may be strongly influenced by the perceptual salience of features of problem information.

In these experiments subjects were shown samples of normally distributed data which varied on three dimensions – mean difference (from 100), sample size and variability. They were told in each case that the numbers represented IQs of a group of people in a given occupation, and asked to estimate the odds in favour of the hypothesis that the occupational group from which they were sampled was above (or below) average in intelligence. The question was always phrased so that the odds would be in favour of the hypothesis (greater than 1).

All else being equal the odds are greater, the greater the difference between the sample mean and 100. However, since samples estimate population parameters more accurately when their size increases and their variability reduces, these variables should also affect judgments. Specifically, subjects' confidence that the hypothesis is correct should increase for samples with larger sizes and reduce for samples with larger variability.

In Experiment I, subjects were presented with all the raw data on a VDU. In one group the sample mean was stated underneath, and in the other it was not. The odds were converted into probabilities for analysis, and the means are shown in Table 5.4.

TABLE 5.4 *Results of Evans and Pollard's experiments expressed as mean subjective probabilities*

	Mean difference*	Sample size*	Variability
Experiment I (tables)	*1* 0·659	*64* 0·659	*8* 0·680
	1·5 0·682	*144* 0·681	*12* 0·681
	2·25 0·695	*324* 0·696	*18* 0·686

	Mean difference*	Sample size	Variability*
Experiment II (histograms)	*1* 0·628	*64* 0·641	*8* 0·659
	1·5 0·650	*144* 0·655	*12* 0·650
	2·25 0·667	*324* 0·650	*18* 0·637

* Significant main effect

Whilst the absolute values of these subjective probabilities are grossly inaccurate, it is their *relative* size that is of interest. Analysis of variance revealed that in Experiment I subjects' judgments were significantly influenced by mean difference and sample size, both in the normative direction. In addition, the statement of sample mean interacted with mean difference – subjects placed more weighting on the mean if it was stated.

On the basis of Experiment I, then, one might conclude that subjects understand the nature of the effect of mean difference and sample size, but *not* variability on sample likelihoods. However, if subjects attach more weight to the sample mean if it is stated, then this suggests that this is not the whole story. On further consideration, it was felt that the method of displaying the data made sample size very salient – larger samples entailed a larger block of numbers on the screen. On the other hand, variability was not salient, even though it is known that subjects can perceive differences in variance in numerical displays (e.g. Beach and Scopp, 1968).

In Experiment II, exactly the same data and instructions were presented to a second group of subjects. The difference was that histograms were used to present the data. This had the effect of increasing salience of variability which was cued by the visual spread of the distribution. Sample size could now be learned only by reading the scale, and thus lost the immediate perceptual salience of Experiment I. The results for main effects are again shown in Table 5.4.

The most striking difference between the results of Experiment II compared with Experiment I is that sample size is no longer significantly influencing judgments, whereas variability is now doing so and in the normatively correct direction. That is, more variance about the sample mean decreases confidence in the hypothesis, and reduces the estimate of its likelihood. Thus the apparent competence of subjects' judgment about these two sample features is reversed with respect to Experiment I.

The perceptual salience hypothesis is strengthened, in retrospect, by consideration of the mean difference factor. In Experiment II the strength of the effect was greater (compare means in Table 5.4) and the interaction with the group factor disappeared. That is, stating the mean did *not* induce any greater attention to this factor as it did in Experiment I. On the histogram displays, a dotted vertical line indicated the expected mean under the null hypothesis. Thus mean difference was perceptually cued by the amount of the distribution which lay to the left or right of this line.

The findings of Experiment II were considerably complicated by a whole set of significant interactions involving the factor above/below population mean. When the sample mean was above that of the population the mode appeared to the right of the vertical line, and when below the mode was shifted to the left. Although the effects of this factor were too complex to discuss here, it is interesting to note that subjects' judgments could be significantly different when statistical distributions were presented in a mirror-image which has no effect on the objective probabilities. Clearly, this is some kind of perceptual effect rather than response bias, since the latter would have produced comparable effects in Experiment I.

The above/below mean factor had no effects at all in the first experiment.

This study, then, provides strong evidence for the influence of attentional factors – cued by perceptual salience – on statistical judgment. There is practical as well as theoretical interest here. Clearly, people's subjective interpretation of sample information is strongly influenced by the manner of its presentation.

Content effects

Most of the research discussed so far has been concerned with artificial reasoning problems utilising 'abstract' content, e.g. letters and numbers. Content factors arise from the manipulation of the *meaning* of the propositions contained in the problems, without changing the formal structure of the task. If subjects reasoned formally such factors should not influence their performance, but in practice reasoning is highly dependent on problem content (cf. Evans, 1982; Pollard, 1982; GRIGGS, this volume).

Space restrictions preclude any specific discussion of content effects in this chapter. However, the effects can be readily interpreted within the framework presented here. That is to say, variations in performance can be attributed to selective attention and direction of thought arising from people's previous experience with realistic content. I entirely agree with GRIGGS (this volume) that there is no general facilitatory effect of making problems realistic rather than artificial and that facilitation of *performance* does not entail facilitation of logical reasoning. If one's previous experience cues one to think about the relevant information it will indeed assist (cf. GRIGGS's discussion of memory-cuing and reasoning-by-analogy on the selection task). Performance may also be inhibited if one's attention is directed to logically inappropriate possibilities (see, for example, Pollard and Evans, 1981 and Pollard, 1982, for discussion of helpful and unhelpful associational cues, and Fillenbaum, 1978 and Evans, 1982, for discussion of pragmatic aspects of conditional inference).

If we follow the idea that reasoners operate in 'problem spaces' (cf. Newell, 1980) then clearly the subjects' previous knowledge of the task environment will exert a considerable influence on the manner in which such a space is constructed and searched.

Conclusions

I have argued elsewhere that reasoning tasks should be treated as specialised problem-solving or decision-making tasks, and that the focus on questions or rationality has distracted attention from full analysis of the thought processes involved (Evans, 1982). For example, the notion that problem-solving errors can arise in representation of problem information has been widely accepted for many years, and strongly supported by the work of Newell and Simon (e.g. 1972). The importance of problem representation is increasingly being recognised in the study of decision making (see, for example, Payne, 1980). Its application to deductive reasoning tasks has been extremely limited, however. Reasoning theorists seem to have been widely influenced by the approach of Henle (1962) and to have focused on misinterpretation of the premises as the sole form of representational error. Such theorists have also been reluctant to admit to any distortion from logic in the processing of stored representations (e.g. Revlis, 1975; Revlin and Leirer, 1978).

If we are to regard reasoners as people solving problems, then we must pay much more attention to the specific nature of the task demands placed on the subject, and less to *a priori* conceptions of rationality and logicality. Reasoning researchers have tended to ask questions about competence – can subjects make modus tollens, appreciate the role of sample size, see the need to eliminate hypotheses, etc. – with perhaps insufficient attention to what determines *performance* on a particular task.

JOHNSON-LAIRD (this volume) has argued that reasoning is a skill which, like other skills, may be learned and may be subject to cognitive limitations. An important limitation which he discusses is that of working memory capacity. The present chapter has focused on an alternative set of factors limiting performance, namely those inducing selective attention and direction of thought.

A rather broad range of examples has been discussed in this chapter to illustrate such phenomena. It has been argued that in some situations subjects fail to solve a problem because they do not attend to the logically relevant information. In other situations, irrational behaviour arises because subjects pay attention to logically irrelevant features. To make progress theoretically, however, we must also analyse the factors which determine where attention will be placed. In the discussion three distinct classes of factor have emerged – *perceptual, linguistic* and *semantic*. It must, however, be admitted that for some of the phenomena, it is not yet clear which type of factor is responsible.

The most basic type of explanation is that of perceptual factors. Quite simply, the perceptual salience of features in the displayed information may determine the amount of attention paid to them. Perhaps the clearest example discussed in this chapter is the recent statistical judgment study of Evans and Pollard. The figural bias in syllogistic reasoning should perhaps be regarded as 'perceptual' also. The point is that the configuration of terms in the syllogism appears to direct thinking, *irrespective* of the mood of the premises. The independence of mood suggests that bias is not dependent upon any linguistic processing of the problem information, and indeed may help to shape the nature of that processing (cf. Johnson-Laird and Steedman, 1978; JOHNSON-LAIRD, this volume).

While a perceptual explanation of 'matching bias' is tempting, it is hard to reconcile with the dependence of the effect on conditional rather than disjunctive rules. In the relevant section a semi-linguistic explanation was offered in terms of a linguistic presupposition of affirmatives coupled with a general preference for thinking in positive terms – the latter being applied also to behaviour on the 2 4 6 and related problems. Linguistic factors certainly do seem to be implicated, for example, in directionality effects of conditional inference. The notion of linguistic presupposition, in particular, seems a likely cause of attentional bias. A simpler type of linguistic effect arises when sheer complexity of wording distracts the subject from encoding the problem information correctly. This was illustrated with reference to one of Kahneman and Tversky's problems.

Semantic factors have been dealt with only briefly in this chapter since the focus has been on artificial reasoning problems. There is little doubt, however, that prior beliefs and expectations will be a major determinant of the information which is heeded by the problem solver in realistic or real-life reasoning. A problem in this area is that such materials may induce subjects to disregard the instruction altogether and respond on the basis of prior belief without attempting to reason at all. Consider, for example, the 'belief bias' effect in which subjects tend to evaluate the validity of syllogisms on the basis of their belief in the truth of the conclusion, rather than its logical necessity from the premises (for reviews, see Revlin and Leirer, 1978; Evans, 1982). This could be due to subjects augmenting their problem spaces with premises derived from prior knowledge, and making deductions from this elaborated data base. Alternatively subjects could be simply failing to comply with instructions and making direct truth judgments of the conclusion. It is hard to discriminate these alternatives in the existing literature.

Pollard (1982) has presented an account of reasoning responses on the basis of 'available' cues. These are determined in the case of thematic problems by previous experience with the content and context, and in the case of abstract problems by salient cues in the presentation. This approach has obvious similarities to the present discussion of semantic and perceptual factors. (Pollard does not deal with linguistic factors or directionality effects.) While the similarities are genuine, there is an important difference between his approach and mine. I have described an active problem solver subject to attentional limitations. Pollard seems less 'cognitive' in approach. For example, like me he regards matching bias and the presentation of hypotheses on the 2 4 6 problem to be related phenomena. His explanation, however, is along the lines of *response priming*; that is, the stimulus cues directly raise the probability of certain responses.

I would argue that the postulation of selective attention as a mediating state has certain advantages, especially in explanation of the *logical* component of performance as well as the biases. Pollard must argue that all correct responses are elicited by available cues rather than strategies. He makes a good attempt to do this for thematic, but not for abstract problems.

The arguments in this chapter suggest that subjects have more understanding of logical and statistical principles than their behaviour often suggests. Procedures which increase attention to the relevant features tend to facilitate performance *without* cuing the right answer. For example, matching bias on truth table tasks (e.g. Evans, 1972) determines whether or not a subject constructs an instance. The nature of that construction (true or false) is, however, determined by its logical significance. Similarly, in the Evans and Pollard statistical inference study, cue salience determines whether or not subjects take account of sample size and variability. It is not, however, clear what 'available' cues tell the subjects to prefer large to small, and less to more variable samples.

I would, however, be extremely cautious about the supposition of any underlying 'competence' system, in the sense of a general set of principles applicable to all situations (see Evans, 1982, Chapter 11, and JOHNSON-LAIRD's discussion of 'mental logic' in this volume). The striking aspect of reasoning research is still the difficulty which intelligent adults have in generating and/or applying appropriate inferential strategies to solve the problems. The manner in which perceptual, linguistic and semantic factors dominate thinking, for example, is irreconcilable with the Piagetian notion of a formal operational thinker. For the present at least, the emphasis in the field must shift away from a search for competence, and towards an explanation of performance.

References

Bar-Hillel, M. (1979), 'The role of sample size in sample evaluation', *Organisational Behavior and Human Performance*, *24*, pp. 245–57.

Beach, L. R. and Scopp, T. S. (1968), 'Intuitive statistical inferences about variances', *Organisational Behavior and Human Performance*, *3*, pp. 109–23.

Bourne, L. E., Dominowski, N. L. and Loftus, E. (1979), *Cognitive Processes*, Englewood Cliffs, New Jersey, Prentice-Hall.

Braine, M. D. S. (1978), 'On the relation between the natural logic of reasoning and standard logic', *Psychological Review*, *85*, pp. 1–21.

Bruner, J. S., Goodnow, J. J. and Austin, G. A. (1956), *A Study of Thinking*, New York, Wiley.

Clark, H. H. and Clark, E. V. (1977), *Psychology and Language*, New York, Harcourt.

Cohen, L. J. (1981), 'Can human irrationality be experimentally demonstrated?', *The Behavioral and Brain Sciences*, *4*, pp. 317–70.

Dickstein, L. S. (1978), 'The effect of figure on syllogistic reasoning', *Memory and Cognition*, *6*, pp. 76–83.

Evans, J. St B. T. (1972), 'Interpretation and "matching bias" in a reasoning task', *Quarterly Journal of Experimental Psychology*, *24*, pp. 193–9.

Evans, J. St B. T. (1975), 'On interpreting reasoning data: a reply to Van Duyne', *Cognition*, *3*, pp. 387–90.

Evans, J. St B. T. (1977), 'Linguistic factors in reasoning', *Quarterly Journal of Experimental Psychology*, *29*, pp. 297–306.

Evans, J. St B. T. (1982), *The Psychology of Deductive Reasoning*, London, Routledge & Kegan Paul.

Evans, J. St B. T. and Beck, M. A. (1981), 'Directionality and temporal factors in conditional reasoning', *Current Psychological Research*, *1*, pp. 111–20.

Evans, J. St B. T. and Dusoir, A. E. (1977), 'Proportionality and sample size as factors in statistical judgment', *Acta Psychologica*, *41*, pp. 129–37.

Evans, J. St B. T. and Lynch, J. S. (1973), 'Matching bias in the selection task', *British Journal of Psychology*, *64*, pp. 391–97.

Evans, J. St B. T. and Newstead, S. E. (1977), 'Language and reasoning: a study of temporal factors', *Cognition*, *8*, pp. 265–83.

Evans, J. St B. T. and Newstead, S. E. (1980), 'A study of disjunctive reasoning', *Psychological Research*, *41*, pp. 373–88.

Fillenbaum, S. (1978), 'How to do some things with IF', in J. W. Cotton and R. L. Klatzky (eds), *Semantic Factors in Cognition*, Hillsdale, New Jersey, Erlbaum.

Frase, L. T. (1966), 'Validity judgments in relation to two sets of items', *Journal of Educational Psychology*, *57*, pp. 539–45.

Griggs, R. A., and Cox, J. R. (1982), 'The elusive thematic materials effect in Wason's selection task', *British Journal of Psychology*, *73*, pp. 407–20.

Henle, M. (1962), 'On the relation between logic and thinking', *Psychological Review*, *69*, pp. 366–78.

Johnson-Laird, P. N. and Steedman, M. (1978), 'The psychology of syllogisms', *Cognitive Psychology*, *10*, pp. 64–98.

Johnson-Laird, P. N. and Wason, P. C. (1970), 'Insight into a logical relation', *Quarterly Journal of Experimental Psychology*, *22*, pp. 49–61.

Kahneman, D. and Tversky, A. (1972), 'Subjective probability: A judgment of representativeness', *Cognitive Psychology*, *3*, pp. 430–54.

Kahneman, D. and Tversky, A. (1973), 'On the psychology of prediction', *Psychological Review*, *80*, pp. 237–51.

Kahneman, D., and Tversky, A. (1982), 'On the study of statistical intuitions', *Cognition*, *11*, pp. 123–41.

Lichtenstein, S., Slovic, P., Fischhoff, B., Layman, M. and Combs, B. (1978), 'Judged frequency of lethal events', *Journal of Experimental Psychology: Human Learning and Memory*, *6*, pp. 551–79.

Luchins, A. S. and Luchins, E. H. (1950), 'New experimental attempts at preventing mechanisation in problem solving', *Journal of General Psychology*, *42*, pp. 279–97.

Lunzer, E. A., Harrison, C. and Davey, M. (1972), 'The four card problem and the generality of formal reasoning', *Quarterly Journal of Experimental Psychology*, *24*, pp. 326–39.

Manktelow, K. I. and Evans, J. St B. T. (1979), 'Facilitation of reasoning by realism: effect or non-effect?', *British Journal of Psychology*, *71*, pp. 227–31.

Miller, G. A. (1967), *The Psychology of Communication*, New York, Basic Books.

Mynatt, C. R., Doherty, M. E. and Tweney, R. D. (1977), 'Confirmation bias in a simulated research environment: an experimental study of scientific inference', *Quarterly Journal of Experimental Psychology*, *29*, pp. 85–96.

Mynatt, C. R., Doherty, M. E. and Tweney, R. D. (1978), 'Consequences of confirmation and disconfirmation in a simulated research environment', *Quarterly Journal of Experimental Psychology*, *30*, pp. 395–406.

Newell, A. (1980), 'Reasoning, problem solving and decision processes: the problem space as a fundamental category', in R. S. Nickerson (ed.), *Attention and Performance VIII*, Hillsdale, New Jersey, Erlbaum.

Newell, A. and Simon, H. A. (1972), *Human Problem Solving*, Englewood Cliffs, New Jersey, Prentice-Hall.

Nisbett, R. E. and Ross, L. (1980), *Human Inference: Strategies and Shortcomings of Social Judgment*, Englewood Cliffs, New Jersey, Prentice-Hall.

Olson, C. L. (1976), 'Some apparent violations of the representativeness heuristic in human judgment', *Journal of Experimental Psychology: Human Perception and Performance*, 2, pp. 599–608.

Payne, J. W. (1980), 'Information processing theory: some concepts and methods applied to decision research', in T. S. Wallstein (ed.), *Cognitive Processes in Choice and Decision Behaviour*, Hillsdale, New Jersey, Erlbaum.

Pollard, P. (1982), 'Human reasoning: some possible effects of availability', *Cognition*, 10, pp. 65–96.

Pollard, P. and Evans, J. St B. T. (1981), 'The effect of prior beliefs in reasoning: an associational interpretation', *British Journal of Psychology*, 72, pp. 73–82.

Popper, K. (1959), *The Logic of Scientific Discovery*, London, Hutchinson.

Revlin, R., and Leirer, V. O. (1978), 'The effect of personal biases on syllogistic reasoning: rational decisions from personalized representations', in R. Revlin and R. E. Mayer (eds), *Human Reasoning*, New York, Wiley.

Revlis, R. (1975), 'Syllogistic reasoning: logical decisions from a complex data base', in R. J. Falmagne (ed.), *Reasoning: Representation and Process*, New York, Wiley.

Rips, L. J. and Marcus, S. L. (1977), 'Suppositions and the analysis of conditional sentences', in M. A. Just and P. A. Carpenter (eds), *Cognitive Processes in Comprehension*, New York, Wiley.

Roberge, J. J. (1978), 'Linguistic and psychometric factors in propositional reasoning', *Quarterly Journal of Experimental Psychology*, 30, pp. 705–16.

Roth, E. M. (1979), 'Facilitating insight into a reasoning task', *British Journal of Psychology*, 70, pp. 265–72.

Tweney, R. D., Doherty, M. E., Warner, W. J., Pliske, D. B., Mynatt, C., Gross, K. A. and Arkkezin, D. L. (1980), 'Strategies of rule discovery in an inference task', *Quarterly Journal of Experimental Psychology*, 32, pp. 109–24.

Tversky, A. and Kahneman, D. (1973), 'Availability: a heuristic for judging frequency and probability', *Cognitive Psychology*, 5, pp. 207–32.

Van Duyne, P. C. (1976), 'Necessity and contingency in reasoning', *Acta Psychologica*, 40, pp. 85–101.

Wason, P. C. (1960), 'On the failure to eliminate hypotheses in a conceptual task', *Quarterly Journal of Experimental Psychology*, 12, pp. 129–40.

Wason, P. C. (1968), 'On the failure to eliminate hypotheses: a second look', in P. C. Wason and P. N. Johnson-Laird (eds), *Thinking and Reasoning*, Harmondsworth, Penguin.

Wason, P. C. (1969), 'Regression in reasoning', *British Journal of Psychology*, *60*, pp. 471–80.

Wason, P. C. (1972), 'In real life negatives are false', *Logique et Analyse*, *19*, pp. 19–38.

Wason, P. C. (1977), 'Self-contradictions', in P. N. Johnson-Laird and P. C. Wason (eds), *Thinking: Readings in Cognitive Science*, Cambridge, Cambridge University Press.

Wason, P. C. (1980), 'The verification task and beyond', in D. R. Olson (ed.), *The Social Foundations of Language and Thought*, New York, Norton.

Wason, P. C. and Brooks, P. G. (1979), 'THOG: the anatomy of a problem', *Psychological Research*, *41*, pp. 79–90.

Wason, P. C. and Evans, J. St B. T. (1975), 'Dual processes in reasoning', *Cognition*, *3*, pp. 141–54.

Wason, P. C. and Golding, E. (1974), 'The language of inconsistency', *British Journal of Psychology*, *65*, pp. 537–46.

Wason, P. C. and Johnson-Laird, P. N. (1969), 'Proving a disjunctive rule', *Quarterly Journal of Experimental Psychology*, *21*, pp. 14–20.

Wason, P. C. and Johnson-Laird, P. N. (1970), 'A conflict between selecting and evaluating information in an inferential task', *British Journal of Psychology*, *61*, pp. 509–15.

Wason, P. C. and Johnson-Laird, P. N. (1972), *Psychology of Reasoning: Structure and Content*, London, Batsford.

Wetherick, N. E. (1962), 'Eliminative and enumerative behavior in a conceptual task', *Quarterly Journal of Experimental Psychology*, *3*, pp. 184–97.

Woodworth, R. S. and Schlosberg, H. (1954), *Experimental Psychology*, London, Methuen.

6 Thinking as a skill*

Philip N. Johnson-Laird

Sir Frederic Bartlett argued that thinking is a skill that evolved from bodily behaviour, and he studied it from this standpoint for many years. In the book in which he reported his investigations, he suggested that thinking begins with environmental information which is incomplete or fragmentary, and develops in a series of interconnected steps (and sometimes intuitive leaps) which eventually reach some terminus. He wrote, 'We should be content to regard thinking as an extension of evidence, in line with the evidence and in such a manner as to fill up gaps in the evidence' (Bartlett, 1958, p. 20). He distinguished three kinds of gap-filling processes, and he claimed that all thinking depends on one or more of them:

> In the first the gap is filled by interpolation, in the second by extrapolation, and the third requires that the evidence given should be looked at from a special, and often an unusual point of view, and that it should be recomposed and reinterpreted to achieve a desired issue. (Bartlett, 1958, p. 22)

What could thinking be if not a skill? One's first reaction is that there is no other possibility. But, perhaps thinking might be a set of mental processes that are inborn rather than learned, that apply universally to any cognitive content, and that are exercised wholly without error. This view seems so contrary to common sense that, as you might suspect, it is held by some philosophers (and some

* This chapter is a slightly revised and shortened version of the Ninth Bartlett Memorial Lecture, originally published by the Quarterly Journal of Experimental Psychology, 1982, 34A, pp. 1–29. Reproduced by permission of the Experimental Psychology Society.

psychologists). Thus, Spinoza's metaphysical dread of illogicality led him to the view that what seemed like an invalid inference was merely a valid inference based on other premises. This doctrine has surfaced more recently in Mary Henle's (1962) explanation of apparent errors of reasoning in terms of the forgetting or reinterpretation of premises, the importation of irrelevant information, and other such processes that lead reasoners to argue from a different set of premises than those explicitly presented to them. From this position it is a short step to the view, which Henle espouses, that the underlying competence of ordinary individuals untutored in logic cannot be at fault – errors may occur in performance, but 'in all such cases some malfunction of an information-processing mechanism has to be inferred' (Cohen, 1981). And this doctrine suggests, in turn, that there is an innate mental logic and indeed that the mind is entirely furnished with innate concepts (Fodor, 1980). Such claims are tendentious with the best of intentions. Their authors are impressed by the fact that human beings invented logic, mathematics, and the very concept of rationality. It follows, they believe, that people must in principle think logically; the laws of thought are indeed the laws of logic.

Curiously, a number of recent investigators have advanced exactly the opposite argument. They have proposed theories of deductive reasoning that render people inherently irrational (e.g. Erickson, 1974; Revlis, 1975; Evans, 1977, 1980; Guyote and Sternberg, 1981). Even if an individual draws a conclusion that happens to be valid, the underlying thought process fails to be logical since these theories preclude a complete examination of the consequences of premises. If you contemplate the follies and fallacies of the human condition, then you might well conclude that these theories are essentially correct. Indeed, if you are of a Romantic cast of mind, you might revel in irrationality like Walt Whitman, who delighted in his capacity for self-contradiction, or you might fear rationality like Tolstoy, who wrote that if human life were ever controlled by reason, then all possibility of spontaneity would be annihilated.

Such views inflate the importance of logic. A valid deduction, of course, is one that follows necessarily from the premises: if the premises are true, then the conclusion must be true. But it is entirely possible to argue validly from false premises and to make valid deductions that proceed from alternative and perhaps incompatible points of view – as Sydney Smith observed of two women shouting at each other from houses on opposite sides of the street: they'll never agree, they're arguing from different premises. Moreover, any set of premises yields an infinite number of valid conclusions. Most of them are wholly trivial, such as a conjunction of all the premises, or a disjunction of all of them. Logic provides only a set of procedures for testing whether a given conclusion follows validly from a set of premises; it does not tell you which particular conclusion you should draw. Hence, when you draw a specific valid conclusion, you must be guided by more than logic: you must follow certain other principles that lead to a conclusion that is not wholly trivial.

There is, in short, a controversy about human reasoning. Some theorists, principally philosophers, argue that we are invariably rational; other theorists, principally psychologists, argue that we are invariably irrational. But these contrary points of view are not exhaustive. There remains a third possibility, which is implicit in Bartlett's writings. If thinking is a skill, then its exercise will vary in expertise: human beings may well be rational in some circumstances, but not in others. These three alternatives – invariable rationality, invariable irrationality, and variable rationality – exhaust the universe of possibilities; my task in this paper will be to try to decide amongst them.

Implicit and explicit inference

For most of us, the paragon of deductive ability is Sherlock Holmes, who was wont to make such remarks as, 'Beyond the obvious facts that he has at some time done manual labour, that he takes snuff, that he is a freemason, that he has been in China, and that he has done a considerable amount of writing lately, I can deduce nothing else.' Here is a rather longer extract from a Holmes story, 'Charles Augustus Milverton', that I would like you to read. All that you need to know is that Milverton is the wickedest man in London, a blackmailer, and that Holmes and Watson are about to burgle his house to recover some compromising letters.

> With our black silk face-coverings, which turned us into two of the most truculent figures in London, we stole up to the silent, gloomy house. A sort of tiled veranda extended along one side of it, lined by several windows and two doors.

"That's his bedroom," Holmes whispered. "This door opens straight into the study. It would suit us best, but it is bolted as well as locked, and we should make too much noise getting in. Come round here. There's a greenhouse which opens into the drawing room."

The place was locked, but Holmes removed a circle of glass and turned the key from the inside. An instant afterwards he had closed the door behind us, and we had become felons in the eyes of the law. The thick warm air of the conservatory and the rich choking fragrance of the exotic plants took us by the throat. He seized my hand in the darkness and led me swiftly past banks of shrubs which brushed against our faces. Holmes had remarkable powers, carefully cultivated, of seeing in the dark. [!] Still holding my hand in one of his, he opened a door, and I was vaguely conscious that we had entered a large room in which a cigar had been smoked not long before. He felt his way among the furniture, opened another door, and closed it behind us. Putting out my hand I felt several coats hanging from the wall, and I understood that I was in a passage. We passed along it, and Holmes very gently opened a door upon the right-hand side. Something rushed out at us and my heart sprang into my mouth, but I could have laughed when I realized that it was the cat. A fire was burning in this new room, and again the air was heavy with tobacco smoke. Holmes entered on tiptoe, waited for me to follow, and then very gently closed the door. We were in Milverton's study, and a portière at the farther side showed the entrance to his bedroom.

It was a good fire, and the room was illuminated by it. Near the door I saw the gleam of an electric switch, but it was unnecessary, even if it had been safe, to turn it on. At one side of the fireplace was a heavy curtain which covered the bay window that we had seen from outside. On the other side was the door which communicated with the veranda.

You may have noticed that Holmes does not make a deduction in this extract, and to compensate for this uncharacteristic lapse, I want you to attempt to make one. Imagine the plan of the house as a square with the veranda running along its lower side. The question is: which way did Holmes and Watson walk along the veranda – from right to left or from left to right?

In my experience very few people are able to make this inference unless they are asked the question before they read the passage, in which case the answer is relatively easy to work out. The crucial evidence occurs, as Bartlett would have said, in disguise. (For those readers who are still perplexed, the answer can be found at the end of the paper.) Yet, it would be a mistake to think, if you were unable to answer the question, that you made no inferences while you were reading the passage. I estimate that you drew about 40 inferences during the process of understanding it. Consider, for example, the way in which you understood the sentences:

The place was locked, but Holmes removed a circle of glass and turned the key from the inside. An instant afterwards he had closed the door behind us. . . .

You inferred that 'the place' refers to the greenhouse, not the drawing room, and that its door was locked. You inferred that Holmes removed a circle of glass from a pane in the door, that he put his hand through the resulting hole in the pane, and turned the key in the lock of the door to unlock it. And you inferred that Holmes opened the door, and that the two men entered the greenhouse. These inferences are so obvious that you may feel that they hardly merit the term. Yet they are inferences none the less, and they play a crucial role in enabling you to build up an integrated representation of the passage. They depend on general knowledge, and if like the Martian in Craig Raine's (1979) poem you lacked that general knowledge, then you would be unable to make the inferences, and the passage would be incomprehensible to you. It was only when workers in Artificial Intelligence attempted to program computers to understand texts in natural language that the ubiquity of these inferential steps was discovered. The computer is the best Martian of all.

What this passage from Conan Doyle has revealed to us is the existence of two sorts of thinking. There are explicit inferences that require a deliberate and conscious effort, and there are implicit inferences that proceed so smoothly and automatically that one is not normally aware of making them. Bartlett would have said that implicit inferences are intuitive leaps.

There is another important difference between implicit and explicit inferences apart from the conscious/unconscious split between them. Generally, when an implicit inference is made, it goes beyond the literal evidence. For example, when you read in the Sherlock Holmes story:

An instant afterwards he had closed the door behind us. . . .

you inferred that Holmes and Watson had entered the house. But the story might have continued:

For at the last moment Holmes had turned us away from the house and from the only criminal act that I had ever known him to contemplate.

At the point at which these interpolations occur they can seldom be definitive: they are plausible inferences based on general knowledge rather than valid deductions. Some psychologists are accordingly tempted to suppose that a probabilistic mechanism underlies them. However, there is no reason to suppose that individuals compute probabilities in determining, say, the reference of a pronoun. The mechanism is more like one that yields a conclusion by default. The conclusion is justified provided that there is no (subsequent) evidence to overrule it. The inference lacks the mental imprimatur of an explicit deduction in which an attempt is made to test the validity of a conclusion.

The ability to make appropriate implicit inferences is a skill that children must acquire – without it, they will be unable to construct an integrated representation of discourse. This claim has been corroborated by a number of experimental studies. Til Wykes, a former student of mine, has shown that young children of about 4 to 5 years of age have considerable difficulty in correctly acting out with glove puppets such pairs of sentences as:

Jane needed Susan's pencil.
She gave it to her.

The task is much easier for them if gender can be used as a cue:

Susan needed John's pencil.
He gave it to her.

In general, the greater the number of pronouns in a sentence, the harder it is for young children to understand. They appear to adopt a syntactically based procedure for assigning referents to pronouns rather than an inferential one. They assume that a pronoun refers to the same entity as the subject of the previous clause (see Wykes, 1978). In a further joint study, we discovered that children are poor at making inferences based on general knowledge in order to work out the meaning of such sentences as,

The Smiths saw the Rocky mountains flying to California.
(Wykes and Johnson-Laird, 1977)

Similarly, children presented with a sentence such as,

The man stirred his cup of tea

tend not to infer spontaneously that the man used a spoon to stir his tea. In all these cases, it was clear from control studies that the children are able to make the relevant inferences if they are explicitly asked to do so. The point is that they do not readily make implicit inferences as a normal part of understanding discourse.

Skill in making implicit inferences is equally important in reading. My student, Jane Oakhill, has shown that an important distinction between excellent and average readers lies precisely in their ability to make such inferences. In one study, Oakhill (1982) gave a sample of 168 children (aged 7 to 8 years) a variety of vocabulary and reading tests. She was then able to select two groups matched on vocabulary and phonic skills, but differing in their ability to understand what they read. In order to eliminate the effects of other possible differences in reading ability, the two groups of children were asked to listen to accounts of simple episodes. Each account consisted of three sentences, such as,

The car crashed into the bus.
The bus was near the crossroads.
The car skidded on the ice.

After the children had heard eight such passages, their memory for them was tested. Those who made implicit inferences in order to build up an integrated representation of an episode should assume that the sentence,

The car was near the crossroads

occurred in the original passage. Given the nature of the episode, it is extremely plausible that the car was near the crossroads, since it crashed into the bus, and the bus was near the crossroads. The assertion,

The bus skidded on the ice

is much less plausibly inferred, since there is no reason to draw this conclusion in building a representation of the events in the passage. The results of the memory test using such sentences showed, as expected, that the good readers tended to make more recognition errors based on plausible inferences than did the average readers. The good readers, however, performed better than the average ones in recognizing the original sentences from the passages, and in rejecting the implausible inferences. It seems that excellent readers are likely to make implicit inferences in order to build up an integrated representation of a story, whereas average readers are less likely to do so. Obviously, this study tells us nothing about causal direction: good readers may be good because they spontaneously make inferences, or they may make such inferences because they are good readers . . . as a result of other factors. However, in a series of additional studies, Oakhill has so far failed to isolate any other major distinction between her two groups of readers.

The doctrine of mental logic

Suppose that you are sitting on a tube train going to Uxbridge, and someone asks you, 'Does this train go to Ickenham?' You look at the map and discover that every train that goes to Uxbridge goes to Ickenham, and so you reply, 'Yes.' At the heart of what you did is a simple valid deduction of the form:

This is an x.
Every x is a y.
Therefore, this is a y.

Of course, you had to know how to obtain the information about the train's route, which in turn probably required an inferential process. Similarly, you may have considered whether or not the train was likely to rush through the station at Ickenham without stopping – an event which, though not strictly bearing on the accuracy of your answer, would be likely to aggrieve your questioner. Nevertheless, your conclusion hinges on a deductive inference that has the abstract form shown above.

Ever since Aristotle, logicians have been sensitive to the form of inferences, and they have proposed formal rules like the one above in order to specify the set of valid inferences. In psychology, there is a tradition culminating in the work of Jean Piaget which holds that there is a mental logic. The mind uses formal rules of inference, which are not consciously accessible, to guide the process of valid deduction. In your inference about the tube train, you could have used such a rule as a kind of abstract template, and, by filling in the specific values of the variables, you could have made the deduction. In Piagetian lore, of course, a complete logic has been acquired once a child has attained the level of formal operations.

When I first began to study thinking, I too subscribed to the doctrine of mental logic, but over the years my doubts about it have gradually grown. They have been fostered by three main problems.

First, there are the problematic phenomena that occur in the well-known 'selection' task invented by Peter Wason, which we jointly investigated (see Wason and Johnson-Laird, 1972). This is a reasoning task in which the *content* of the problem affects the likelihood of success (see chapters by WASON and by GRIGGS, this volume). The effects on performance certainly cast doubt on the doctrine of mental logic, which should be indifferent to content. Faced with a complex situation,

> the subject will ask himself two kinds of questions: a) whether fact x implies fact y. . . . To verify it, he will look in this case to see whether or not there is a counterexample x and non-y. b) he will also ask whether, on the contrary, it is y which implies x. . . . (Piaget, in Beth and Piaget, 1966, p. 181)

The subjects in the selection task do, indeed, search for counterexamples, but their search is more likely to be complete with realistic materials – a phenomenon that is difficult to reconcile with the notion that it is directed by formal rules of inference, since, by definition, they are neutral with respect to content.

The second source of my doubts about mental logic is the question of its acquisition. It would seem that in order to learn a logic you might have to be able to reason validly, but if you can reason validly then you might not need a logic, and certainly what would require an explanation would be the origin of your logical ability. In fact, several conjectures have been made in the literature about how the mind acquires its logic, but none of them is completely satisfactory.

Some theorists such as Falmagne (1980) have drawn a parallel between learning logic and learning language. Children encounter valid deductions in verbal guise and, it is said, they abstract rules of inference from them in the same way that they learn grammatical rules. Adults, alas, are not noted for sustained public demonstrations of logical thinking, and so this conjecture presumes that children can tell the difference between valid and invalid inferences, or else begs the question by assuming that adults have learned the difference. Although such teaching procedures may be useful in extending logical competence to new patterns of inference, they can hardly account for its original acquisition.

Piaget attempted to explain the development of logical thinking without relying on the conventional principles of learning theory. He argued that children construct logic by internalizing their own actions and by reflecting upon them. The mastery of logical thinking ultimately grows from the mental operations created by this reflective process. Unfortunately, Piaget never described this theory in a form that is completely explicit and at a level of detail that would allow it to be modelled by a computer program. The vagueness of his account masked its inadequacies from Piaget himself and later proponents; the effort required to understand it is so great that to succeed exhausts one's critical faculties. Consider just one difficulty: if thought is internalized action, then what is it that controls such action in the first place? The answer can hardly be simple reflex arcs, since there is no way in which internalizing reflexes and their effects can give rise to the notion of truth or to the formal rules of the propositional calculus. Moreover, what is the underlying mechanism for this mysterious process of internalization? An ability to internalize events might turn out to be nothing else than the ability to think. Hence, if one were to maintain, contrary to Piaget, that action is externalized thought, how in principle could the issue be decided? In making these highly critical comments about Piaget's theory, I do not wish to impugn his genius for asking the right questions or his inventiveness as an experimenter. Thinking may be a form of internalized action, but the nature of this claim remains to be clarified.

Faced with the difficulty of explaining the learning of logical competence, there is a natural temptation to suppose that it is inborn (Fodor, 1980), just as the principles of universal grammar are supposedly innate. The trouble with this view is that the best argument in its favour is the current failure of other approaches to the problem: if no one has succeeded in explaining how an ability could be learned, then perforce it must be inborn. Positive arguments that the ability to reason is innate are as hard to come by as positive arguments that it arises from divine intervention.

The third and severest problem for mental logic is that people make mistakes. They draw invalid inferences that should not occur if deduction is guided by rules of inference. The main response to this discrepancy is an heroic denial of the phenomenon. Mary Henle (1978) bravely declares, 'I have never found errors which could unambiguously be attributed to faulty reasoning. If they are found under clear conditions, I will be forced to a drastic revision of my view of the relation of logic to thinking.' As I have already mentioned, she suggests that mistakes arise because people misunderstand or forget premises, and because they import additional and unwarranted premises into their reasoning. They fail to stick to the original logical problem. Even with the most charitable interpretation of my own and others' errors in inferential performance, I believe that this defence is mistaken. However, there are no generally agreed criteria by which to make an independent assessment of whether an error violates logic. It is easy – all too easy – to explain errors away. My claim is accordingly that the notion that logical errors never occur is either false or else lacking in empirical content. In order to demonstrate errors in reasoning under clear conditions, let us consider the process of syllogistic inference.

Experiments with syllogisms

Imagine that there is a roomful of people, including some scientists, parents, and drivers, and that you are told the following facts about them:

Some of the scientists are parents.
All of the parents are drivers.

What conclusion would you draw? The reader may care to pause for a moment to consider what follows from the premises. The majority of subjects given this problem in the laboratory draw the valid conclusion,

Some of the scientists are drivers.

Only a few subjects draw the equally valid converse conclusion,

Some of the drivers are scientists.

I will call this asymmetry in the responses, the 'figural bias', for reasons that will become clear presently (this phenomenon is also discussed by EVANS, this volume). The point to be emphasized is that this syllogism is very easy: nearly every subject makes the correct response with a latency that is typically around four to five seconds. Here is a very much harder syllogism:

All the beekeepers are artists.
None of the chemists are beekeepers.

Once again, the reader should imagine a roomful of people including beekeepers, artists, and chemists, and attempt to decide what, if anything, follows from the premises. One sample of highly intelligent university students produced the following responses to this problem:

None of the chemists are artists.	60% of the subjects
None of the artists are chemists.	10% of the subjects
'There's no valid conclusion'.	20% of the subjects
Some of the chemists are not artists.	10% of the subjects

Not a single subject drew the correct conclusion: Some of the artists are not chemists (see Johnson-Laird and Steedman, 1978). The result is entirely typical of performance with this sort of syllogism, and there are no grounds for supposing that the subjects forgot a premise or distorted a meaning, since they had both premises in front of them throughout their attempt to make an inference. Indeed, I see no possibility of explaining away the mistakes that does not also empty the doctrine of logical infallibility of all its empirical content. One final defence might be to claim that,

Syllogisms are highly artificial problems.
Psychologists should not study artificial problems.
Therefore, psychologists should not study syllogisms.

In fact, as Kate Ehrlich has shown in an unpublished study, exactly the same phenomena occur if the formal dress of the syllogism is abandoned in favour of a more naturalistic presentation of premises with the same underlying logic. There appears to be no option but to conclude that individuals are capable of thinking logically in some cases but make genuine deductive errors in other cases. It should also be noted that there are marked differences from one individual to another in inferential skill. I therefore propose to abandon the doctrine of mental logic in favour of an alternative approach.

Reasoning with mental models

The theory of reasoning which I wish to propose is based on the concept of a mental model – a notion that was originally introduced by Bartlett's protégé, Kenneth Craik (1943). What is assumed here is that a knowledge of the language enables speakers to construct a model of the state of affairs corresponding to a description: connected discourse can be mentally represented, not only in a linguistic way, but also in a form that is similar to a model based on perceiving or imagining the events instead of merely reading or hearing about them (Johnson-Laird, 1970). The thesis of a 'procedural semantics', which derives from work in Artificial Intelligence (Woods, 1967; Davies and Isard, 1972; Longuet-Higgins, 1972), has inspired theoretical work on the nature of the mental lexicon

(Miller and Johnson-Laird, 1976); and it is natural to assume that such procedures are used in the construction, manipulation, and interrogation of mental models (Johnson-Laird, 1980, 1981). There is also experimental evidence to support the hypothesis that individuals can represent discourse both in a superficial linguistic format and in the form of mental models (Mani and Johnson-Laird, 1982). The fundamental principle of the present theory is that reasoning consists in the construction of mental models on the basis of the premises, and the search for alternative models that might render putative conclusions false. The theory is based on six principal assumptions.

1. Reasoners interpret premises by constructing an integrated mental model of them. This process, of course, is not peculiar to reasoning but can occur whenever individuals interpret coherent discourse. However, the assumption leads to an important but subtle claim: the logical properties of an expression are not directly represented in the mind (except perhaps in the case of logicians) but emerge naturally as a consequence of the use of the expression in the construction and search processes. This point should become clearer by considering what the theory has to say about the two example problems (the easy syllogism and the hard syllogism). In the case of the first premise of the easy syllogism

Some of the scientists are parents

the reasoners' knowledge of the language enables them to imagine some arbitrary number of scientists:

scientist
scientist
scientist

and to mentally tag them in some way to indicate that some of them are identical to parents:

scientist = parent
scientist = parent
(scientist) (parent)

The parenthetical items indicate that there may be scientists who are not parents, and parents who are not scientists. The information from the second premise, 'All the parents are drivers', can then be directly added to this model to yield an integrated representation of both premises:

$$
\begin{array}{ccc}
\text{scientist} & = & \text{parent} = \text{driver} \\
\text{scientist} & = & \text{parent} = \text{driver} \\
(\text{scientist}) & & (\text{parent} = \text{driver}) \\
& & (\text{driver})
\end{array}
$$

where again there is an arbitrary number of parenthetical items representing the possibility of drivers who are not parents.

2. The conclusion that is drawn from a mental model is based on novelty and parsimony: it interrelates those items that have not been explicitly related in the premises, i.e. that have not been directly used in setting up the model. A valid deduction adds nothing to the semantic content of the premises, but reasoners are not immediately aware of the consequences of that content. Hence, they draw conclusions that bring out these new relations but refrain from restating the premises, which can be taken for granted.

3. The order in which information is expressed in a conclusion follows the principle that working memory operates on a 'first-in first-out' basis. It is easier, for example, to recall the premises in the order in which they were presented than in the opposite order. Likewise, it is easier to formulate a conclusion in which the terms occur in the order in which they entered working memory.

The consequences of Assumptions 2 and 3 lead to an overwhelming bias for the following conclusion to the easy syllogism

Some of the scientists are drivers

where the two terms that were not related in the premises are now interrelated in the order in which they entered the mental model.

An inference depends on forming an integrated model of the premises. The arrangement, or 'figure', of the terms in a syllogism may readily permit this process of integration. With premises in the figure:

$$
\begin{array}{c}
A - B \\
B - C
\end{array}
$$

the two occurrences of the middle term, B, are temporarily adjacent, and it is a straightforward matter to construct a mental model of the first premise and then to integrate within it the information from the second premise. The conclusion will then take the form:

$$A - C$$

4. If the premises are in a figure that does not permit an immediate integration, then additional operations have to be carried out to make it possible. It is easy to spell out these operations in a systematic way (see Johnson-Laird and Bara, 1982); they are closely related to Hunter's (1957) classic account of three-term series problems. There is an increase in the number of operations required to form a mental model over the four figures.

5. The greater the load on working memory, the harder it will be to make an inference. One factor that should plainly increase the load on working memory is the need to carry out the additional operations required to form an integrated model in certain figures. Table 6.1 presents the relevant results from three experiments. In Experiment 1, 20 American students were given all 64 possible pairs of premises with a sensible everyday content and asked to state what followed from each pair of premises (see Johnson-Laird and Steedman, 1978). Experiments 2 and 3 are part of an unpublished investigation carried out by Bruno Bara and myself; Experiment 2 consisted of a replication of the American study carried out with 20 Italian students at the University of Milan; Experiment 3 was a further replication with another group of 20 subjects who were given only 10 seconds in which to make their response to each problem. In all three experiments, the figure of the problems produced the predicted trend in the difficulty of drawing a valid conclusion.

TABLE 6.1 *The percentages of valid conclusions as a function of the figure of the premises in three experiments*

| | Figure of the premises | | | |
	A – B B – C	B – A C – B	A – B C – B	B – A B – C
Experiment 1	60	50	53	49
Experiment 2	51	48	35	22
Experiment 3	40	27	33	16

The explanation of the effects of the figural arrangement of terms has received further empirical support. In Experiment 2, we recorded the latencies of the subjects' responses. Table 6.2 presents the mean latencies of the correct valid conclusions for the one-model problems – the only sort that produced enough correct responses for the latencies to be analysed.

TABLE 6.2 *The mean latencies (sec.) to produce the correct valid conclusions to one-model syllogisms in Experiment 2. The results are shown as a function of figure*

	Figure of the premises			
	A – B B – C	B – A C – B	A – B C – B	B – A B – C
Mean latencies	11·6	12·9	18·7	22·1

Even with the one-model problems some subjects failed to produce any correct responses in some figures, but we were able to rank order the mean correct latencies for 14 subjects as a function of figure. The mean ranks for the four figures were 1·7, 2·3, 2·6 and 3·4 (Page's L = 387, p<0·0005). This trend is exactly what is predicted by the number of additional operations required for each figure.

6. Ordinary individuals who have not been taught logic do not make use of rules of inference in order to make valid deductions. They have instead one essential piece of semantic information. They know that an inference is valid if the conclusion is true in every state of affairs in which the premises are true. In other words, a putative conclusion follows validly from a set of premises, if it is true when the premises are true and there is no way of interpreting the premises so as to render it false. Because there is no such way of reinterpreting the premises in the easy syllogism, the conclusion that was derived above is a valid one. But, consider now the second, more difficult, syllogism. Its premises are,

All of the beekeepers are artists.
None of the chemists are beekeepers.

Since the two occurrences of the middle term, 'beekeepers', are not adjacent, the figure demands that the initial model is constructed on the basis of the second premise. This negative premise can be interpreted by forming a model in which the two classes are isolated from each other:

chemist
chemist
— — — — — — — — — — — — — —
                    beekeeper
                    beekeeper

The force of the dotted line is to indicate that no chemist is, or can subsequently be represented as, identical to a beekeeper. A more explicit notation would indicate that no chemist is identical with any beekeeper, and vice versa. There would be a relation of the following sort:

Chemist ≠ beekeeper

between each possible pairing of chemist and beekeeper. One way in which the information from the first premise can be added to the model is as follows:

chemist
chemist
— — — — — — — — — — — — — — — — —
            beekeeper = artist
            beekeeper = artist
                         (artist)
                         (artist)

This model suggests the conclusion, 'None of the chemists are artists', drawn by 60 per cent of the subjects in the American experiment. Reasoners who attempt to search for an alternative interpretation of the premises may succeed in finding a second integrated model of the premises:

chemist
chemist   =   artist
— — — — — — — — — — — — — — — — — — —
            beekeeper   = artist
            beekeeper   = artist
                             (artist)

This model shows that the previous conclusion is false, and suggests instead the conclusion, 'Some of the chemists are not artists', which was drawn by 10 per cent of the American subjects. There is, however, a third possible model of the premises:

chemist	=	artist
chemist	=	artist
	beekeeper	= artist
	beekeeper	= artist

which suggests that even the last conclusion is invalid. At this point, it is tempting to respond that there is no valid conclusion interrelating the chemists and artists – a response that was made by 20 per cent of the subjects. However, there is one relation that is common to all three models of the premises: 'Some of the artists are not chemists.' The difficulty of this response, as reflected in the fact that not a single subject made it, is a consequence of having to construct three different models of the premises and to evaluate each model in an order that violates the 'first-in first-out' principle of working memory.

Some syllogistic premises yield only a single mental model, others yield two alternative models, and still others yield three alternatives. On the assumption that a greater number of models will place a greater load on working memory, a trend in difficulty can obviously be predicted. The relevant results from Experiments 1, 2, and 3 are summarized in Table 6.3.

TABLE 6.3 *The percentages of correct valid conclusions in three experiments on syllogistic reasoning. The percentages are shown as a function of the number of mental models that have to be constructed to yield the correct conclusion*

	One model	Two models	Three models
Experiment 1	92	46	28
Experiment 2	80	20	9
Experiment 3	62	20	3

In each experiment, there was a highly reliable trend: the greater the number of models that have to be constructed, the poorer the performance. In fact, we have yet to test a subject who does not perform best on the one-model problems.

Reasoning without logic

A formal logic is a calculus for proving the validity of an inference. It provides us with a systematic method for establishing in effect that there is no interpretation of the premises that is consistent with a denial of the conclusion. In fact, logicians have developed a variety of such methods. I will not discuss these methods, but turn directly to the claim that the manipulation of mental models enables valid inferences to be made without recourse to rules of logic. This claim, as I know from the reaction of audiences to whom it has been addressed, is both hard to understand and hard to believe – it is viewed as almost on a par with the Pelagian heresy in some quarters.

The crux of the matter is that a system of inference may perform in an entirely logical way even though it does not employ rules of inference, inferential schemata, meaning postulates, or any other sort of machinery conventionally employed in a logical calculus. The rest of the argument is simple once this point is grasped, and so I will labour it awhile. The theory applies to any sort of deductive inference though I have illustrated it here only with respect to syllogisms (see Johnson-Laird, in press, for a general account).

During the course of developing the theory of mental models, I have written several computer programs (in the high-level list-processing language, POP-10) that model the process of syllogistic inference. The most recent of these programs constructs a model of one premise, adds the information from the second premise, and then draws a conclusion interrelating the end items according to the assumptions described above. It then searches for an alternative model of the premises that would render the conclusion false. If the conclusion is affirmative, it examines the model for tokens representing the middle term that are not linked to both end terms. On finding such a token, it then breaks a link that is part of a chain that identifies two end items, and uses the free middle item in order to construct a new model that is true to the premises. For example, the following sort of model:

$$a = b = c$$
$$a = b = c$$
$$(b)$$
$$(b)$$

can be reconstructed as:

$$a = b = c$$
$$a = b$$
$$b = c$$
$$(b)$$

where both are models of the premises of the form:

All the A are B.
All the C are B.

The program uses a similar method for attempting to destroy negative models. At each step, it produces whatever conclusion is currently warrantable, and it continues to try to reconstruct the model so as to falsify a conclusion until it has run out of any further possibilities – a point at which it always arrives since the models have only a finite number of entities in them. Nowhere in the program are there any rules of inference, or inferential schemata, that are employed to guide the search process. The program searches in a way that resembles Bartlett's (1958) account of the sectional map-reader: it is not random but guided by a goal. It embodies merely a knowledge of the truth conditions of syllogistic premises, and the principles of searching for models that refute conclusions – the principle that likewise underlies, without being directly represented in, any logical calculus or formal system of deduction.

Such is the scepticism of certain defenders of the doctrine of mental logic that they refuse to believe that the program does not employ rules of logic. What about the machinery for searching for end items, destroying identities, and testing truth conditions? They argue that it must surely embody logical rules; indeed, they say, a computer programming language has such rules built into it. If what they mean is that the program, or programming languages in general, make use of rules of inference, then the claim is false. If the program was governed by rules of inference, then it would not be able to model the errors that people make. It is easy to write a program that makes invalid deductions, and indeed the first stage in the output of my program is often to produce an invalid conclusion. The power of programs comes from the computational machinery of recursive functions that they realize, and this machinery suffices for developing algorithms for both logical and illogical inference.

The theory of mental models assumes that human reasoners construct models and search for alternatives, not necessarily in a random way, but certainly not in a wholly systematic way, either. Moreover, since even the most intelligent individuals have difficulty with certain syllogisms, and are aware of it, they have an obvious motivation to try to externalize and to systematize the search for alternative models of the premises. Hence, the theory suggests an obvious reason for the development of logic as an intellectual discipline.

Individual differences

My aim was to decide amongst three mutually exclusive hypotheses about reasoning: that it was invariably logical, that it was invariably illogical, that it was sometimes logical and sometimes illogical. Only the last of these alternatives appears to conform with the facts; it is the only one of them that truly treats thinking as a skill. Skills, of course, have to be acquired, and individuals differ in their mastery of them. Reasoning is no exception. In the studies of syllogistic reasoning that my colleagues and I have carried out, the extent of individual differences has been painfully apparent. The best subject that we have tested responded correctly to 85 per cent of the premises that yield a valid conclusion interrelating the end items; the worst subject that we have tested responded correctly to only 15 per cent of them. In fact, one subject might be thought to have done still worse: she abandoned the experiment on the grounds that she was not personally acquainted with the individuals referred to in the premises. However, this reaction reflects, not necessarily an inability to reason, but a reluctance to engage in the laboratory 'game' of reasoning – a reaction common among people who live in a non-literate culture (see Scribner, 1977; Luria, 1977).

What causes individuals to differ in their ability to make inferences? No certain answer is as yet known. In the past, psychologists have often been content to correlate performance in a particular reasoning task either with scores on intelligence tests or with factors postulated to underlie test performance (e.g. Guilford, 1959; Frandsen and Holder, 1969). They have been happy to treat 'general intelligence', or some such notion derived from a factor analysis of test data, as a primitive and unanalysed commodity that gives rise to observed differences in ability. Whatever the general merit of investigating 'individual differences' by way of mental tests, their use is of little value in the study of thinking. The data they yield are too gross to elucidate differences in mental processes from one individual to another.

The theory of mental models offers an explanatory framework that helps to make sense of differences in reasoning ability. It specifies the separate components underlying inferences and places several constraints on the possible differences amongst individuals. The theory assumes that syllogistic inference, for example, depends on three component skills: (1) an ability to form an integrated model of the premises; (2) an appreciation that an inference is only sound if there are no counter-examples to it, together with a capacity to put this principle into practice; (3) an ability to put into words the common characteristics of a set of mental models. Bruno Bara and I have begun to explore the differences in the detailed performance of subjects carrying out syllogistic reasoning, and I will describe some of our preliminary findings in the light of the three main abilities postulated by the theory.

The main difficulty in constructing an integrated model is that a representation of one premise must be held in working memory while information from the other premise is combined with it. Although all the subjects that we have tested performed best with one-model problems, we have tested two subjects who failed to perform reliably better than chance with these problems. (They were quite unable to cope with premises that required more than one model.) The figural arrangement of terms had a striking effect on their performance: they could only form a model from premises in the two theoretically easier figures:

$$
\begin{array}{cc}
A - B & B - A \\
B - C & C - B
\end{array}
$$

With premises in the other more difficult figures, they either declared erroneously that there was no valid conclusion or forgot one of the end terms and mistakenly replaced it with the middle term so as to form a conclusion that was blatantly inconsistent with the premises. Their tendency to assert that there was no valid conclusion in these figures gave rise to a spuriously good performance with invalid syllogisms.

Only where a valid inference depends on constructing alternative models of the premises are genuine differences in inferential ability to be observed. A reasoner must appreciate the need to construct and to evaluate different models, and must be able to carry out this procedure within the processing limitations of working memory. Some subjects seem not to perceive the need to consider alternatives. The hallmark of their performance is a string of erroneous conclusions combined with a reluctance to respond that there is no valid conclusion interrelating the end items. Three of the subjects that we have tested failed disastrously with premises that required more than one model to be constructed and responded correctly to invalid problems on less than one in five occasions. Other subjects evidently perceive the need to consider alternative models, but are wholly incapable of assessing them correctly. The hallmark of their performance is a tendency to respond 'No valid conclusion' whenever there is more than one model of the premises. They, too, do spuriously well with the class of problems that have no valid conclusions, but they make this same response to the two- and three-model premises that have a valid conclusion. Any subject who performs better with invalid syllogisms than with valid syllogisms is showing signs of this syndrome.

Most of the subjects that we have tested are able to construct some alternative models, but from time to time they fall down in assessing their implications. They are particularly prone to error in those figures that are theoretically more difficult, failing to detect either that a putative conclusion is violated by one alternative model or else that there is a conclusion common to all the alternatives. It is noteworthy that only one subject that we have tested showed any competence with the most difficult syllogisms of all, namely, those with three models where the conclusion runs counter to the figural bias.

There are a number of other differences in performance between the subjects, including their susceptibility to figural effects, which

I will not discuss here. My aim has been to establish that the theory of mental models provides a framework suitable for describing individual differences, and suggests one important clue to their cause. Apart from a knowledge of the semantic principle of refutations, perhaps the single biggest factor in reasoning is the processing capacity of working memory, since the effects of both the number of models and the figure of the premises appear to arise as a consequence of its limitations. The same point has emerged from studies of other sorts of inference. In an experiment carried out by Johnson-Laird and Wason (1970), for example, the task was to check whether a description of the contents of an envelope was correct (see also WASON, this volume). The subjects selected diagrams one at a time from a set laid out in front of them. As they selected a diagram, the experimenter told them whether or not the same diagram was in the envelope. A sensible strategy in this task is to choose diagrams that do not fit the description on the envelope: if such a diagram is in the envelope, then plainly the description is false. Some subjects, however, choose diagrams that fit the description. This choice is uninformative once it is known that the envelope is not empty, because there is no reason why a diagram that fits the description cannot be outside the envelope. What was unexpected was that a complex disjunctive description had a striking effect on subjects' insight into the task. A subject would perform perfectly with one description, only to lose that insight on the very next trial when the disjunction occurred. The point to be stressed is that the content of the particular description has no bearing on the 'logic' of the task, yet it had a considerable impact on performance. As Johnson-Laird and Wason commented, 'it is possible that this [complex disjunctive description] occupies a greater amount of short-term memory than a single complex rule, and thus leaves a smaller amount of "computing space" available for handling the selection of the diagram.' More recently, Baddeley and his colleagues have made a comprehensive examination of the role of working memory in simple verbal inferences. They have found that when subjects are asked to hold in mind a string of digits, then their performance in reasoning tasks is adversely affected (see, e.g. Baddeley and Hitch, 1974; Hitch and Baddeley, 1976).

Some practical implications

In a modern society, it is advantageous to be able to think logically. That might seem a surprising claim; let me give just one illustration to support it. We are all governed by rules and regulations that confer upon us certain rights and duties. The government and its agencies issue numerous leaflets to keep us informed. These leaflets are, however, notoriously difficult to understand. A decade ago, A. R. Jonckheere, Sheila Jones, Peter Wason, and others, introduced the technique of converting complicated rules into 'logical trees'. A typical passage from an official leaflet reads as follows:

> The earliest age at which a woman can draw a retirement pension is 60. On her own insurance she can get a pension when she reaches that age, if she has then retired from regular employment. Otherwise she has to wait until she retires or reaches age 65. At age 65 pension can be paid irrespective of retirement. On her husband's insurance, however, she cannot get a pension, even though she is over 60, until he has reached age 65 and retired from regular employment, or until he is 70 if he does not retire before reaching that age.

The same information is much more easily understood (see Wason, 1968; Jones, 1968) when it is presented as a logical tree, such as:

1. Are you under 60 years of age?   If YES, you are not entitled to a pension.
   If NO, read item 2.
2. If you are claiming on your own insurance, read question 3.
   If you are claiming on your husband's insurance, read question 5.
3. Are you under 65 years of age?   If YES, read question 4.
   If NO, you are entitled to a pension.
4. Are you working?   If YES, you are not entitled to a pension.
   If NO, you are entitled to a pension.
5. If your husband's age is:
   (a) less than 65, you are not entitled to a pension.

(b) between 65 and 69, read question 6.
(c) 70 or more, you are entitled to a pension.
6. Has your husband   If YES, you are entitled to a
    retired?   pension.
                                If NO, you are not entitled to
                                a pension.

One of the leaflets that Wason and Jones successfully rendered comprehensible concerned the eligibility of widows for death grant. I recently read the new leaflet (NI.49 issued in 1979) on this topic to see what lessons Whitehall had learned. The crucial extract runs as follows:

Death grant is payable where either of the following conditions is satisfied by the person on whose contributions the grant is claimed:
     The contributor must have paid or been credited with at least 25 contributions of any class at any time between 5 July 1948 or the date of entry into insurance, if later, and 5 April 1975, or the date on which he reached 65 (60 for a woman), or died under that age, whichever is the earliest; or
     Since 6 April 1975 the contributor must have actually paid contributions in any one tax year (6 April to the following 5 April) before the relevant year, on earnings of at least 25 times the lower earnings limit for that year. The relevant year is usually the income tax year in which the death occurred, but if immediately before the date of death, the person on whose contributions the grant is claimed was himself dead or over 65 (60 for a woman), it is either the year in which he reached that age, or the year in which he died, whichever is earlier.

I hope that that clears up any confusions the reader might have had about the matter. On a flying visit to University College, London, the late Richard Crossman told Jonckheere, Jones and me that there were dangers in clarity – people would get what they were entitled to and that would cost the government a lot of money. I used to think that he said it as a joke.

What is needed, evidently, are ways of improving reasoning ability, and educationalists have developed a variety of methods that are supposed to do so. They include the pedagogical use of stories illustrating logical principles (Lipman and Sharp, 1978), practice with special reasoning problems (Feuerstein, Hoffman and Miller, 1980), and courses on thinking and problem solving (e.g. Whimbey and Lochhead,1980). Psychologists have become increasingly involved in such matters, especially since the start of the project to raise the intelligence of the entire population of Venezuela. (The International newsletter, *Human Intelligence*, has published several reports on this project, which includes work carried out by researchers at Harvard University, Bolt, Beranek and Newman, Inc., and many other research organizations.)

My own work suggests that the most common cause of difficulty in reasoning for individuals living in a literate society is the limited processing capabilities of working memory. Its effects have been apparent in every subject that we have tested. However, it must be emphasized that there appears to be a spontaneous improvement in reasoning ability simply as a consequence of practice (with no knowledge of results). The subjects in Experiment 1 (see Table 6.1) were tested again one week later. They were given no forewarning that they would be retested, but their overall performance increased by 10 per cent, and 19 out of the 20 subjects returned an improved score. One striking differential effect of practice occurred with the valid conclusions drawn in the most difficult figure, B – A, B – C. Here, there was an overall improvement of 20 per cent, and half of it was due to a decline in erroneous responses that there was no valid conclusion. The effect of practice must in part be to increase the efficiency of the encoding operations of working memory. Experience with the task may also produce a growing awareness of the logical properties of the problems. Some subjects may begin to notice, for example, that two negative premises never yield an interesting valid conclusion.

Several people have suggested to me that diagrams of mental models might serve a useful pedagogical function in teaching the principles of deduction. Although the prospect is appealing, it may be dangerous. Whenever I have presented a reasoning problem informally, I have noticed the difficulties that people get themselves into if they use Euler circles. The problem is that there is no simple algorithm for using them that one can learn like one learns, say, the algorithm for long multiplication. Merely drawing circles does not guarantee that all their possible combinations will be considered exhaustively. The same problem applies to the notation that I have invented for depicting the structure of mental models – if there were a simple algorithm, then doubtless most of us would have mastered it when we first learned to reason. Educators are probably better advised to ensure that their students understand the fundamental principle of deductive inference and get plenty of opportunities to put it into practice.

Conclusions

Bartlett believed that thinking is a high-level skill. He considered only a restricted variety of thought processes, and I have restricted myself to a still narrower aspect of what he would have called, 'closed system thinking'. I have argued that such thinking consists of three essential skills:

1.   The ability to construct mental models of the situations described by sentences. This is part of the process of verbal comprehension, and implicit inferences are nothing more than the use of pieces of general knowledge to aid this process of constructing a single mental model. They are rapid and automatic because no attempt is made to test their validity.
2.   The ability to search for different models of the same premises in order to check whether an inference is valid. Most people appear to be aware of the principle at stake, here, but there are marked differences in individual skill at putting it into practice. A major cause of the difficulty of making explicit deductions is the need to form integrated models, and to search for alternatives, within the processing capacity of working memory. The sequence and timing of operations integrating the premises are critical: they show up in the effects of figure on the form of conclusions, on the time that it takes to make an inference, and on the chances of drawing the correct conclusion.
3.   The ability to put into words the common characteristic of a set of mental models. Here, again, people differ in skill. It is a rare individual indeed who can cope with the assessment of a set of models that have to be evaluated in violation of the 'first-in first-out' principle of working memory.

There is no need to postulate rules of logic in the mind. There is no need to suppose that human beings are intrinsically irrational. Logical thinking is a skill that is exercised with varying degrees of success. Logic itself is a consequence of our happy ability to search for refutations, not the cause of the ability.

Note

The solution to the Sherlock Holmes riddle is that Watson and he must have gone along the veranda from right to left (given that it runs along the lower side of the plan). The reason is because they entered the house from one end of the veranda, passed from room to room, and then turned right into Milverton's study with its door opening on to the veranda. By a nice coincidence, Sheila Jones lives in the house in Hampstead that is generally believed to be Conan Doyle's model for the story.

Acknowledgments

This research was supported by a grant from the Social Science Research Council. Many individuals have helped me, and I am particularly grateful to Bruno Bara, Kate Ehrlich, Alan Garnham, Dave Haw, Janellen Huttenlocher, Maria Legrenzi, Paolo Legrenzi, Kannan Mani, George A. Miller, Jane Oakhill, Mark Steedman, Patrizia Tabossi, Peter Wason and Til Wykes for some fruitful collaborations over the years. Alan Garnham, Leslie Henderson, Jane Oakhill and Keith Oatley very kindly read an earlier version of this paper and made many helpful criticisms of it. I also thank my colleagues Steve Isard, Christopher Longuet-Higgins and Stuart Sutherland for ideas, encouragement and advice. Finally, I am grateful to the Experimental Psychology Society and to its officers for the invitation to give this lecture and for helping to make its occasion a pleasure (for me) rather than a duty.

References

Baddeley, A. D. and Hitch, G. (1974), 'Working memory', in G. H. Bower (ed.), *The Psychology of Learning and Motivation, Vol. 8*, New York, Academic Press.

Bartlett, F. (1958), *Thinking: An Experimental and Social Study*, London, Allen & Unwin.

Beth, E. W. and Piaget, J. (1966), *Mathematical Epistemology and Psychology*, Dordrecht, Reidel.

Cohen, L. J. (1981), 'Can human irrationality be experimentally demonstrated?', *The Behavioral and Brain Sciences*, *4*, pp. 317–70.

Conan Doyle, Arthur (1905), *The Return of Sherlock Holmes*, London, Murray.

Craik, K. (1943), *The Nature of Explanation*, Cambridge, Cambridge University Press.

Davies, D. J. M. and Isard, S. D. (1972), 'Utterances as programs', in D. Michie (ed.), *Machine Intelligence*, *7*, Edinburgh, Edinburgh University Press.

Erickson, J. R. (1974), 'A set analysis of behavior in formal syllogistic reasoning tasks', in R. Solso (ed.), *Theories in Cognitive Psychology: The Loyola Symposium*. Potomac, Maryland, Erlbaum.

Evans, J. St B. T. (1977), 'Toward a statistical theory of reasoning', *Quarterly Journal of Experimental Psychology*, *29*, pp. 621–35.

Evans, J. St B. T. (1980), 'Current issues in the psychology of reasoning', *British Journal of Psychology*, *71*, pp. 227–39.

Falmagne, R. J. (1980), 'The development of logical competence: a psycholinguistic perspective', in R. H. Kluwe and H. Spada (eds), *Developmental Models of Thinking*, New York, Academic Press.

Feuerstein, R., Hoffman, M. B. and Miller, R. (1980), *Instrumental Enrichment*, Baltimore, University Park Press.

Fodor, J. A. (1980), 'Fixation of belief and concept acquisition', in Piatelli-Palmarini, M. (ed.), *Language and Learning: The Debate between Jean Piaget and Noam Chomsky*, Cambridge, Mass., Harvard University Press.

Frandsen, A. N. and Holder, J. R. (1969), 'Spatial visualization in solving complex verbal problems', *Journal of Psychology*, *73*, pp. 229–33.

Guilford, J. P. (1959), 'Three faces of intellect', *American Psychologist*, *14*, pp. 469–79.

Guyote, M. J. and Sternberg, R. J. (1981), 'A transitive-chain theory of syllogistic reasoning', *Cognitive Psychology*, *13*, pp. 461–525.

Henle, M. (1962), 'On the relation between logic and thinking', *Psychological Review*, *69*, pp. 366–78.

Henle, M. (1978), Foreword to R. Revlin and R. E. Mayer (eds), *Human Reasoning*, Washington, D.C., Winston.

Hitch, G. J. and Baddeley, A. D. (1976), 'Verbal reasoning and working memory', *Quarterly Journal of Experimental Psychology*, *28*, pp. 603–21.

Hunter, I. M. L. (1957), 'The solving of three-term series problems', *British Journal of Psychology*, *48*, pp. 286–98.

Johnson-Laird, P. N. (1970), 'The perception and memory of sentences', in J. Lyons (ed.), *New Horizons in Linguistics*, Harmondsworth, Penguin.

Johnson-Laird, P. N. (1980), 'Mental models in cognitive science', *Cognitive Science*, *4*, pp. 71–115.

Johnson-Laird, P. N. (1981), 'Comprehension as the construction of mental models', *Proceedings of the Royal Society of London*, Series B, *295*, pp. 353–74.

Johnson-Laird, P. N. (in press), *Mental Models*, Cambridge, Cambridge University Press, and Cambridge, Mass., Harvard University Press.

Johnson-Laird, P. N. and Bara, B. (1982), 'The figural effect in syllogistic reasoning', unpublished paper, Laboratory of Experimental Psychology, University of Sussex.

Johnson-Laird, P. N. and Steedman, M. J. (1978), 'The psychology of syllogisms', *Cognitive Psychology, 10*, pp. 64–99.

Johnson-Laird, P. N. and Wason, P. C. (1970), 'Insight into a logical relation', *Quarterly Journal of Experimental Psychology, 22*, pp. 49–61.

Jones, S. (1968), *Design of Instruction*, London, HMSO.

Lipman, M. and Sharp, A. M. (1978), *Growing Up with Philosophy*, Philadelphia, Temple University Press.

Longuet-Higgins, H. C. (1972), 'The algorithmic description of natural language', *Proceedings of the Royal Society*, Series B, 182, pp. 255–76.

Luria, A. R. (1977), *The Social History of Cognition*, Cambridge, Mass., Harvard University Press.

Mani, K. and Johnson-Laird, P. N. (1982), 'The mental representation of spatial descriptions', *Memory and Cognition, 10*, pp. 181–7.

Miller, G. A. and Johnson-Laird, P. N. (1976), *Language and Perception*. Cambridge, Cambridge University Press, and Cambridge, Mass., Harvard University Press.

Oakhill, J. (1982), 'Constructive processes in skilled and less-skilled comprehenders' memory for sentences', *British Journal of Psychology, 73*, pp. 13–20.

Raine, C. (1979), *A Martian Sends a Postcard Home*, Oxford, Oxford University Press.

Revlis, R. (1975), 'Two models of syllogistic reasoning: feature selection and conversion', *Journal of Verbal Learning and Verbal Behavior, 14*, pp. 180–95.

Scribner, S. (1977), 'Modes of thinking and ways of speaking: culture and logic reconsidered', in P. N. Johnson-Laird and P. C. Wason (eds), *Thinking: Readings in Cognitive Science*, Cambridge, Cambridge University Press.

Wason, P. C. (1968), 'The drafting of rules', *New Law Journal, 118*, pp. 548–9.

Wason, P. C. and Johnson-Laird, P. N. (1972), *Psychology of Reasoning: Structure and Content*, London, Batsford, and Cambridge, Mass., Harvard University Press.

Whimbey, A. and Lochhead, J. (1980), *Problem Solving and Comprehension: A Short Course in Analytical Reasoning*, 2nd Edition, Philadelphia, The Franklin Institute Press.

Woods, W. A. (1967), 'Semantics for a question-answering system', Mathematical Linguistics and Automatic Translation Report NSF-19, Cambridge, Mass., Harvard Computational Laboratory.

Wykes, T. (1978), 'Inference and children's comprehension of prose', unpublished DPhil thesis, University of Sussex.

Wykes, T. and Johnson-Laird, P. N. (1977), 'How do children learn the meanings of verbs?', *Nature*, *268*, pp. 326–7.

7 Mental imagery in thinking and problem solving

John T. E. Richardson

It is not surprising that psychologists interested in the nature of thinking should pay particular attention to the phenomenon of mental imagery. Of all the various experiences, events and processes which might be reckoned among the constituent elements of conscious experience, mental images are certainly among the most ubiquitous, the most intriguing, and the most striking. It is of course notoriously difficult to submit such private episodes to rigorous scientific investigation. Nevertheless, over the last twenty years a substantial amount of careful experimental research seems to have established mental imagery as an empirical phenomenon of considerable predictive importance and as a major representational system underlying human cognitive processing. This research has been hailed as symptomatic of a fundamental change in the direction of experimental psychology, and as a reaction against the excesses of the behaviourist tradition (Holt, 1964; Kessel, 1972; Neisser, 1972a; 1972b).

Mental images possess certain characteristic properties which are of particular relevance to an analysis of their role in thinking and problem solving. First, at least some mental images are intentionally constructed so as to represent certain ideas or concepts in a symbolic manner. Second, although these representations can normally be described or labelled, the creation and maintenance of mental images do not appear to be functionally dependent upon the use of language. Third, these representations may be maintained over a definite period of time, and they may be manipulated and transformed in various ways. In terms of the information-processing perspective which is prevalent in contemporary cognitive psychology, these considerations have been taken to imply that 'mental

197

imagery constitutes a non-verbal, short-term, working memory in which information may be pictorially represented and spatially transformed' (Richardson, 1980, p. 43; see also Baddeley *et al.*, 1974). Such a mechanism is likely to be a powerful mediator of performance in a variety of cognitive tasks. It should be noted, however, that these characteristics apply specifically to mental images which can be created and manipulated under the conscious control of the person who has them. For the purposes of this chapter, I am excluding other categories of phenomenal experience, such as after-imagery, dreaming imagery, and hallucinations. These forms of mental imagery have been discussed in detail by Richardson (1969, Chapters 2 and 5), but their relevance to an understanding of the processes of conscious thought is highly questionable. Accordingly, I shall confine my attention to what I have elsewhere described as the 'constructive' uses of mental imagery (Richardson, 1980, p. 43).

I shall begin by considering the attitudes towards mental imagery and its role in thinking and problem solving which have been expressed at various points in the historical development of cognitive psychology. I shall then consider in somewhat more detail the two prevalent theoretical positions, the dual coding theory of imagery and verbal processes and the common coding theory of propositional representations. This discussion will bring out certain fundamental conceptual problems which have to be recognized before an adequate appreciation of the research literature is possible. Finally, I shall review the relevant empirical findings under two different headings. On the one hand, one must consider the role of mental imagery in cognitive tasks where the subjects are explicitly required to represent, to maintain, and to manipulate information concerning the spatial location, the spatial orientation, and the physical properties of perceptual objects. On the other hand, in order to demonstrate the general relevance of mental imagery to the study of thinking, one must also consider its role in cognitive tasks which do not explicitly require the subjects to process this sort of information.

Historical background

The basic position that human thought is essentially based upon the formation and appreciation of mental images has always been an attractive idea in the Western intellectual tradition. Historically, it extends back at least to the Ancient Greeks. For instance, Aristotle held that 'images exist in the mind in the absence of external objects, and thinking consists in a contemplation of these images' (Mandler and Mandler, 1964, p. 9). More recently, the conception of mental images as the primary symbols of thinking was a central premise of the British empiricist movement, as exemplified by Hobbes, Locke, Berkeley and Hume. These philosophers held that the fundamental constituents of rational thought had to be based upon perceptual experience, and hence that they must be either actual sensations or else proxies or replicas of those sensations in the form of mental images.

This theoretical scheme was very influential in the early development of scientific psychology. During this period, towards the end of the nineteenth century and the beginning of the present century, psychology tended to be defined as the study of the mind and its contents. The primary source of information and evidence in this study was introspection, the careful observation of one's own mental processes; and mental images were regarded as the most obvious elements or constituents into which the process of thought might be introspectively analysed (Holt, 1964). Although the introspectionist approach produced a considerable amount of research activity, it also received a number of serious criticisms, and went into a severe decline. A detailed account of these criticisms has been given by Kaufmann (1979, pp. 16–24), but two points deserve special mention. First, the introspective method seemed reasonably satisfactory in studying simple cognitive events, but it appeared to be quite inadequate to handle complex problem-solving situations. In some cases, the subjects were unable to report any conscious episodes at all; *a fortiori*, the cognitive processing involved seemed to be completely imageless. Second, the introspective reports which were produced appeared to be inadequate as objective scientific data, since only the subject himself could observe, describe, or quantify his cognitions.

The reaction against introspectionism took an extreme form in the behaviourist movement. The behaviourists claimed that mental phenomena could not be the object of scientific investigation, and so the study of behaviour should be the sole purpose of psychogy. Moreover, they argued that even the very words which were used to describe mental experience could not be rigorously defined in terms of behaviour, and so they should be excluded from all scientific discussion. Consequently, concepts such as 'attention', 'sensation' and 'image' were systematically excluded from both theory and research in experimental psychology, and cognitive states, episodes and processes were virtually ignored. These attitudes dominated research in human experimental psychology for a considerable portion of this century, and continue to exert a powerful influence upon conceptual, theoretical, and methodological discussions even today.

Nevertheless, the late 1950s witnessed an apparent change in these attitudes, and concepts relating to mental experience began to reappear in the experimental literature. Superficially, these developments involved a resurgence of interest in all kinds of cognitive states and processes, and especially a reconsideration of the role of mental imagery. However, the approach to mental phenomena which is prevalent nowadays is quite different from that of the introspectionist period. As Neisser (1972a) pointed out, 'What contemporary . . . psychologists mean by "the mind", however, is very different from what their predecessors meant. The definition is no longer in terms of conscious, introspectively given phenomena. Instead, it is in terms of a flow of information in the organism.' Holt (1964) suggested that the methodological approach of behaviourist psychology had changed so that it became possible to conceptualize subjective phenomena as part of the inner workings of a theoretical model. Richardson (1980, p. 7) tried to describe the contemporary attitude more precisely in the following way:

> The crucial point about contemporary information-processing or cognitive approaches in psychology is that they do not identify mental concepts as empirical phenomena to be investigated in their own right; rather, they are introduced as explanatory constructs incorporated into theories of the processes which are hypothesized to be responsible for other, purely behavioural phenomena.

Contemporary cognitive psychology thus restates the traditional problem of how to carry out an objective, scientific investigation of a subjective, private experience as a question about the connection between observable behaviour and a hypothetical mechanism. The problem is handled by specifying experimental operations or procedures which define a theoretical entity in terms of observable and measurable changes in behaviour. In particular, mental imagery is typically interpreted as a theoretical construct with behavioural, operational indicators (Paivio, 1975b). Several different operational procedures have been used in the relevant experimental research; in each case, correlated changes in performance are taken to reflect the involvement of mental imagery as a theoretical construct in the task under consideration:

1   the use of instructions to experimental subjects to employ mental imagery in carrying out psychological tasks;
2   the comparison of different samples of stimulus material in terms of the extent to which they are reported to evoke mental imagery by the experimental subjects;
3   the comparison of different experimental subjects in terms of their reports of the subjective vividness of experienced mental imagery, in terms of their performance in tests of spatial manipulation ability, or in terms of their preferred strategies in the relevant cognitive tasks;
4   the use of concurrent perceptual or spatial tasks in order to interfere in a selective manner with the use of mental imagery in the criterion tasks.

The individual adequacy of each of these operational indicators is to be evaluated by demonstrating meaningful correlations between the particular operation or procedure and performance in various psychological tasks. The question of whether a set of operational indicators is adequate to define a single theoretical construct is more complicated. It is usually suggested that the various logically independent procedures be demonstrated to 'converge' on the theoretical construct (Kosslyn and Pomerantz, 1977). This concept of convergence is typically never explained in any unequivocal manner, but it includes the idea that the various operational indicators should show meaningful interactions in terms of their observable effects (Richardson, 1980, p. 10). In short, then, the adequacy of a theoretical construct in contemporary cognitive psychology is sup-

ported by the demonstration of reliable and meaningful main effects
and interactive relationships among the operational indicators defining the construct.

Theoretical positions

Serious experimental research and theorizing on mental imagery
began to be carried out during the early 1960s. It was then presented
as a radical alternative to the prevalent associationistic account of
human cognition which assumed that learning and remembering,
thinking and reasoning were carried out by means of operations
upon a single, verbal form of representation. This new approach
gave rise to a theoretical framework involving two different forms
of cognitive representation which might be employed in a variety
of psychological tasks:

> The theory assumes that cognitive behavior is mediated by two
> independent but richly interconnected symbolic systems, which
> are specialized for encoding, organizing, transforming, storing,
> and retrieving information. One (the *image* system) is
> specialized for dealing with perceptual information concerning
> nonverbal objects and events. The other (the *verbal* system) is
> specialized for dealing with linguistic information. (Paivio,
> 1979)

There are two important assumptions in this 'dual coding' theory
(Paivio, 1978b). The first is that of the 'independence-interconnec-
tedness' of the two symbolic systems. On the one hand, they are
supposed to be functionally independent, so that in principle it is
possible to manipulate either system experimentally in isolation of
the other. On the other hand, the two systems are supposed to be
richly interconnected, so that in practice they interact continuously
in a specific experimental situation. The second important assumption is that the two symbolic systems are supposed to be different
in terms of the internal organization of the represented information.
The imaginal system is taken to represent information in a syn-
chronous or spatially parallel manner, which enables the subject to
process simultaneously different components of a complex thing or
scene. However, the verbal system is assumed to represent infor-

mation in the sequential manner which is characteristic of linguistic utterances.

This research was generally taken to present crucial problems for models of human cognition based upon the assumption of a single, verbal code. It was therefore not surprising that the dual coding theory was initially accepted by most cognitive psychologists investigating mental imagery as providing essentially the correct framework for subsequent research. Nevertheless, most of the work which had been carried out during the 1960s was concerned with human learning and memory, and relatively little attention had been paid to thinking and problem solving. Paivio (1971) made only two connections with these latter issues. First (pp. 301, 324), he referred to a much earlier suggestion by Reed (1918) that paired-associate learning could be regarded as a problem-solving situation; specifically, the associative learning of arbitrarily chosen pairs of items can be regarded as a concept-learning task in which the solution is to discover an effective mediator or associative aid (see also Earhard and Mandler, 1965). Second (pp. 529–30), he pointed out that there existed some results which implicated mental imagery in traditional concept-formation tasks. While Paivio's suggestions are interesting ones, and while one should in general encourage the theoretical integration of research using different experimental paradigms, it can scarcely be claimed that paired-associate learning and concept formation are central cases of problem-solving situations. Moreover, the findings from the latter paradigm which are mentioned by Paivio indicate that mental imagery is only involved in concept formation when the task requires the effective use of long-term memory.

A more fundamental problem is that a number of alternative theories have been proposed in order to handle the empirical findings on mental imagery within a single cognitive system, in a manner which is not subject to the limitations of the traditional verbal coding model. These theories were originally devised to explain the comprehension and retention of narrative on the assumption that information is represented at an abstract semantic level by networks of propositions (for example, Anderson and Bower, 1973; Bower, 1970; 1972; Rumelhart, Lindsay and Norman, 1972). However, it soon became obvious that it would be parsimonious to represent both linguistic and perceptual information in a common propositional base which would be neutral with regard to the original source of that information. In this approach, mental imagery is not regarded as implicating a qualitatively distinct form of mental code, and all cognitive processes are explained in terms of a single system of abstract propositional representations.

It is agreed by both sides to the current debate over dual coding versus common coding that the two classes of theory are quite different explanatory frameworks which contradict each other at various fundamental points. Normally, of course, one would expect that such a situation could be resolved by carrying out an appropriate programme of experimental research to decide between the two different theories in terms of their conflicting empirical predictions. However, this particular debate has become much more complicated, and the recent research has concentrated upon two more complex and less tractable issues. First, those theorists who have championed a common coding or propositional approach have tried to attack the dual coding theory on conceptual, rather than empirical grounds, by claiming that mental imagery does not constitute a theoretically adequate form of representation. Second, there has been some controversy over the last four or five years as to whether *any* experimental results would serve to distinguish between the two approaches.

The first detailed and extensive critique of mental imagery as an explanatory construct in contemporary cognitive psychology was put forward by Pylyshyn (1973). Although Pylyshyn accepted the existence and importance of mental imagery both as a possible source of scientific evidence and as a possible object of scientific investigation, he argued that it could not be employed to give a coherent theoretical account of human cognition. His original paper contained a whole series of interrelated arguments to support the proposition that the functional origin of mental imagery lies in a system of knowledge which is 'essentially *conceptual* and *propositional*, rather than sensory or pictorial, in nature'. These conceptual criticisms of mental imagery have been restated in two recent papers by Pylyshyn (1979a, 1981), but he does not appear to have appreciably modified or extended his arguments in the intervening period. I have attempted to assess the adequacy of these arguments elsewhere (Richardson, 1980, pp. 16–19).

A considered reaction to Pylyshyn's criticisms from the dual coding point of view was given by Kosslyn and Pomerantz (1977;

see also Kosslyn, 1980, Chapter 2; 1981; Kosslyn *et al.*, 1979), who came to the following conclusion:

> We have found no reason to discard imagery as an explanatory construct in psychology, either on structural or functional grounds. There are no convincing arguments that images are not represented in a distinct format, nor can imagery phenomena be easily accounted for by appealing to propositional representations.

Nevertheless, Kosslyn and Pomerantz described a compromise between the standard dual coding theory, which assumes that imaginal and verbal codes are jointly sufficient for the representation of information, and the standard common coding theory, which argues that the hypothesized imaginal code is either redundant or incoherent. This alternative theoretical position accepts the necessity of propositions as a representational medium, but holds that mental imagery may also make a contribution, since mental images possess emergent properties which systems of propositions lack. This 'weaker' position on the relationship between mental imagery and cognitive representation is more tenable, since it recognizes the fundamental role which propositional structures play in integrating information obtained from different perceptual modalities. Moreover, Kosslyn and Pomerantz argued for the functional usefulness of mental imagery on empirical grounds, on the basis of a wide variety of experiments concerned with the construction, maintenance, and transformation of mental images.

However, Anderson (1978) attempted to evaluate these empirical findings, and was led to question the whole relevance of empirical research to the controversy over dual coding versus common coding. He concluded that in each case what had been taken as evidence for a particular cognitive representation was actually evidence for one possible process operating upon the representation, where there was really no good reason to associate that specific process with that particular representation:

> One can show that, given a set of assumptions about an image representation and a set of processes that operate upon it, one can construct an equivalent set of assumptions about a propositional representation and its processes. Or one can be

given a propositional theory and construct an equivalent imagery theory. In fact, it is possible to establish a more general claim: Given any representation-process pair it is possible to construct other pairs with different representations whose behavior is equivalent to it. These pairs make up for differences in representation by assuming compensating differences in the processes.

Thus, Anderson argued that it was not possible to decide between imaginal and propositional representations strictly on the basis of behavioural data. He considered various alternative criteria for discriminating among different hypothesized representations, but rejected each of these criteria as unsatisfactory. He concluded, therefore, that psychological theories of cognitive representation were inherently *non-identifiable*, in the sense that no set of empirical findings would unambiguously favour a particular theory over its competitors.

Anderson's arguments were subsequently criticized and discussed by Hayes-Roth (1979) and by Pylyshyn (1979b), but his replies essentially amount to a restatement of his original position (Anderson, 1979). I have recently argued that most contemporary psychologists would find Anderson's conclusion unacceptable, and would especially object to his belittling of the importance of physiological and neuropsychological research in discriminating among alternative psychological theories:

The purpose of psychology is to investigate human faculties, and the role of psychological theories is to specify putative mechanisms which underlie those faculties. This will involve ascribing properties to those structures which are causally responsible for the behaviour being studied, in particular the structures of the human brain. Any adequate theory must therefore postulate hypothetical entities which must be considered at least as candidates for objective existence among the physiological structures of the central nervous system. This entails that physiological data and neuropsychological research will be of immense value in discriminating among alternative theories. Moroever, since these theories are offering putative descriptions of the real mechanisms responsible for behaviour, the truth or falsehood of those descriptions must in principle be demonstrable.

In addition, I pointed out that Anderson's own account of an experiment on cerebral asymmetries in face recognition rested upon the assumption that neuropsychological evidence is relevant to deciding among different theories of cognitive representation. However, Anderson's original paper was both important and timely, in that it pointed to the necessity for theorists in cognitive psychology to be clear and specific about both the representations which they were postulating and the processes which were assumed to be operating upon those representations.

Conceptual issues

The controversy described above has tended to focus upon the theoretical question of the representation or format in terms of which a subject's knowledge is realized and employed when he is carrying out various cognitive tasks, including learning, remembering, thinking, and problem solving. A somewhat different issue, one which is conceptual rather than theoretical in nature, is whether the experience of mental imagery and a subject's reports of his imaginal experiences constitute a valid means of understanding the processes and functions which are involved in carrying out such tasks. In terms of the 'neomentalist' framework developed by Paivio and his colleagues, mental imagery is conceptualized as a theoretical entity defined by observable, behavioural operations. It is not therefore usually characterized as a conscious experience or mental episode, nor is it defined by reference to conscious introspection (Paivio, 1975b, 1978b). Moreover, whether or not mental imagery is, as a matter of empirical fact, a conscious mental process is normally regarded as an open question, and one which is irrelevant to the importance and adequacy of mental imagery as a theoretical construct (Paivio, 1971, pp. 135–6). Some researchers do consider that a subject's introspective reports may provide useful data on the question of the involvement of mental imagery in a particular cognitive task. For instance, it was suggested by Doob (1972) that psychologists might carry out experimental investigations of either *reported* images which are 'mentioned or described verbally by the subjects experiencing them', or *inferred* images which are ascribed to the subjects on the basis of variations in their objective performance. Nevertheless, most cognitive psychologists remain suspicious of introspective reports and sceptical of their value as empirical data (Richardson, 1980, p. 11).

In the specific context of mental imagery, this position on the methodological value of introspective reports often reflects merely a naive acceptance of the behaviourist legacy. Independent of this, however, some psychologists have recently come to the conclusion that verbal reports are in general quite irrelevant to an understanding of higher-order cognitive processes. Such scepticism had been expressed by Pylyshyn (1973), for example, in his original critique of mental imagery:

While most psychologists are willing to concede that not all important psychological processes and structures are available to conscious inspection, it is not generally recognized that the converse may also hold: that what is available to conscious inspection may not be what plays an important causal role in psychological processes.

The most incisive (and the most extreme) attack upon the value of introspective reports in both cognitive psychology and social psychology was presented by Nisbett and Wilson (1977; also discussed by BYRNE, this volume) who stated their position in the following manner:

1. People often cannot report accurately on the effects of particular stimuli on higher order, inference-based responses. . . . The accuracy of subjective report is so poor as to suggest that any introspective access that may exist is not sufficient to produce generally correct or reliable reports.
2. When reporting on the effects of stimuli, people may not interrogate a memory of the cognitive processes that operated on the stimuli; instead, they may base their reports on implicit, a priori theories about the causal connection between stimulus and response. . . .
3. Subjective reports about higher mental processes are sometimes correct, but even the instances of correct report are not due to direct introspective awareness. Instead, they are due

to the incidentally correct employment of a priori causal theories.

Nisbett and Wilson did not consider any recent research in the psychology of thinking, but they did discuss the traditional literature on creative problem solving. As in their general conclusions on the validity of introspective reports, they argued in this specific case that subjects have no special access to the cognitive processes underlying their own problem solving, but will, if required, generate possibly accurate accounts based upon implicit, subjective theories of the processes involved. Whether or not these accounts are valid will depend upon whether or not they concur with the explanations educed by other people (including research psychologists) on the basis of purely behavioural evidence. Obviously, this entails that introspective reports are formally redundant for the purposes of the construction and evaluation of psychological theories of cognitive function, since the behavioural evidence is always available (cf. Evans, 1980a; 1980b).

The approach of Nisbett and Wilson appears to reduce all verbal reports to the status of informal (and possibly inaccurate) conjectures on the underlying causes of behaviour. Not surprisingly, many cognitive psychologists find such a general condemnation of introspective reports unacceptable, especially when it is applied to significant mental episodes such as thoughts, feelings, sensations and mental images. The replies to Nisbett and Wilson's paper have attempted to specify the conditions under which accurate introspective judgments may be elicited. For instance, Smith and Miller (1978) suggested that the validity of verbal reports would depend upon 'the degree to which the subject is asked to report on tasks that are novel and of interest'. More crucial, however, is the point made by Ericsson and Simon (1980) that Nisbett and Wilson specifically excluded from their critique introspective reports concerning thoughts, feelings and intentions. The relevant passage from the latter paper is as follows:

> The individual knows a host of personal historical facts; he knows the focus of his attention at any given point in time; he knows what his current sensations are and has what almost all psychologists and philosophers would assert to be 'knowledge'

at least quantitatively superior to that of observers concerning his emotions, evaluations, and plans.

If this catalogue of mental episodes is taken to include the phenomenal experience of mental imagery, then Nisbett and Wilson would appear to have left open the question of whether introspective reports of mental imagery are of any value in understanding the cognitive processes underlying thinking and problem solving.

An adequate answer to this question would require a serious and detailed analysis of the concept of mental imagery, and I have attempted to provide such an analysis in detail elsewhere (Richardson, 1980, Chapter 3). This involves the crucial distinction between a capacity and its *vehicle*: the physical properties of the object which possesses that capacity, by virtue of which that object exhibits or embodies the capacity (Kenny, 1972). The essential point to realize is that the hypothetical states and processes which are ascribed to the vehicle which underlies a human cognitive capacity are the putative physical states and processes of the central nervous system, and not the mental states and processes of the person who possesses that capacity. That is, one must carefully distinguish both between psychological states and human dispositions, and between a cognitive capacity and its vehicle. Contemporary research in cognitive psychology commits the fundamental error of conflating these categories, in taking expressions which have an established, everyday employment as the names of psychological states, and using them in theoretical descriptions of the vehicles underlying human cognitive capacities (cf. Evans, 1980b). This move is especially obvious in research on mental imagery, which employs a term which is normally used to describe a conscious mental episode in order to refer to a hypothetical form of coding or representation. Nevertheless, it is also apparent in the equivocal use of the expression 'mental process' in the paper by Nisbett and Wilson (1977). This is used in opposition to the phrase 'private fact' in order to delimit those cognitive events which are not available to introspection; however, why such events should still be regarded as 'mental' is not made clear (cf. Smith and Miller, 1978). In fact, they are 'mental' only in the sense that they are hypothetical episodes intended to explain a capacity of a conscious being (cf. Kenny, 1972). This and other serious conceptual confusions can be avoided only by distinguishing in a careful and rigorous manner between the empirical phenomenon of mental imagery and any hypothetical construct or representation which is postulated to explain human cognitive faculties.

Nevertheless, one may enquire whether there is any connection, either empirical or conceptual, between the two types of entity which I have described. The research literature on mental imagery suggests an obvious empirical relationship: that the voluntary arousal of relevant and appropriate mental imagery constitutes a strategy which has causal implications for the cognitive representation employed in a particular psychological task. This proposition is supported by the wealth of experimental evidence on the effects of imagery mnemonic instructions and on the manipulation of stimulus imageability in human learning and memory (Richardson, 1980, Chapters 6 and 7). It should be noted, however, that this evidence entails that the use of mental imagery gives rise to a more effective mnemonic representation, but not that it gives rise to a qualitatively different form of representation. The latter assumption lay behind the totally invalid and misleading identification of the phenomenal experience of mental imagery with the hypothetical representation which was supposedly engendered by its use as a cognitive strategy (cf. Evans, 1980a; 1980b).

The logical connection between mental imagery and the system of cognitive representations is rather more complicated. As was pointed out by Pylyshyn (1973), mental images are not like raw sensory impressions; rather, they come to mind already interpreted. Indeed, it is an important conceptual property of mental imagery that the *object* of a mental image (what it is an image of) is determined by how it is intended, not by what it resembles. The notion of intentionality is a difficult philosophical concept, though there have been a few recent discussions of its relevance to cognitive psychology (Fodor, 1975, Chapter 4; Malcolm, 1977, pp. 147–53 *et passim*; Richardson, 1980, pp. 39–41). Accordingly, the object of a mental image is not defined by any of the pictorial properties of the image itself, but is carried by the abstract propositional description under which the image is intended. This suggests, as Pylyshyn (1973) argued, that the functional origin of mental imagery lies in a system of knowledge which is 'essentially *conceptual* and *propositional*, rather than sensory or pictorial in nature' (see also Yuille and Catchpole, 1977).

The latter conclusion seems to indicate that the experience of mental imagery is purely epiphenomenal, and some writers believe that this is the appropriate attitude to adopt towards the study of mental experience (Evans, 1980b). Nevertheless, there seem to be at least two respects in which the construction of mental images might be helpful (Fodor, 1975, p. 191; Richardson, 1980, p. 40). The first point is that, if mental images depict spatial properties and relationships in a quasi-pictorial form, then they may constitute a more efficient basis for carrying out certain tasks than discursive, verbal descriptions. Successive cross-modal similarity judgments seem to be an example of such a task (Posner *et al.*, 1969). Second, the intentional description according to which a mental image is produced does not exhaustively specify all of the properties of the image; equivalently, a mental image may be determinate under several different descriptions other than that according to which it was constructed. It follows that any mental image may manifest *emergent* properties which were not included in the original intentional description and which could not be readily computed from the original description by means of normal deductive reasoning (Kosslyn and Pomerantz, 1977). An example of this would be counting the number of windows in one's house by 'reading off' the information from a mental image (Shepard, 1966). In those cognitive tasks which make use of the emergent properties of images, therefore, mental imagery will deserve a role in psychological investigation as a distinctive mode of thinking (Richardson, 1980, p. 41).

Empirical findings

The representation of spatial information

The findings of experiments in which subjects are required to construct, to manipulate, and to interrogate mental images of three-dimensional scenes suggest that mental imagery constitutes a literal, isomorphic model of spatial information. That is, the spatial relationships between the objects in an imaged array appear to correspond to the relationships which would hold between the same objects in an actual array (Pinker and Kosslyn, 1978). Since mental images can be maintained over a definite period of time, they appear to be especially useful in tasks which require the short-term retention of spatial information (Richardson, 1980, p. 45).

An extended research programme was undertaken by Shepard and his colleagues on the question of whether the objects in an imaged array are manipulated in a manner which corresponds to that in which actual objects might be manipulated (Shepard and Podgorny, 1979). Their original study found that the time taken to match two different views of the same three-dimensional object was linearly related to the angle between the two views (Shepard and Metzler, 1971). Subsequently, a similar pattern of results was obtained in matching actual and imaged forms of rotated alphanumeric characters (Cooper and Shepard, 1973). In both cases, it was concluded that the subjects were mentally rotating a visual image at a constant rate until it was in the same orientation as the test stimulus. Indeed, all of the subjects reported using mental imagery in order to carry out this process of mental rotation. The results of these and other, similar experiments have been discussed by Cooper and Shepard (1979).

Mental comparisons

Thus far, I have only considered the findings of experiments in which the subjects are explicitly required to represent information concerning the spatial properties of physical objects. Nevertheless, if it is to be claimed that mental imagery has a general role in human thinking and problem solving, then one must consider experimental tasks in which the subjects are not explicitly required to deal with this sort of information. One research paradigm which has been extensively employed involves the comparison of pairs of objects along some dimension when the objects are presented in a symbolic form (for example, as their names or as pictures).

Three basic findings have been consistently demonstrated in this reasearch. First, the reaction time to compare two named objects or concepts is inversely proportional to the magnitude of the difference between the actual items along the relevant dimension. (For instance, the time taken to say which of two named animals is larger decreases as the difference between the actual sizes of the animals increases.) This has been called the 'symbolic distance effect'; it seems to arise when subjects make mental comparisons along any ordered dimension whatsoever, and is generally taken to mean that the relevant information is represented in a continuous, analogue form in the underlying cognitive system (Banks, 1977; Friedman, 1978; Kerst and Howard, 1977; Paivio, 1975c; 1978a; 1978c; Richardson, 1980, pp. 47–9). Second, the reaction time to compare two pictured objects is faster than that to compare two named objects. Obviously, this comparison can only be made in the case of concrete objects, but the superiority of pictorial presentation occurs with both physical and abstract properties of such objects (Paivio, 1975c; 1978a; 1978c; Richardson, 1980, pp. 49–51). Third, the reaction time to compare two named objects is inversely proportional to the subject's performance in tests of spatial thinking. This relationship also seems to occur when concrete objects are compared along either physical or abstract dimensions (Paivio, 1978a; 1978b; 1978c; Richardson, 1980, pp. 51–2). These last two effects suggest that the relevant comparisons are made in terms of a cognitive representation which is accessed more easily by pictorial stimuli than by verbal stimuli, and which underlies performance in tests of spatial thinking. Subjects' verbal reports indicate that mental imagery is employed in making mental comparisons among concrete objects in terms of both physical properties and abstract properties, but not in making mental comparisons among abstract concepts in terms of abstract properties, nor in making mental comparisons among individual words in terms of non-semantic properties (Richardson, 1979). A conceptual problem in this research is that some of the original experiments employed dimensions such as apparent physical size which must be carried by the intentional descriptions according to which any mental images might be constructed (Banks, 1977); however, many subsequent studies have used dimensions which are almost certainly emergent properties which would only be manifest in mental images of the relevant objects (Richardson, 1980, p. 53).

Selective interference

Earlier in this chapter, I mentioned that one line of research into mental imagery had employed concurrent perceptual or spatial tasks which might interfere with the ability to create and use mental images. For example, Brooks (1967) investigated the extent of competition or functional overlap between reading, listening, and imagery, and concluded that reading interfered with the visualization of spatial relationships. This was subsequently confirmed by studies in which subjects give introspective reports on the time taken to construct a mental image in response to a verbal description (Beech, 1977). Other research has shown that the processing of spatial information interferes in a selective manner with the maintenance of mental images during an interpolated retention interval (Healy, 1975), and that making a visually guided response interferes in a selective manner with the retrieval of spatial information from mental images (Brooks, 1968).

Some investigators have assumed that the effect of concurrent perceptual tasks upon mental imagery should not only be *selective*, in the sense that they disrupt mental imagery disproportionately more than other cognitive faculties, but it should also be *modality-specific*, in the sense that visual tasks disrupt visual imagery more than auditory imagery. However, Brooks (1968) himself demonstrated that a pointing response was equally disruptive of the recall of spatial information whether it was monitored visually or tactually; and more recent experiments by Baddeley and Lieberman (1980) showed that performance on Brooks's visualization tasks could be disrupted by a concurrent, auditory, spatial task, but not by a concurrent, visual, non-spatial task. These results suggest that such concurrent activities have an effect by disrupting a general spatial system (Baddeley, 1976, pp. 230–1; Richardson, 1980, pp. 55–7). However, other research by Phillips and Christie (1977) criticized the adequacy of the control conditions in Brooks's experiments, and indicated that visualization might be disrupted by any concurrent activity which is not preprogrammed and overlearned, but which might therefore compete for the resources of a central, amodal, executive system or working memory.

Transitive inference

In discussing the dual coding position earlier, I made the observation that very little research on mental imagery had been concerned with thinking and problem solving. Moreover, the relevant experimental evidence on the subject of human reasoning has virtually been restricted to one specific task, that of transitive inference. Although this task is formally very similar to that involved in making mental comparisons, there has unfortunately been very little attempt to relate these two areas of research.

A transitive inference is a valid deduction based upon comparative sentences which define the ordering of items along some dimension. A typical problem of this type (variously known as a linear syllogism or a three-term series problem) would be: John is better than Bill; Jim is worse than Bill; who is best? The idea that mental imagery might be implicated in this task was first suggested by DeSoto, London and Handel (1965). They supposed that subjects constructed a directionally marked mental axis or array in which the three terms were placed; the solution to the linear syllogism could then be 'read off' the mental picture by inspecting the relative positions of the three terms along the relevant axis. This account of transitive inference was subsequently developed by Handel, DeSoto and London (1968) and by Huttenlocher (1968). An opposing theory was put forward by Clark (1969), who argued that transitive inference was based upon abstract linguistic interpretations of the two premises. Originally, these researchers attempted to evaluate their respective positions by considering the error rates and response latencies on linear syllogisms of different forms. Subsequent reviews of this controversy have tended to conclude that such data are not adequate to discriminate between the two theories in a satisfactory manner (Johnson-Laird, 1972; Shaver, Pierson and Lang, 1975). However, Potts and Scholz (1975) argued that differential predictions could be derived if one measured separately the time required to encode the two premises of a three-term series problem and the time required to generate an answer to the test question from the resulting internal representation. Their results indicated that subjects tend to integrate the two premises into a single unified representation, rather than simply storing the functional relations underlying each of the two premises separately. This outcome is consistent with the theory that transitive inference is based upon a composite mental image, and inconsistent with Clark's linguistic model. Nevertheless, the experiments reported by Potts and Scholz provide no evidence to suggest that the unified representation which they postulated was in any way based upon the use of mental imagery. Accordingly, other sorts of evidence are needed if mental imagery is to be implicated in the solution of three-term series problems.

The initial research on transitive inference yielded three sorts of findings which supported the imagery model. First, the subjects' introspective reports suggested that relevant mental imagery some-times accompanied the solution of three-term series problems (Hut-tenlocher, 1968; see also Shaver *et al.*, 1975). Second, when children attempt to solve such problems by arranging concrete objects in an actual spatial array, they produce a similar pattern of results to adults attempting to reason without such aids (Huttenlocher *et al.*, 1970). Finally, when the subjects are required to write down the elements of a linear syllogism in a spatial array, the arrangement of the three terms tends to correspond to that predicted to occur in the postulated imaginal array (DeSoto *et al.*, 1965). However, a more detailed analysis by Jones (1970) showed that the spatial assignment of the elements of a linear syllogism and the subsequent relative difficulty of the task could be better predicted by Clark's (1969) deep-structure theory. Moreover, Huttenlocher's comparison of children and adults shows only that similar cognitive processes underlie both mental problem solving and spatial manipulation tasks, not that mental imagery is specifically involved. Since most psychologists would regard introspective reports by themselves as an inadequate basis for a theory of problem solving, the original evidence for the imagery model was clearly unsatisfactory.

A systematic experimental analysis of the role of mental imagery in transitive inference was undertaken by Shaver *et al.* (1975), who related performance on linear syllogisms to each of the four types of operational procedure which are normally taken to define mental imagery as a theoretical construct. Their first experiment involved three types of linear syllogism, chosen so as to manipulate the likelihood of evoked mental imagery. Following Brooks (1968), the problems were presented both visually and auditorily, in order to manipulate the amount of selective interference with visual-spatial imagery. Finally, each subject completed a set of psychometric tests in order to yield a measure of spatial ability (see below). Each of these variables showed a significant relationship with reasoning performance in the expected direction: thus, performance was better on imageable material, with auditory presentation, and in the case of subjects of high spatial ability. The latter effect occurred with male subjects, but not with females; this is explicable on the as-sumption that male experimenters inhibit the use of mental imagery and of other optional strategies on the part of subjects of the opposite sex (Gralton, Hayes and Richardson, 1979; Richardson, 1980, p.

146). In the second experiment reported by Shaver *et al.*, half of the subjects were given specific training in the use of visual-spatial imagery, and were instructed to use it in solving a series of linear syllogisms, chosen so as to minimize the likelihood of spontaneous mental imagery among the non-instructed control subjects. The instructions to use mental imagery produced a significant improvement in reasoning performance.

This study contains a number of serious methodological problems, which have been enumerated and discussed by Evans (1980b). However, the most serious difficulty arises out of the claim by Shaver *et al.* that they were approaching the problem of the role of mental imagery in problem solving by the use of converging operations. All of the procedural variables which they employed did show statistically significant relationships with reasoning scores. Nevertheless, the demonstration that each of a set of operational indicators individually correlates with performance in a particular task does not rule out the possibility that the different indicators are affecting quite separate components of the total cognitive system. As is quite clear from other research on mental imagery (Richardson, 1980, p. 10) and from the specific study by Brooks (1968), to which Shaver *et al.* refer, the conclusion that different operational indicators define a single theoretical construct and affect a single component of the total cognitive system can only be based upon the demonstration of meaningful and significant interactions among those operational indicators in terms of their effects upon performance (Evans, 1980b). Unfortunately, Shaver *et al.* did not look for any interactions involving the manipulation of imagery instructions in the design of their second experiment, and none of the relevant interactions in their first experiment achieved statistical significance. The selective interference produced by reading the problems did tend to be greater with imageable material; and, at least with male subjects, the correlation between spatial ability and reading performance tended to be more pronounced with less imageable material and with auditory presentation. There was also a tendency for the correlation with spatial ability on less imageable material to be increased by practice on imageable problems. However, further research is clearly needed to establish whether these different operations really 'converge' on a single theoretical construct. If an unpublished experiment mentioned by Evans (1980b) is any indication, then the findings of this research may well prove to be negative; at present, it is certainly safest to accept Evans's conclusion that 'there does not appear to be any good evidence that visual imagery is either a necessary or useful explanatory construct for transitive inference.'

Individual differences

The study of how individual subjects differ in terms of their cognitive strategies and abilities has always formed a significant part of psychological research, and it is thus not surprising that the investigation of individual differences is one of the oldest approaches to the understanding of mental imagery. However, most of the relevant literature has been concerned with human learning and memory (Richardson, 1980, Chapter 9), and there has been relatively little research on individual differences in other cognitive faculties (though see Ernest, 1977). There are two main topics of interest: the study of spatial ability and the study of creativity. In both cases, experimental research has been concerned to develop formal psychometric tests and to correlate the results of these tests with introspective reports of experienced mental imagery.

In an analysis of the factors underlying human cognitive abilities, Thurstone (1938) defined the space factor as the ease with which a subject employs spatial and visual imagery. This is measured by tests of spatial thinking, many of which are quite similar to the mental rotation tasks devised by Shepard and his colleagues. Such tests correlate moderately well with one another, they load on the same factor or factors in investigations which have employed factor analysis, and they have had some success as general predictors of cognitive efficiency (Ernest, 1977). The neuroanatomical basis of this sort of faculty is fairly well understood: impaired performance in spatial tasks tends to be produced by damage to the posterior regions of the brain, and especially to the parietal lobes of the cerebral cortex (Miller, 1972, Chapter 4). The relative frequency of deficit in patients with damage to the right cerebral hemisphere compared to patients with damage to the left cerebral hemisphere appears to vary from task to task (Benton, 1969).

Formal questionnaires on the qualities of experienced mental imagery have been used extensively in psychological research, and typically demonstrate considerable variation among individual subjects in terms of their introspective reports. However, they do not seem to show any consistent relationship with performance in tests of spatial thinking, and the two sorts of test usually load on different factors in the solutions obtained by means of factor analysis (Ernest, 1977; Richardson, 1977). Unfortunately, formal introspective questionnaires are subject to a variety of conceptual and methodological problems, of which two are especially important: first, introspective reports of experienced mental imagery appear to be particularly vulnerable to experimenter effects and to variations in perceived demand characteristics (Berger and Gaunitz, 1977; Neisser, 1972b; Richardson, 1980, pp. 121–3); second, many of the items contained in introspective questionnaires on experienced mental imagery do not, on serious conceptual analysis, appear to be legitimate or meaningful questions to ask (Richardson, 1980, pp. 124–5). It should be noted that performance in tests of spatial ability may be equally vulnerable to experimenter effects, though there is little evidence on this point (Ernest, 1977).

The literature on creative thinking contains many subjective and informal accounts of the importance of mental imagery (Forisha, 1978). This applies both to the study of literary creativity (Havelka, 1968), and to the study of scientific creativity (Paivio, 1971, p. 531). It has been suggested that the value of mental imagery arises out of the fact that it combines freedom of association with richness of organization (Rugg, 1963, p. 311). However, studies of the relationship between creativity and introspective reports of experienced mental imagery have been inconclusive (Durndell and Wetherick, 1976; Forisha, 1978; Schmeidler, 1965). The effect is dependent upon the specific imagery questionnaire employed (Durndell and Wetherick, 1976) and upon the sex of the subjects (Forisha, 1978), and in any case is subject to the conceptual and methodological problems mentioned above. Further research is clearly necessary in this area.

Conclusions

I began this chapter by pointing out that mental imagery is an aspect of personal experience that is especially ubiquitous, intriguing, and striking. Nevertheless, psychological research on mental imagery has proved to be especially complex, and the results which it has generated have been notably inconclusive. There does seem to be at least a *prima facie* case for the position that an appreciation

of the role of mental imagery will prove to be important in understanding human thinking and problem solving. However, any advance beyond this vague generalization will require serious
developments of a conceptual, theoretical and methodological nature. The research to date has largely served merely to define the
immediate problems to be tackled in each of these three directions.

First, confusion and unclarity in psychological research on mental
imagery can only be avoided by the apposite employment of sophisticated conceptual analysis. Researchers must specify unambiguously the criteria for the application of the central concepts
with which they are concerned, whether those concepts are taken
from ordinary language with their normal everyday use, or whether
some novel employment is stipulated for the purpose of scientific
investigation. They must recognize the salient categorical differences which exist in the language used to describe human beings
and their behaviour, especially the distinction between psychological states and human dispositions, and the distinction between
capacities and their vehicles. Correspondingly, they must carefully
differentiate between the use of an expression to refer to a conscious
mental episode and its use as a hypothetical construct in an articulated theory of cognitive structure. Future research must clarify the
relationship between descriptions of mental experience and descriptions of behaviour, and the status of these two categories of statement as scientific evidence. Still to be resolved are central questions
concerning the relevance of introspection to an understanding of
human thinking and problem solving, and the status of intentional
and emergent properties in the apprehension of mental images.

Second, the development of incisive theoretical accounts of human thinking and problem solving demands an adequate amount
of attention to the question of the testability, the falsifiability, and
the identifiability of psychological theories of cognitive representation. It is clear that the original models of human cognition which
incorporated the use of mental imagery were inadequately specified,
inadequately tested, and inadequately differentiated from possible
alternatives. The potential of propositional theories has still to be
fully explored: in particular, they have yet to be properly applied
to the description of the spatial configurations employed in experiments on mental rotation, and to the integration of semantic information of the sort required in experiments on transitive inference.
On the other hand, we also need more sophisticated accounts of

possible pictorial representations; the recent work of Kosslyn (1981) in this direction appears to be most promising.

Finally, future experimental research on human thinking and problem solving must employ methods and procedures which are appropriate to the object of the investigation. If this research is to be cast in terms of hypothetical constructs and defining operations, then experimental design must focus upon the question of the validity of those operations as predictors of human behaviour, and the question of their convergence upon a single putative system. This requires fairly complicated factorial designs in which a variety of main effects and interactions can be examined simultaneously. On the other hand, if this research is intended to focus upon the subjective experience of mental imagery and other 'private' episodes, then the questions which are addressed to experimental subjects concerning such episodes must be appropriate, legitimate, and meaningful. Nevertheless, the main criticism which can be levelled at previous research on mental imagery and human cognition is that it has been concerned with a very restricted range of highly artificial experimental situations. Future investigations must reflect the diversity and richness of human thinking, and be prepared to consider the wide variety of respects in which mental imagery might be involved.

References

Anderson, J. R. (1978), 'Arguments concerning representations for mental imagery', *Psychological Review, 85*, pp. 249–77.

Anderson, J. R. (1979), 'Further arguments concerning representations for mental imagery: a response to Hayes-Roth and Pylyshyn', *Psychological Review, 86*, pp. 395–406.

Anderson, J. R. and Bower, G. H. (1973), *Human Associative Memory*, Washington, D.C., Hemisphere Press.

Baddeley, A. D. (1976), *The Psychology of Memory*, New York, Basic Books.

Baddeley, A. D., Grant, S., Wight, E. and Thomson, N. (1974), 'Imagery and visual working memory', in P. M. A. Rabbitt and S. Dornic (eds), *Attention and Performance V*, London, Academic Press.

Baddeley, A. D. and Lieberman, K. (1980), 'Spatial working memory', in R. S. Nickerman (ed.), *Attention and Performance VIII*, Hillsdale, New Jersey, Erlbaum.

Banks, W. P. (1977), 'Encoding and processing of symbolic information in comparative judgments', in G. H. Bower (ed.), *The Psychology of*

Learning and Motivation: Advances in Research and Theory, vol. 11, New York, Academic Press.

Beech, J. R. (1977), 'Effect of selective visual interference on visualization', *Perceptual and Motor Skills*, 45, pp. 951–4.

Benton, A. L. (1969), 'Constructional apraxia: some unanswered questions', in A. L. Benton (ed.), *Contributions to Clinical Neuropsychology*, Chicago, Aldine Publishing.

Berger, G. H. and Gaunitz, S. C. B. (1977), 'Self-rated imagery and vividness of task pictures in relation to visual memory', *British Journal of Psychology*, 68, pp. 283–8.

Bower, G. H. (1970), 'Imagery as a relational organizer in associative learning', *Journal of Verbal Learning and Verbal Behavior*, 9, pp. 529–33.

Bower, G. H. (1972), 'Mental imagery and associative learning', in L. W. Gregg (ed.), *Cognition in Learning and Memory*, New York, Wiley.

Brooks, L. R. (1967), 'The suppression of visualization by reading', *Quarterly Journal of Experimental Psychology*, 19, pp. 289–99.

Brooks, L. R. (1968), 'Spatial and verbal components in the act of recall', *Canadian Journal of Psychology*, 22, pp. 349–68.

Clark, H. H. (1969), 'Linguistic processes in deductive reasoning', *Psychological Review*, 79, pp. 387–404.

Cooper, L. A. and Shepard, R. N. (1973), 'Chronometric studies of the rotation of mental images', in W. G. Chase (ed.), *Visual Information Processing*, New York, Academic Press.

Cooper, L. A. and Shepard, R. N. (1979), 'Transformations on representations of objects in space', in E. C. Carterette and M. Friedman (eds), *Handbook of Perception. Vol. VIII: Space and Object Perception*, New York, Academic Press.

DeSoto, C. B., London, M. and Handel, S. (1965), 'Social reasoning and spatial paralogic', *Journal of Personality and Social Psychology*, 2, pp. 513–21.

Doob, L. W. (1972), 'The ubiquitous appearance of images', in P. W. Sheehan (ed.), *The Function and Nature of Imagery*, New York, Academic Press.

Durndell, A. J. and Wetherick, N. E. (1976), 'The relation of reported imagery to cognitive performance', *British Journal of Psychology*, 67, pp. 501–6.

Earhard, B. and Mandler, G. (1965), 'Mediated associations: paradigms, controls, and mechanisms', *Canadian Journal of Psychology*, 19, pp. 346–78.

Ericsson, K. A. and Simon, H. A. (1980), 'Verbal reports as data', *Psychological Review*, 87, pp. 215–51.

Ernest, C. H. (1977), 'Imagery ability and cognition: a critical review', *Journal of Mental Imagery*, 2, pp. 181–216.

Evans, J. St B. T. (1980a), 'Current issues in the psychology of reasoning', *British Journal of Psychology*, 71, pp. 227–39.

Evans, J. St B. T. (1980b), 'Thinking: experiential and information processing approaches', in G. Claxton (ed.), *Cognitive Psychology: New Directions*, London, Routledge & Kegan Paul.

Fodor, J. A. (1975), *The Language of Thought*, New York, Thomas Y. Crowell.

Forisha, B. L. (1978), 'Mental imagery and creativity: review and speculations', *Journal of Mental Imagery*, 2, pp. 209–38.

Friedman, A. (1978), 'Memorial comparisons without the "mind's eye"', *Journal of Verbal Learning and Verbal Behavior*, 17, pp. 427–44.

Gralton, M. A., Hayes, Y. A. and Richardson, J. T. E. (1979), 'Introversion-extraversion and mental imagery', *Journal of Mental Imagery*, 3, pp. 1–10.

Handel, S., DeSoto, C. B. and London, M. (1968), 'Reasoning and spatial representation', *Journal of Verbal Learning and Verbal Behavior*, 7, pp. 351–7.

Havelka, J. (1968), *The Nature of the Creative Process in Art*, The Hague, Martinus Nijhoff.

Hayes-Roth, F. (1979), 'Distinguishing theories of representation: a critique of Anderson's "Arguments concerning mental imagery"', *Psychological Review*, 86, pp. 376–82.

Healy, A. F. (1975), 'Coding of temporal-spatial patterns in short-term memory', *Journal of Verbal Learning and Verbal Behavior*, 14, pp. 481–95.

Holt, R. R. (1964), 'Imagery: the return of the ostracized', *American Psychologist*, 19, pp. 254–64.

Huttenlocher, J. (1968), 'Constructing spatial images: a strategy in reasoning', *Psychological Review*, 75, pp. 550–60.

Huttenlocher, J., Higgins, E. T., Milligan, L. and Kaufman, B. (1970), 'The mystery of the "negative equative" construction', *Journal of Verbal Learning and Verbal Behavior*, 9, pp. 334–41.

Johnson-Laird, P. N. (1972), 'The three-term series problem', *Cognition*, 1, pp. 57–82.

Jones, S. (1970), 'Visual and verbal processes in problem-solving', *Cognitive Psychology*, 1, pp. 201–14.

Kaufmann, G. (1979), *Visual Imagery and its Relation to Problem Solving: A Theoretical and Experimental Inquiry*, Bergen, Universitetsforlaget.

Kenny, A. J. P. (1972), 'To mind via syntax', in A. J. P. Kenny, H. C. Longuet-Higgins, J. R. Lucas and C. H. Waddington (eds), *The Nature of Mind*, Edinburgh, Edinburgh University Press.

Kerst, S. M. and Howard, J. H., Jr. (1977), 'Mental comparisons for ordered information on abstract and concrete dimensions', *Memory and Cognition*, 5, pp. 227–34.

Kessel, F. S. (1972), 'Imagery: a dimension of mind rediscovered', *British Journal of Psychology*, 63, pp. 149–62.

Kosslyn, S. M. (1980), *Image and Mind*, Cambridge, Mass., Harvard University Press.

Kosslyn, S. M. (1981), 'The medium and the message in mental imagery: a theory', *Psychological Review*, 88, pp. 46–66.

Kosslyn, S. M., Pinker, S., Smith, G. E. and Schwartz, S. P. (1979), 'On the demystification of mental imagery', *The Behavioral and Brain Sciences*, 2, pp. 535–48.

Kosslyn, S. M. and Pomerantz, J. R. (1977), 'Imagery, propositions, and the form of internal representations', *Cognitive Psychology, 9*, pp. 52–76.

Malcolm, N. (1977), *Memory and Mind*, Ithaca, New York, Cornell University Press.

Mandler, J. M. and Mandler, G. (1964), *Thinking: from Association to Gestalt*, New York, Wiley.

Miller, E. (1972), *Clinical Neuropsychology*, Harmondsworth, Penguin.

Neisser, U. (1972a), 'A paradigm shift in psychology', *Science, 176*, pp. 628–30.

Neisser, U. (1972b), 'Changing conceptions of imagery', in P. W. Sheehan (ed.), *The Function and Nature of Imagery*, New York, Academic Press.

Nisbett, R. E. and Wilson, T. D. (1977), 'Telling more than we can know: verbal reports on mental processes', *Psychological Review, 84*, pp. 231–59.

Paivio, A. (1971), *Imagery and Verbal Processes*, New York, Holt, Rinehart & Winston.

Paivio, A. (1975a), 'Imagery and synchronic thinking', *Canadian Psychological Review, 16*, pp. 147–63.

Paivio, A. (1975b), 'Neomentalism', *Canadian Journal of Psychology, 29*, pp. 263–91.

Paivio, A. (1975c), 'Perceptual comparisons through the mind's eye', *Memory and Cognition, 3*, pp. 635–47.

Paivio, A. (1978a), 'Comparisons of mental clocks', *Journal of Experimental Psychology: Human Perception and Performance, 4*, pp. 61–71.

Paivio, A. (1978b), 'Dual coding: theoretical issues and empirical evidence', in J. M. Scandura and C. J. Brainerd (eds), *Structural/Process Models of Complex Human Behavior*, Leiden, Nordhoff.

Paivio, A. (1978c), 'Mental comparisons involving abstract attributes', *Memory and Cognition, 6*, pp. 199–208.

Paivio, A. (1979), 'The relationship between verbal and perceptual codes', in E. C. Carterette and M. P. Friedman (eds), *Handbook of Perception. Vol. IX: Perceptual Processing*, New York, Academic Press.

Phillips, W. A. and Christie, D. F. M. (1977), 'Interference with visualization', *Quarterly Journal of Experimental Psychology, 29*, pp. 637–50.

Pinker, S. and Kosslyn, S. M. (1978), 'The representation and manipulation of three-dimensional space in mental images', *Journal of Mental Imagery, 2*, pp. 69–83.

Posner, M. I., Boies, S. J., Eichelman, W. H. and Taylor, R. L. (1969), 'Retention of visual and name codes of single letters', *Journal of Experimental Psychology, 79* (1, Part 2).

Potts, G. R. and Scholz, K. W. (1975), 'The internal representation of a three-term series problem', *Journal of Verbal Learning and Verbal Behavior, 14*, pp. 439–52.

Pylyshyn, Z. W. (1973), 'What the mind's eye tells the mind's brain: a critique of mental imagery', *Psychological Bulletin, 80*, pp. 1–24.

Pylyshyn, Z. W. (1979a), 'Imagery theory: not mysterious – just wrong', *The Behavioral and Brain Sciences, 2*, pp. 561–3.

Pylyshyn, Z. W. (1979b), 'Validating computational models: a critique of Anderson's indeterminacy of representation claim', *Psychological Review*, *86*, pp. 383–94.

Pylyshyn, Z. W. (1981), 'The imagery debate: Analogue media versus tacit knowledge', *Psychological Review*, *88*, pp. 16–45.

Reed, H. B. (1918), 'Associative aids: III. Their relation to the theory of thought and to methodology in psychology', *Psychological Review*, *25*, pp. 378–401.

Richardson, A. (1969), *Mental Imagery*, New York, Springer.

Richardson, A. (1977), 'The meaning and measurement of memory imagery', *British Journal of Psychology*, *68*, pp. 29–43.

Richardson, J. T. E. (1979), 'Subjects' reports in mental comparisons', *Bulletin of the Psychonomic Society*, *14*, pp. 371–2.

Richardson, J. T. E. (1980), *Mental Imagery and Human Memory*, London, Macmillan Press.

Rugg, H. (1963), *Imagination*, New York, Harper & Row.

Rumelhart, D. E., Lindsay, P. H. and Norman, D. A. (1972), 'A process model for long-term memory', in E. Tulving and W. Donaldson (eds), *Organization of Memory*, New York, Academic Press.

Schmeidler, G. R. (1965), 'Visual imagery correlated to a measure of creativity', *Journal of Consulting Psychology*, *29*, pp. 78–80.

Shaver, P., Pierson, L. and Lang, S. (1975), 'Converging evidence for the functional significance of imagery in problem solving', *Cognition*, *3*, pp. 359–75.

Shepard, R. N. (1966), 'Learning and recall as organization and search', *Journal of Verbal Learning and Verbal Behavior*, *5*, pp. 201–4.

Shepard, R. N. and Metzler, J. (1971), 'Mental rotation of three-dimensional objects', *Science*, *171*, pp. 701–3.

Shepard, R. N. and Podgorny, P. (1979), 'Cognitive processes that resemble perceptual processes', in W. K. Estes (ed.), *Handbook of Learning and Cognitive Processes*, Hillsdale, New Jersey, Erlbaum.

Smith, E. R. and Miller, F. D. (1978), 'Limits on perception of cognitive processes: a reply to Nisbett and Wilson', *Psychological Review*, *85*, pp. 355–62.

Thurstone, L. L. (1938), 'Primary mental abilities', *Psychometrika Monographs*, no. 1.

Yuille, J. C. and Catchpole, M. J. (1977), 'The role of imagery in models of cognition', *Journal of Mental Imagery*, *1*, pp. 171–80.

8 Protocol analysis in problem solving

Richard Byrne

Protocol analysis, in psychological rather than diplomatic circles, refers to the use of some blow-by-blow record of an individual's behaviour, while engaged on a cognitive task, as a source of psychological data. It may be used either along with or instead of the traditional techniques of reaction time and error analysis. The purpose of this chapter is to evaluate the contribution that this methodology can make to our understanding of human problem solving, and to identify the pitfalls to be avoided when using the method. First, though, it is necessary to clarify what is meant by the term 'protocol analysis'.

Whilst protocols are usually verbal – obtained by asking subjects to 'think aloud' during problem solving – they need not be; nor are all verbal reports to be regarded as protocols in the sense that I shall use the term. The essential ingredient of a protocol analysis is that it examines *patterns* and *sequences* in a continuous stream of behaviour, which need not be verbal. For example, it is reasonable to regard a sequence of eye-movements made in scanning a chess board (De Groot, 1966) or of moves of an object in a child's attempt at a Piagetian seriation task (Baylor and Gascon, 1974), as 'protocols'. On the other hand, analysing the *content* of verbal reports, often collected retrospectively in order to explain other behaviour, is *not* to be regarded as protocol analysis. Some attention will, however, be given to problems arising from the latter technique, which is not always clearly distinguished from protocol analysis proper. (For a discussion of the problems of introspective reports, with reference to mental imagery, see RICHARDSON, this volume.)

A protocol often consists of a stream of verbal comments constituting a part of the solution path, but in some cases the protocol may *be* the solution. For instance, Linde and Labov (1975) asked residents of apartments to explain their layout. They found that descriptions were never in the form of existential statements of where rooms are, nor of maps viewed from above, but were 'tours', saying what you come to when you do such-and-such. The tours followed rules: at each branch point, one-roomed branches were mentioned first but not entered; longer branches were entered; at the end of each branch the tour moves back 'instantaneously' to the origin of the branch, and does not retrace steps. Linde and Labov describe the results as showing rules of linguistic discourse, though they can be treated as showing the form of representation of the information (Byrne, 1982). Either way, the analysis is one of describing pattern regularities in a stream of (verbal) behaviour: protocol analysis. By contrast, although Burgoyne (1975) asked subjects to think aloud while coming to evaluative judgments about their learning experiences, the 'inductive analysis of content' made by the experimenter is not helpfully termed by him 'the methodology of protocol analysis'.

Although the technique is not new (it was first used by Duncker in 1945), it is still viewed with suspicion in psychology (see Ericsson and Simon, 1980, for examples) and is indeed often not even mentioned in elementary textbooks (Hilgard, Atkinson and Atkinson, 7th edition, 1979; Haber and Fried, 1975; Silverman, 1979; and many others). Yet in applied psychology it is now quite widely used. Since the use of protocol analysis in artificial, quasi-mathematical problems is familar (see Newell and Simon, 1972, for a review) two of these more applied cases will be used to introduce it here.

The first concerns the process of coming to a decision when choosing between alternatives. Payne (1976) studied choice of apartments, and also made explicit the pattern in which pieces of information (cost, size, noise level, etc.) were examined by presenting the data base as an array of cards, to be turned face-up one at a time by the subject. This method was first used by Pask (1973) to study the learning strategies of individuals: some, his 'serialists', explored one dimension or category exhaustively; others, his 'holists', followed complex hypotheses which cut across dimensions and categories. Payne prefers to say that this method, like verbal protocol analysis, is a 'process tracing technique' rather than another form of protocol analysis but in any case he finds the results of both agree. If only two apartments are to be compared, subjects balance one asset against another fault, typically searching *all* the information, or at least equal amounts in each case. With six alternatives, this compensatory strategy is dropped and the number quickly reduced by ruling out any which don't meet pre-set criteria, examining only partial information in each case. When only two remain, a compensatory strategy is used. Olshavsky (1979) replicated this with choice of condominiums and stereo receivers, finding that in addition as the number of attributes of each item was increased, subjects began to differentially weight their importance: again, a subtle, balancing strategy was preceded by a 'quick and dirty' screening if the task was too complex. He found that the results of verbal protocol analysis were consistent with the times taken to make the decisions. Crow, Olshavsky and Summers (1980) studied industrial buyers requesting quotations and selecting final suppliers for electrical components. None of their tasks had only two alternatives, and they found no compensatory strategies: all buyers used a sequential elimination of 'unworthy' candidates on the basis of single attributes, and the verbal protocols could be closely matched by the stages in output of a computer simulation. Varying the number of vendors (from 7 to 15) and the time pressure had no detectable effects. However, the authors are perhaps naive to state that protocol analysis 'permits direct observation of decision processes' and to assume implicitly that thinking aloud has no effect on the structure of the search. We will return to these issues later.

Some studies do not merely employ problems *like* those encountered in daily life, but actually record protocols 'in the field', of people solving genuine problems they *have* encountered. A fine example is Rasmussen and Jensen (1974), who worked on skilled 'trouble-shooters' of electronic faults as they repaired instruments at a nuclear research establishment. They stress the need for the analyst to fully appreciate the task in order to interpret the protocols properly: they themselves had engineering backgrounds. Their expectations were also realistic: they note that, with the very many parameters influencing the behaviour, 'reliable quantitative information is not to be expected' and that a formal comparison of a man with a model covering all possible strategies 'is impracticable in real-life conditions'. Unlike many studies, they give details of technique: men were asked to use everyday terms and just to give hints when working fast, then the record was typed immediately and the men asked to correct mistakes and fill in missing points while they still sat in front of the faulty instrument. Analysis began by 'extracting the most obvious and frequent routines, leaving for later analysis the complicated and more idiosyncratic parts of the records'. The experimenters felt that verbalisation sometimes forced a process which was parallel, like visual recognition, to be reported as a serial scan, or an automatic routine to become conscious and so interfere with other mental activities. Nevertheless, their main findings are interesting and probably not invalidated by these artifacts. Trained technicians use a stream of simple good/bad decisions in an exhaustive, informationally inefficient but *fast* manner. These are organised by viewing the system as a hierarchy of subunits, and search controlled by using the circuit diagram as a topographic map. The workers are quite *capable* of using the circuit diagram to understand the system's internal functioning, and would do so if measurements would have serious consequences, for instance if the circuit were live or radioactive waste might be spilled; otherwise, procedures are quick and simple, not 'clever', and seem to be very effective in minimising time spent on the task and mental load.

By examining these current uses of the method, we can see a number of questions of theoretical importance arise. What are verbal protocols a record of? What can protocol analysis be used to study? What can we, in principle, discover with it? What is the best technique in practice? How should the data be treated? In many cases, clear-cut answers cannot be given yet, but the account which follows is an attempt to synthesise our present knowledge, concentrating on areas least well covered in the literature (see, especially, Ericsson and Simon, 1980).

Where do verbal protocols come from?

Beliefs about what the verbalisations of subjects are reports *of* are varied. On the one hand, thinking aloud is claimed to be a direct output of inner speech (Benjafield, 1969) and to permit observation of the processes of decision making (Crow, Olshavsky and Summers, 1980); on the other, all verbal reports (implicitly including protocols) are treated as epiphenomena, generated by independent processes of rationalisation which do not also control other behaviour (Nisbett and Wilson, 1977). No doubt the truth lies in between, but not necessarily in a half-hearted compromise in which protocol analysis is used but the results distrusted unless they tell us what was already eminently probable. As Ericsson and Simon (1980) have argued, such lukewarm acceptance leads to sloppy methodology. It would be more useful to distinguish the *particular* cases in which verbal reports should be used, the *sort* of verbal reports that should be taken and *precisely* what status the data should be accorded in those instances. With the aim of doing this, we will distinguish two very different uses of verbal data: for content analysis in order to explain other behaviour, and for pattern analysis in order to suggest and test models. Each kind of analysis can use concurrent or retrospective verbalisations. Of course, these categories are not mutually exclusive.

Verbal reports as explanations

In social psychology, people are often asked why they did certain things (chose a career or a detergent, voted the way they did; see Nisbett and Wilson, 1977, for many references), and this is routine in social psychology experiments; some researchers have even argued for replacing experiments, and consequent deception, with straightforwardly asking how subjects *would* have behaved had the experiment been done. Nisbett and Wilson (1977) have shown clearly that this will not do. They catalogue many reasons for scepticism: subjects may be unaware of any change in their beliefs and behaviour, even when the changes are reliably and deliberately produced by an experimenter, and don't report the mental processes which *can* explain their actions (e.g. most cognitive dissonance work); they may be quite unaware of stimuli which demonstrably influence behaviour (e.g. the effect of other bystanders on helping); they may be sure of the influence of stimuli which are actually quite ineffectual. Nisbett and Wilson's examples are many and they even deliberately set up a series of experiments (see also Wilson and Nisbett, 1978) in which subjects are shown to be unaware of true influences on their actions and to cite instead just those same influences which observers, not asked to take part, predict *would* be influential. Clearly the many fluent claims subjects make do not reflect privileged introspection of their mental processes, but are better seen as private theories of behaviour based on general knowledge and cultural stereotypes. One would be rash to treat them as 'explaining' the behaviour, without proper experimental support. Nisbett and Wilson also cite creative people's memories in later life of their 'unconscious' problem solving, and Maier's (1931) experimental work in which hints on how to solve problems were often not mentioned later by subjects, though they clearly helped. This is odd, since they consider that this work helps to demonstrate lack of *awareness* of mental events, yet they themselves (1977, p. 251) note that removal in time from the actual occurrence reduces the accuracy of the report. Consequently, we can hardly take such demonstration at face value. Indeed, Ericsson and Simon (1980) have shown that all the available evidence indicates that these reports are unreliable. If protocol analysis, instead of retrospective probing, were used, intermediate steps in creative thought (including use of hints) might be shown up.

It is important, therefore, to keep concurrent protocols conceptually separate from retrospective reports; though they have much in common, protocols are not simply 'subjective reports . . . slightly disguised' (Shallice, 1972). Nisbett and Wilson (1977, pp. 255–6) believe that one has privileged and fairly accurate access to 'the focus of his attention at any given point in time', 'knowledge at least quantitatively superior to that of observers concerning his emotions, evaluations and plans' and the 'intermediate results of a series of mental operations'. This is not enough for the sort of analyses social psychologists need, but it is fine for protocol analysis in cognitive psychology – pattern analysis of verbal reports, generated while engaged in problem solving, as a form of data. Thus Nisbett and Wilson have shown that if one is interested in underlying motives and influences on behaviour then introspective methods, such as content analysis of retrospective reports (and likely enough also of concurrent protocols, although they did not use this technique) are not advisable. If, as a cognitive psychologist, one is interested in the mechanics and immediate control of problem solving, introspective methods may be very useful. The appropriate method is to analyse patterns, not content, and there is no doubt that a pattern analysis of a concurrent protocol will give far higher quality data than that of a retrospective report.

Verbal reports as data

Radford (1974) gives a useful taxonomy of introspective methods, and distinguishes three categories: thinking aloud; self-report, in which the subject simply attempts to describe his experiences with no attempt at objectivity; and self-observation, or introspection proper, in which trained non-naive subjects attempt accurate objective observation of their own mental life. He notes that in the latter technique systematic introspectionists such as Tichener believed that inner experience could be observed, just as behaviourists would observe an animal's behaviour. On this basis, we should properly be treating systematic introspection as an ethological, data-collecting technique; however, few would now wish to do so. Use of the verbal reports of small numbers of practised observers, often psychologists, lives on in psychophysics and in this case the success of the field needs no apologia. Self-report, when used wisely, can prove to be a useful technique for the experimentalist. For instance, in a discrimination task, Karpf and Levine (1971) found asking subjects to state their current hypothesis at each trial to give identical results to the time-consuming procedure of interpolating test-only trials; and Kroll and Kellicutt (1972) showed that when subjects indicated by button-press each time they covertly rehearsed a list in a short-term memory task, this correlated *better* with long-term learning than when rehearsal was manipulated indirectly by backward counting. Thus all three of Radford's categories have uses in current psychology and emphasis, as here, on protocol analysis should not be taken as dismissal of all other kinds of introspective method.

Protocol analysis is closely related to the kinds of fine-grain observation of behaviour used so successfully by ethologists (Tinbergen, 1963), and treats verbalised mental events simply as pieces of behaviour, not as a form of explanation; as such it does not even conflict with Skinner's (1974) position on the status of verbal reports. What it can provide, as well as simply a greater 'density of observations' than other techniques (Simon, 1978), is information on the structure of planning, goals and sub-goals, methods and the criteria for their selection, criteria for assessment of success, and routes and codes of information. But like any other ethological method of recording, it must be carried out without disrupting the process under study, without introducing systematic errors of recording (Altmann, 1974) and in an objective and replicable manner.

When is it appropriate to use protocol analysis?

Among the many tasks which are sufficiently extended in time to allow possible use of protocol analysis not all are suitable for its application; use in inappropriate circumstances is likely to give misleading results and bring the method into disrepute, so is important to avoid.

Evidently, *verbal* protocols can only be obtained from those who are fluent and confident verbalisers; thus animals, children and certain clinical patients are excluded. Protocols of other kinds are not likewise restricted, for instance Baylor and Gascon (1974) used a transcribed record of actions made by children in attempting Piaget's weight seriation task. They were able to construct production systems which modelled each stage of competence, as well as variants for individual differences between children. Young (1978) went further in studying children's length seriation, devising a set of productions which, if all were present, simulated adult competence, and if some were missing but a certain critical subset were present, simulated children's errors. For each particular set of 'missing' productions, behaviour was simulated which exactly matched a certain child's errors; thus, development could be described by adding productions one by one. This shows clearly the essential weakness of any 'stage' theory of development: what causes the quantum jumps, and where do the new skills come from? It has been argued that, for diagnosis of the presence of a Piagetian structure, correct verbal explanations should be given by the child, as well as correct behaviour. But Brainerd (1973) shows that since structures are logical, not linguistic, this is inappropriate and Piagetian work can be done entirely 'behaviouristically' by relying on competence and sequences of behaviour for data.

A major issue has always been, under what circumstances does verbalisation disrupt or affect the primary behaviour under study, hence giving misleading results? In any multiple processor, but limited central capacity model of human behaviour (e.g. Neisser, 1963; Shallice, 1972) this is liable to be the case, and De Groot (1965) believed that verbalisation made thought more organised and less intuitive. However, Ericsson and Simon (1980) and Payne, Braunstein and Carroll (1978) review attempts to check the effect of the secondary task and conclude that only a slight slowing of performance is produced when subjects are expected to verbalise information that would be 'heeded in the normal course of processing'. Ericsson and Simon use a minimally contentious, 'lowest common denominator' of models of human thought and verbal output to deduce which information normally passes through the focus of attention, and which does not. This successfully formalises the intuitions and 'common sense' of many psychologists, and shows clearly that these intuitions are thoroughly sensible and consistent with current theory. However, only empirical testing can show if their rules are sufficient, since current theories of thinking may well be inadequate. For instance, Kearins (1981) tested the abilities of aboriginal and white Australian children at reconstructing spatial arrays from memory. Most white children verbalised spontaneously while committing the array to memory, actively examined the materials, and worked with urgency on the reconstruction task. Aboriginals sat still and silent, staring at the array, and on the reconstruction worked deliberately and slowly. They were also *much* better at the task. It is likely that concurrent verbalisation would have disrupted the aboriginals but not the white children, yet how could this have been deduced *a priori*? Perhaps in the end it will prove better to resort to the atheoretical recommendation that tasks cannot be disrupted when subjects *would rather think aloud than not* (Byrne, 1977) and, in general, that analysis should be restricted to cases where subjects find it *easy* to verbalise.

In certain circumstances, even these guidelines *may* not be sufficient. Wason and Evans (1975) examined the justifications (*not* concurrent verbal protocols) of subjects attempting various versions of the Wason four-card problem of inference (see also WASON, this volume). They showed that justifications are not from the same source as the actual behaviour in those subjects who fail the harder versions. Subjects in fact choose cards *matching* the words of the question, ignoring the logically critical presence or absence of negatives (see EVANS, this volume). In tasks where these happen also to be correct, subjects refer to the need for falsification rather than verification as if they really understood the logic. Yet they do not: on tasks where they fail, they argue for the need to verify. Clearly these are rationalisations, yet they are apparently given readily. More recently, Evans (1980) has suggested that the non-logical, non-verbal process which governs the (faulty) behaviour, and the logical, verbal process which rationalises that behaviour, may even be due to processes arising in the two hemispheres of the brain. Admittedly, taking subjects' justifications at face value would involve a content analysis of retrospective reports, but the possible dangers must also be borne in mind when dealing with protocols: evidently there exist tasks which, like motor skills, are quite un-available to conscious monitoring but which may *appear* to be re-portable. Evans (1976a) argues that statistical ability is in this category and that this accounts for the difficulty of teaching it – verbal instruction addresses processes which in fact are irrelevant to the real skill.

Ideally, of course, the effect or lack of it of collecting protocols should always be tested by collecting some of the data unmonitored, and theories devised with the help of protocol analysis tested experi-mentally without relying on verbal report. However, this is not to imply that protocol analysis should be relegated to the status of an informal adjunct to 'proper' study, for the reasons discussed above.

What can analysis of protocols, in principle, tell us?

Perhaps we should ask, rather, what would it be unrealistic to expect protocol analysis to give? An analogy may be useful to make the issues more concrete without being too particular. Certain com-puter languages possess a facility called 'trace mode' to help users find the bugs in their programs. In trace mode, instead of simply printing out a result or failing mutely, the machine prints brief descriptions of each step it takes when running the program, and this often enables the point at which it goes amiss to be seen. In complex programs, this facility can be a real boon. For our purposes, the machine is analogous to a person solving a problem, and trace mode to thinking aloud. Clearly, the print-out is still not *complete*, it is simply *more* complete; it may well be, for instance, that the machine repeatedly adds in order to multiply, but reports only the end product of this. Byrne (1977) called the analogous lower bound on the level of detail reported by a human subject their 'comment-level'.

Comment-level is likely to vary across individuals and across tasks, and with it the relative completeness of the protocol. In addition, with human subjects, momentary variations in effort and lapses of attention will cause omissions even of comments about items which are above the subject's comment-level. So protocols contain both random and systematic omissions and in general the absence of some item from a protocol proves *nothing*.

In fact, most cases where the absence of a verbal report is treated as 'evidence' come from studies relying on retrospective comment. The reports of 'incubation' in the thought processes of creative people, mentioned above, are a case in point. Ericsson and Simon (1980) cite several studies showing a gradual progression of logical thoughts before the 'sudden' insight, and suggest that the surprising nature of the success deletes the short-term memory of the steps that led to it from the focus of attention; this contrasts with explanations of the effect in terms of parallel computing processes (e.g. Shallice, 1972; Norman and Bobrow, 1976).

The former explanation gains support from a study of real-world problem solving (Byrne, 1975) in which items, part of the solution, were omitted at their proper stage yet remembered later in the midst of 'unrelated' problem solving. But the detailed protocols always show close semantic relatedness to the immediately adjacent verbalisations: the relationship is just not remarked by the subject, or at most considered a 'reminder'. For instance, on a task of designing the decor of a small apartment, S1 first completes the kitchen but omits any mention of radiators, then moves on to the living room. Here, she mentions the colour of the radiators, pauses for 8 secs and adds, 'Oh yeah, there wouldn't be a radiator for central heating in the kitchen, I don't think you need one.' (In all quoted protocols, a comma represents a pause of under 1 sec. and ... represents a pause of 1–2 secs.) She then completes the bedroom in shades of pink but again omits mention of radiators. Later, dealing with the bathroom which she decorates in orange and chocolate, she comments, 'That would have a radiator in it too, I mean it'd all be – everywhere'd have radiators except the kitchen ... er, light pinky coloured too, the radiator would be ... er, no, in the bedroom, sorry ... (4 secs) ... the radiator in the bathroom would be a chocolatey colour.' The complete search is shown in Figure 8.1 as a diagrammatic representation called an Object Transition Graph. An OTG is related to the familiar Problem Behaviour Graph of Newell and Simon (1972) but more useful with planning which

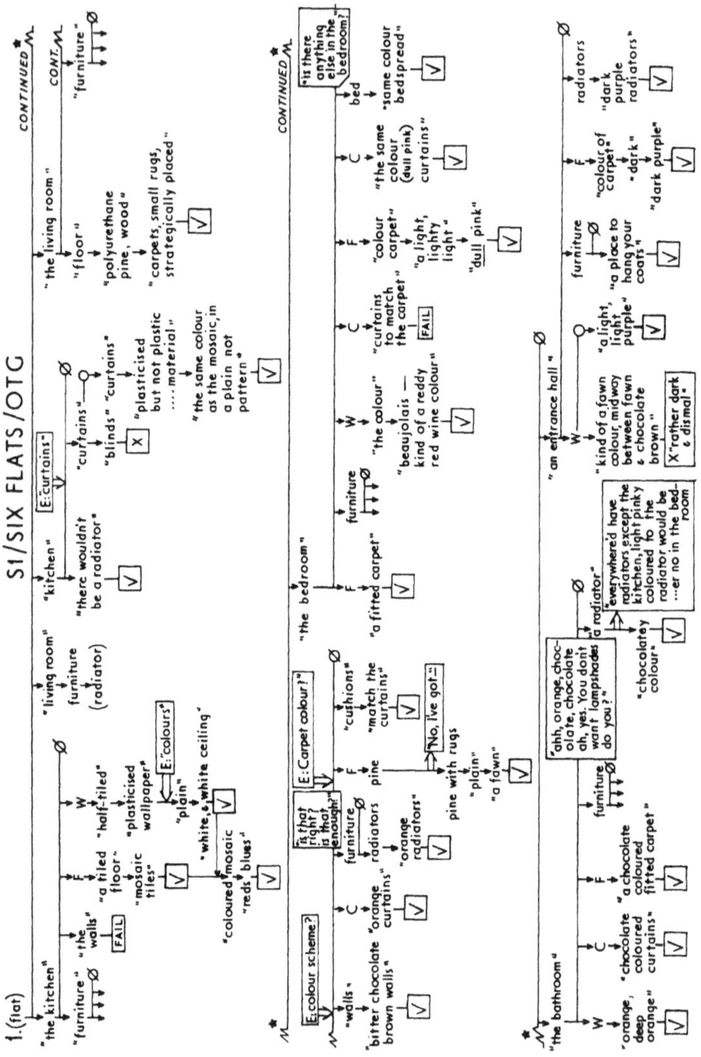

FIGURE 8.1 An 'object transition graph' of S1 solving the first in a series of apartment design tasks. Time flows downwards and to the right, and each terminal branch is defined by an item which makes up part of the final solution to the task. The conventions are explained in the key on page 239. All items in quotes are literal fragments of protocol; those without are inferred

Key to Object Transition Graph

<u>CURRENT OBJECTS</u>

"text"	verbatim from protocol
text	assumed from context
C1, C2, C3	courses of meal, serving order
P, C, V, L	"parts" of C2, roughly :—
	P: protein or main part
	C: carbohydrate often potato
	V: vegetable, salad etc.
	L: liquid, sauce etc.
M_i T_i	main part & trimmings of course (i)

abbreviated assumed objects

<u>TRANSITIONS</u>

"replace-by-a-subset" (one object, one result)

"evaluation" "expand-into-parts"
(one object, N results)

—∅ implicit acceptance, or evaluation of "no more required"

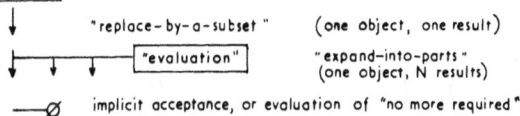

<u>EVALUATIONS OF OBJECTS AT ACCEPTABLE LEVEL OF DETAIL</u>

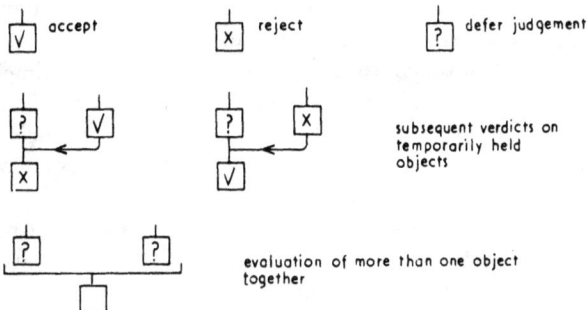

[√] accept   [X] reject   [?] defer judgement

[?] [√]
[X]

[?] [X]
[√]

subsequent verdicts on temporarily held objects

[?]   [?]
[ ]

evaluation of more than one object together

<u>INTERACTIONS WITH EXPERIMENTER</u>

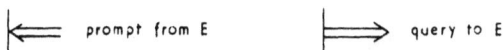

⇐ prompt from E   ⇒ query to E

<u>BREADTH-FIRST PROCESSING</u>

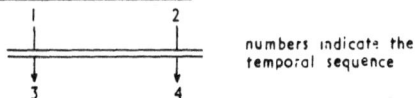

1   2

3   4

numbers indicate the temporal sequence

does not show continual errors and back-up; a PBG of this design task would typically be little more than a straight line, representing a steady accretion of the 'solution'. S1's search is evidently orderly and systematic, treating rooms one at a time, with only the items mentioned above 'out of sequence'. Yet their relationship to the immediately previous items in the protocol is clear. Other examples, from S2 engaged on the same task, illustrate this further:

(i) (immediately after bathroom curtains) 'Um, and I wouldn't have any curtains in the kitchen' (completed two rooms before).

(ii) (immediately after hall newspaper rack) '. . . oh and in the bathroom, want a heated towel rail' (completed one room before).

(iii) (during the bathroom of the second apartment designed) 'Ah! and in *both* of the flats, in the *bathroom*, there must be a long mirror.'

These *reminder* patterns present a real problem for cognitive psychology: how can the relationship to a previously omitted item be 'noticed', when the omission was not apparent at the time? The fact that there *is* a relationship argues against independent, parallel computation; yet if the subjects merely recalled the incidents afterwards, they might easily fail to remember their exact position in the sequence of thought, and mistakenly claim 'incubation'. Paradoxically, it may be a *success* of protocol analysis that it hardly ever discovers mysterious 'incubation' phenomena: the category is a waste-bucket of the unexplained, and protocol analysis may explain too much!

What are the best techniques to use?

A number of 'prescriptions' for use in verbal protocol analysis arise from this discussion:

(i) use of naive subjects who are not asked to theorise about their behaviour;

(ii) use with tasks where subjects find it easy to think aloud and prefer to do so rather than work silently, or where, for good

theoretical reason, it is likely that subjects will be able to verbalise useful material without disrupting the primary task;
(iii) use of silent problem solving as a corroboration of the lack of distortion, and of subsequent experimental tests to check deductions from protocol analysis;
(iv) analysis of pattern rather than merely content:
(v) avoidance of retrospective reporting.

The latter also applies to 'prompting' subjects when they fall silent; this may be necessary to get subjects into the habit of thinking aloud, but what they say when prompted will not be of much use. Written 'protocols' will suffer continually from this problem, and are seldom likely to be worth collecting. However, if subjects ask the experimenter for information it seems wise to provide it, else the subject will presumably resort to some 'default value' which the experimenter will not then know (Byrne, 1977).

At transcription, protocols are normally segmented into convenient, short phrases on the basis of the experimenter's assessment of single task references (Newell and Simon, 1972) and these can then be numbered. If this is done, it is possible to enlist the help of the subject in clarifying obscure referents and deciphering unclear words (e.g. Rasmussen and Jensen, 1974); obviously the subject should not be allowed to add new comments which might be rationalisations or in any case inaccurate. Thus, Quillian's (1966) procedure of asking subjects to transcribe their own protocols, adding comments as they feel inclined, is a dangerous one.

A quite different technique was used by Byrne (1977) in which the transcription was segmented by any pause greater than a certain length: 500 ms, well above the typical hesitation pauses in spontaneous speech which can indicate rapid planning of subsequent discourse (Butterworth, 1975). In this study, no real *use* was made of the pause-segmentation. However, Byrne (1981) used even longer (>2 secs) pauses in subjects' recall of lists of items to deduce the structure of mental information underlying the recall. When people are asked for the ingredients of dishes they can cook, they generate them in an order which exactly mirrors the order which they themselves would use them in cooking: for instance, one subject, who was in the habit of squeezing and grating lemons for a lemon meringue pie *before* starting to make pastry, 'recalled' this ingredient first. Priming does not occur; the fact that the word 'lemon' occurs in the instructions to the subject does not cause it to tend to be recalled first. Analysis of the long pauses during the listing of ingredients (Table 8.1) shows that they occur at the same point in the lists of different subjects, and that most subjects either pause or make some comment between ingredients used for pastry and those used for the lemon filling. Examining the logical structure of a plan

TABLE 8.1 *Interspersed utterances and pauses longer than two seconds in the lists of ingredients of lemon meringue pie*

Position in list	Utterance or pause	Subject
Before pastry[a]	for the pastry	2
	the pastry	4
	for the pastry	8
	the pastry	9
	you'd need ingredients for pastry	10
Within pastry	None	
Between pastry and filling	... (3s) ...	1
	for the lemon mixture	2
	... (4s) ... and the quick filling	4
	... (6s) ...	6
	... (3s) ...	7
	then for the filling	8
	the filling	9
	... (3s) ... you'd need lemon-meringue mixture (which you can buy in a packet) and you can make your own	10
Within filling	None	
Between filling and meringue	for the meringue	2
	you'd use the white for the meringue	4
	then for the meringue	8
After meringue	for the meringue	10

[a] Time before speaking not recorded

or program to cook the dish (Figure 8.2) shows that this corresponds to the major branch point. It seems that experienced cooks can mentally 'simulate' their cooking in order to answer list-generation questions; interestingly for our purposes, their retrospective reports of imagery all concerned themselves, or someone, in a kitchen preparing the dishes. Reports of certain kinds of imagery, of course, would not alone constitute evidence about the underlying process (see RICHARDSON, this volume).

Since subjects vary in their comment-level (see above), selection of the best and most revealing protocol is tempting and greatly simplifies presentation of the results (Newell and Simon, 1972; Byrne, 1977; etc.). But it is essential to analyse other subjects' data

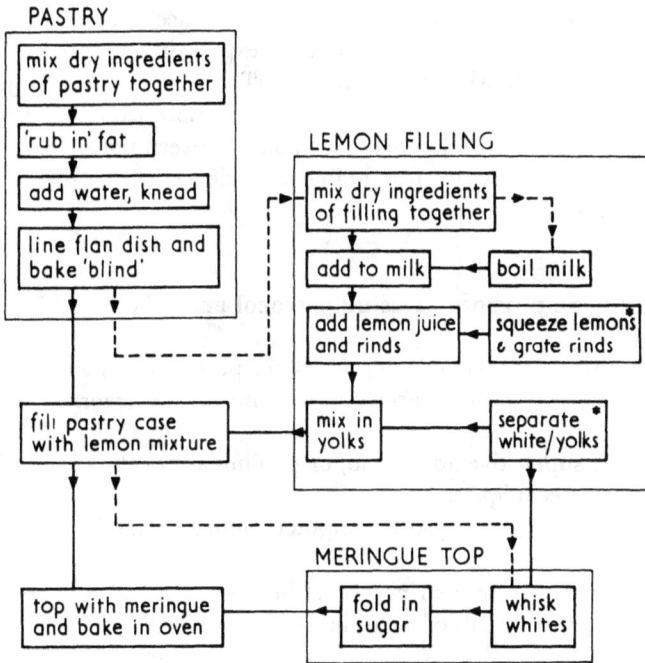

PASTRY

| mix dry ingredients of pastry together |
| 'rub in' fat |
| add water, knead |
| line flan dish and bake 'blind' |

LEMON FILLING

| mix dry ingredients of filling together |
| add to milk | ◄── | boil milk |
| add lemon juice and rinds | | squeeze lemons* & grate rinds |

| fill pastry case with lemon mixture | ──► | mix in yolks | ◄── | separate* white/yolks |

MERINGUE TOP

| top with meringue and bake in oven | ◄── | fold in sugar | ◄── | whisk whites |

FIGURE 8.2 A possible flow diagram for making a lemon meringue pie, to show the branched and modular structure of the process. The real-time path of operations follows the dashed lines, while the logical structure is shown by solid lines; operations with an asterisk are sometimes performed as preliminaries

as fully as possible to ensure that results are not biased by ease of analysis: it may be misleading to 'concentrate on particularly suggestive episodes' (Gick and Holyoak, 1980) or 'select subjects who verbalise easily' (De Groot, 1965, p. 380).

A related issue is that, with practice at a task, we gradually change towards greater automaticity of processing, and correspondingly lose the ability to report introspectively on what we are doing: practice 'makes the conscious unconscious' (Lundh, 1979). This has long been known (Woodworth, 1938) and is sometimes explained as reflecting a change from an 'interpreted' to a 'compiled' mental program (Ericsson and Simon, 1980). This analogy is closely tied to current computer systems and liable to import unintended connotations. In any case, automatic processing is faster and more reliable than controlled, but does not produce useful protocols: compare responses of a learner and an expert driver, asked, 'What exactly do you do when you turn right off a major road?' A subject's comment-level rises as he or she becomes more expert at a task. Researchers will therefore have to choose between inexpert, revealing subjects and expert, inscrutable ones, depending on the aims of the research.

What is the purpose of using protocol analysis?

Aims of researchers employing any of the process-tracing techniques which generate protocols seem to fall into three categories:

  (i) as a supportive adjunct to, or preliminary exploration before other techniques;
 (ii) in order to construct a computer simulation model of some behaviour;
(iii) simply as a very stringent test between theories, relying on the great wealth of detail in a protocol.

(See also discussion in Payne, Braunstein and Carroll, 1978.) The categories are not mutually exclusive, but will be discussed in turn.

Cases where protocol analysis is used only to supplement other data, often in a minor role, are commonplace. Like similar uses of introspection and self-report in general, they go unremarked, since the claims are backed by conventional data like reaction times so the status of introspections is not questioned. Thus, reaction times validate subjects' claims to mentally fold paper (Shepard and Feng, 1972), rotate 3-D objects (Shepard and Metzler, 1971), scan pictures in their mind's eye (Kosslyn, Ball and Reiser, 1978) and run through the alphabet (Hamilton and Sanford, 1978); it is sometimes hard to be sure to what extent the explanatory model depends on the introspections, though the data are often fascinating in any case. The same applies to cases where verbal protocols are used to suggest or interpret experimental manipulations. For instance, Thorndyke and Stasz (1980) gave novice and expert subjects maps to learn, thinking aloud as they did so, and tested them with drawing and navigational problems. Protocols showed good learners systematically selecting items to learn on the basis of those which they already knew least well, and other methods; poor learners seemed unsystematic. The authors do not consider the possibility that thinking aloud may have changed the behaviour for some subjects, which is possible in view of Kearins's (1981) results. However, they do validate their findings to some extent, finding that training in the methods used spontaneously by good learners is more beneficial than with those of poor learners, or no instruction.

To take another example, Quinton and Fellows (1975) used verbalised strategies of subjects solving three-term series problems to divide them into 'thinking' (i.e. structural representations) and 'perceptual' (i.e. simple short-cuts) solutions, finding that practice tended to effect a change to the latter and that when this occurred there was a corresponding decrease in solution times. Evans (1976b) points out that this correlation does not prove causality, and suggests that the verbal reports may come from a rationalisation process unrelated to that governing the behaviour (see above) which is entirely possible since Quinton and Fellows make no attempt to corroborate their explanation independently. Wood, Shotter and Godden (1974), in an equivalent case, gave unexpected supplementary tests which required a structural representation to answer, and found 'thinking' subjects to be faster than 'perceptual' ones. Fellows (1976) argues that there is no need to do this, since it would only 'affirm what we already know from subjects' introspections'; this is, of course, ingenuous, especially in view of the problems of using protocols as explanation rather than data, discussed earlier in this chapter.

Many of the most familiar uses of protocol analysis are associated with the construction of simulation programs to model the planning behaviour of individual subjects (see Newell and Simon, 1972). Programs differ, just as individuals differ, but the *theory* of the process can be identified with 'representative' programs which capture the general mechanisms (Simon, 1978). Typically a great deal of data is used by the experimenter to construct the program, and it is not easy to devise a fair test of the theory, as a program may give behaviour different from a human for many trivial reasons. Although it is sometimes imagined that the complexity of the simulation program allows any amount of underhand 'fitting' to observed protocols, practitioners assert that this is not the case (e.g. Simon, 1978). The major advantage of computer simulation, historically, was that it demonstrated the *adequacy* of the possible explanations offered for human thought, once and for all (Newell, Shaw and Simon, 1958). It may be argued that, now that psychologists are more familiar with criteria for adequacy and with computing in general, it is no longer necessary for every model and theory to be backed by a simulation in some particular high-level language, although they should all be *potentially* couchable in such terms. This would avoid misleading connotations being imported by the conventions of the language and the need to specify every detail, however unimportant and unknown.

In conclusion, the true value of protocol analysis will remain in its ability to provide moment to moment detail, whether of verbal report or observed behaviour, which forms such a severe test of a theory's predictive ability. In many cases, of course, there is in any case no other means of collecting data, but even where statistical analysis of errors and solution times can be done, it remains useful to employ protocol analysis as a check on possible theories. The very wealth of detail produced will function, for an inadequate theory, as the rope in the saying, 'Give a crook enough rope and he'll hang himself.'

References

Altmann, J. (1974), 'Observational study of behaviour: sampling methods', *Behaviour*, *49*, pp. 227–65.
Baylor, G. W. and Gascon, J. (1974), 'An information processing theory of aspects of the development of weight seriation in children', *Cognitive Psychology*, *6*, pp. 1–40.

Benjafield, J. (1969), 'Evidence that "thinking aloud" constitutes an externalisation of inner speech', *Psychonomic Science, 15*, pp. 83–4.

Brainerd, C. J. (1973), 'Judgments and explanations as criteria for the presence of cognitive structures', *Psychological Bulletin, 79*, pp. 172–9.

Burgoyne, J. G. (1975), 'The judgement process in management students' evaluation of their learning experiences', *Human Relations, 28*, pp. 543–69.

Butterworth, B. (1975), 'Hesitation and semantic planning in speech', *Journal of Psycholinguistic Research, 4*, pp. 75–87.

Byrne, R. W. (1975), 'Memory in complex tasks', unpublished PhD thesis, University of Cambridge.

Byrne, R. W. (1977), 'Planning meals: problem-solving on a real data-base', *Cognition, 5*, pp. 287–332.

Byrne, R. W. (1981), 'Mental cookery: an illustration of fact retrieval from plans', *Quarterly Journal of Experimental Psychology, 33A*, pp. 31–7.

Byrne, R. W. (1982), 'Geographical knowledge and orientation', in A. Ellis (ed.), *Normality and pathology of cognitive functions*, London, Academic Press.

Crow, L. E., Olshavsky, R. W. and Summers, J. O. (1980), 'Industrial buyers' choice strategies: a protocol analysis', *Journal of Marketing Research, 17*, pp. 34–44.

De Groot, A. D. (1965), *Thought and choice in chess*, The Hague, Mouton.

De Groot, A. D. (1966), 'Perception and memory versus thinking', in B. Kleinmuntz (ed.), *Problem Solving*, New York, Wiley.

Duncker, K. (1945), 'On problem solving', *Psychological Monographs, 58*, p. 5 (whole no. 270).

Ericsson, K. A. and Simon, H. A. (1980), 'Verbal reports as data', *Psychological Review, 87*, pp. 215–51.

Evans, J. St B. T. (1976a), 'Teaching statistics: some theoretical considerations', *Bulletin of the British Psychological Society, 29*, pp. 172–4.

Evans, J. St B. T. (1976b), 'A critical note on Quinton and Fellows' observation of reasoning strategies', *British Journal of Psychology, 67*, pp. 517–18.

Evans, J. St B. T. (1980), 'Thinking: experiential and information processing approaches', in G. Claxton (ed.), *Cognitive Psychology – New Directions*, London, Routledge & Kegan Paul.

Fellows, B. J. (1976), 'The role of introspection in problem-solving research: a reply to Evans', *British Journal of Psychology, 67*, pp. 519–20.

Gick, M. and Holyoak, K. J. (1980), 'Analogical problem-solving', *Cognitive Psychology, 12*, pp. 306–55.

Haber, R. N. and Fried, A. H. (1975), *An Introduction to Psychology*, New York, Holt, Rinehart & Winston.

Hamilton, J. M. and Sanford, A. J. (1978), 'The symbolic distance effect for alphabetic order judgments: a subjective report and reaction time analysis', *Quarterly Journal of Experimental Psychology, 30*, pp. 33–41.

Hilgard, E. R., Atkinson, R. L. and Atkinson, R. C. (1979), *Introduction to Psychology*, 7th edn, New York, Harcourt Brace Jovanovich.

Karpf, D. and Levine, M. (1971), 'Blank-trial probes and intro-tacts in human discrimination learning', *Journal of Experimental Psychology, 90*, pp. 51–5.

Kearins, J. M. (1981), 'Visual spatial memory in Australian aboriginal children of desert regions', *Cognitive Psychology, 13*, pp. 434–60.

Kosslyn, S. M., Ball, T. M. and Reiser, B. J. (1978), 'Visual images preserve metric spatial information: evidence from studies of imagery scanning', *Journal of Experimental Psychology: Human Perception and Performance, 4*, pp. 47–60.

Kroll, N. E. A. and Kellicutt, M. H. (1972), 'Short-term recall as a function of covert rehearsal and of intervening tasks', *Journal of Verbal Learning and Verbal Behaviour, 11*, pp. 196–204.

Linde, C. and Labov, W. (1975), 'Spatial networks as a site for the study of language and thought', *Language, 51*, pp. 924–39.

Lundh, L. G. (1979), 'Introspection, consciousness and human information processing', *Scandinavian Journal of Psychology, 20*, pp. 223–38.

Maier, N. R. F. (1931), 'Reasoning in humans: II. The solution of a problem and its appearance in consciousness', *Journal of Comparative Psychology, 12*, pp. 181–94.

Neisser, U. (1963), 'The multiplicity of thought', *British Journal of Psychology, 54*, pp. 1–14.

Newell, A., Shaw, J. C. and Simon, H. A. (1958), 'Elements of a theory of human problem solving', *Psychological Review, 65*, pp. 151–66.

Newell, A. and Simon, H. A. (1972), *Human problem solving*, Englewood Cliffs, New Jersey, Prentice-Hall.

Nisbett, R. E. and Wilson, T. D. (1977), 'Telling more than we can know: verbal reports on mental processes', *Psychological Review, 84*, pp. 231–59.

Norman, D. A. and Bobrow, D. G. (1976), 'On the role of active memory processes in perception and cognition', in C. N. Cofer (ed.), *The structure of human memory*, San Francisco, Freeman.

Olshavsky, R. W. (1979), 'Task complexity and contingent processing in decision making: a replication and extension', *Organisational Behaviour and Human Performance, 24*, pp. 300–16.

Pask, G. (1973), 'Educational methods using information about individual styles and strategies of learning', SSRC Project HR 1424/1, interim report.

Payne, J. W. (1976), 'Task complexity and contingent processing in decision making: an information search and protocol analysis', *Organisational Behaviour and Human Performance, 16*, pp. 366–87.

Payne, J. W., Braunstein, M. L. and Carroll, J. S. (1978), 'Exploring pre-decisional behaviour: an alternative approach to decision research', *Organisational Behaviour and Human Performance, 22*, pp. 17–44.

Quillian, M. R. (1966), 'Semantic memory', unpublished PhD thesis, Carnegie Institute of Technology. Shortened version in M. Minsky (ed.), *Semantic information processing*, Cambridge, MIT Press.

Quinton, G. and Fellows, B. J. (1975), 'Perceptual strategies in the solving of three-term series problems', *British Journal of Psychology, 66,* pp. 69–78.

Radford, J. (1974), 'Reflections on introspection', *American Psychologist, 29,* pp. 245–50.

Rasmussen, J. and Jensen, A. (1974), 'Mental procedures in real-life tasks: a case study of electronic trouble shooting', *Ergonomics, 17,* pp. 293–307.

Shallice, T. (1972), 'Dual functions of consciousness', *Psychological Review, 79,* pp. 383–93.

Shepard, R. N. and Feng, C. (1972), 'Mental paper folding', *Cognitive Psychology, 3,* pp. 228–43.

Shepard, R. N. and Metzler, J. (1971), 'Mental rotation of three-dimensional objects', *Science, 171,* pp. 701–3.

Silverman, R. E. (1979), *Essentials of psychology,* Englewood Cliffs, New Jersey, Prentice-Hall.

Simon, H. A. (1978), 'Information processing theory of human problem solving', in W. K. Estes (ed.), *Handbook of learning and cognitive processes, 5,* Hillsdale, New Jersey, Erlbaum.

Skinner, B. F. (1974), *About behaviourism,* New York, Knopf.

Thorndyke, P. W. and Stasz, C. (1980), 'Individual differences in procedures for knowledge acquisition from maps', *Cognitive Psychology, 12,* pp. 137–75.

Tinbergen, N. (1963), 'On aims and methods of ethology', *Zeitschrift für Tierpsychologie, 20,* pp. 410–33.

Wason, P. C. and Evans, J. St B. T. (1975), 'Dual processes in reasoning?', *Cognition, 3,* pp. 141–54.

Wilson, T. D. and Nisbett, R. E. (1978), 'The accuracy of verbal reports about the effects of stimuli on evaluations and behaviour', *Social Psychology, 41,* pp. 118–31.

Wood, D. J., Shotter, J. D. and Godden, D. (1974), 'An investigation of the relationships between problem solving strategies, representation and memory', *Quarterly Journal of Experimental Psychology, 26,* pp. 252–7.

Woodworth, R. S. (1938), *Experimental psychology,* New York, Holt.

Young, R. (1978), 'Strategies and structure of a cognitive skill', in G. Underwood (ed.), *Strategies of information processing,* New York, Academic Press.

Index

For Product Safety Concerns and Information please contact our EU
representative GPSR@taylorandfrancis.com
Taylor & Francis Verlag GmbH, Kaufingerstraße 24, 80331 München, Germany

www.ingramcontent.com/pod-product-compliance
Lightning Source LLC
Chambersburg PA
CBHW070355270326
41926CB00014B/2563